LUKE-ACTS

TEXTS@CONTEXTS

Edited by
James P. Grimshaw

BLOOMSBURY ACADEMIC
LONDON • NEW YORK • OXFORD • NEW DELHI • SYDNEY

BLOOMSBURY ACADEMIC
Bloomsbury Publishing Plc
50 Bedford Square, London, WC1B 3DP, UK
1385 Broadway, New York, NY 10018, USA

BLOOMSBURY, BLOOMSBURY ACADEMIC and the Diana logo
are trademarks of Bloomsbury Publishing Plc

First published in Great Britain 2019
Paperback edition first published 2020

A catalogue record for this book is available from the British Library.

Library of Congress Cataloging-in-Publication Data
Names: Grimshaw, James P., 1963–editor.
Title: Luke-Acts / edited by James P. Grimshaw.
Description: 1 [edition]. | New York: Bloomsbury Academic, 2018. |
Series: Texts@contexts | Includes bibliographical references and index.
Identifiers: LCCN 2017053722 | ISBN 9780567675705 (hardback) |
ISBN 9780567675712 (epdf)
Subjects: LCSH: Bible. Luke–Criticism, interpretation, etc. |
Bible. Acts–Criticism, interpretation, etc.
Classification: LCC BS2589. L8289 2018 | DDC 226.4/06–dc23 LC record available at
https://lccn.loc.gov/2017053722

ISBN: HB: 978-0-5676-7570-5
PB: 978-0-5676-9397-6
ePDF: 978-0-5676-7571-2
eBook: 978-0-5676-7573-6

Series: Texts@Contexts, volume 7

Typeset by Deanta Global Publishing Services, Chennai, India

To find out more about our authors and books visit
www.bloomsbury.com and sign up for our newsletters.

LUKE-ACTS

Texts@Contexts

Series Editors

Nicole Wilkinson Duran
James P. Grimshaw
Daniel Patte

Fortress Press

Old Testament
Joshua and Judges
Leviticus and Numbers
Exodus and Deuteronomy
Genesis

New Testament
Mark
1 & 2 Corinthians
Matthew

T&T Clark
Old Testament
Samuel, Kings and Chronicles I
The Five Scrolls

CONTENTS

Part III
READING WITH THE CHURCH

NOTES ON CONTRIBUTORS

Amy Lindeman Allen is Assistant Professor of New Testament at Christian Theological Seminary in Indianapolis, Indiana. She received her MDiv from the Lutheran School of Theology at Chicago and her PhD in New Testament and Early Christianity from Vanderbilt University in 2016. She specializes in childist biblical criticism and contextual hermeneutics and is a regular contributor to *Political Theology*'s blog 'The Politics of Scripture'.

Esa Autero (ThD, University of Helsinki, Finland) is the dean of faculty at South Florida Bible College and Theological Seminary. He is the author of *Reading the Bible Across Contexts: Luke's Gospel, Socio-Economic Marginality, and Latin American Biblical Hermeneutics* as well as numerous articles on Contextual Hermeneutics in the Gospels and Epistle of James. He is also the president of Missio Dei International, a non-profit organization that develops biblical and ministerial materials for the purpose of community transformation.

Sharon Betsworth is professor of religion at Oklahoma City University in Oklahoma City, Oklahoma. Betsworth received her PhD from the Graduate Theological Union in 2007, and her research focuses upon children in the Gospels and the ancient world. She is the author of *The Reign of God Is Such as These: A Socio-Literary Analysis of Daughters in the Gospel of Mark (2010)* and *Children in Early Christian Narratives* (2015). Betsworth co-chairs the Children in the Biblical World section of the Society of Biblical Literature (SBL).

A. Francis Carter, Jr is a visiting assistant professor of religion at the University of North Carolina, Greensboro. He received a MDiv from Colgate Rochester Crozer Divinity School in 2007 and PhD in New Testament and Early Christian Literature from Vanderbilt University in 2016. With interests in contextual biblical criticism and the socio-cultural nature of historiography, his research is interdisciplinary in its focus on early Christian identity, Black Atlantic discourse, (post)colonialism and theories of diaspora. Carter is a member of SBL and the Institute for Signifying Scriptures.

Rosinah Mmannana Gabaitse is a lecturer in biblical studies at the University of Botswana within the Department of Theology and Religious Studies. She received her PhD at the University of KwaZulu-Natal and is currently a Humboldt Postdoctoral Fellow at the University of Bamberg, Germany. She has published papers in the field of biblical hermeneutics, Luke-Acts and Pentecostalism, among others. Gabaitse's research focuses on the interface between teaching/researching in a university and grassroots communities; hence, some of her publications focus on the Bible and the spread of HIV and AIDS, gender-based violence, and masculinities.

James P. Grimshaw is associate professor of religion at Carroll University in Waukesha, Wisconsin. He received his MDiv from Christian Theological Seminary and his PhD from Vanderbilt University. He is the co-editor of *Matthew* in this same Texts@Contexts series and is co-editor with Nicole Wilkinson Duran for the series volumes on Paul's Letters, Revelation, and Contextual Biblical Methodology. Grimshaw serves on the steering committee for the SBL Contextual Biblical Interpretation section.

James A. Metzger received his PhD in religion from Vanderbilt University (2006) and his MA in English from East Carolina University (2012). He is the author of *Consumption and Wealth in Luke's Travel Narrative* (2007), *Dim: A Novel* (2011), and *The Tub & Other Strange Tales* (2013). For the past several years, he has taught religious studies, ethics, and critical thinking at the college level.

Néstor O. Míguez is professor emeritus in the areas of Bible (New Testament) and Systematic Theology, in the I. U. ISEDET (Buenos Aires). He has been a guest lecturer at various universities and centres of theological education worldwide and has more than 200 publications including books, chapters of books, and academic articles. He received his ThD from ISEDET (1988) and completed his post-graduate studies in Social and Political Anthropology. Some recent publications include *Jesús del Pueblo* (Buenos Aires, La Aurora, 2015), *The Practice of Hope* (Ausburg/Fortress Press, 2012), and *Beyond the Spirit of the Empire* (Co-authored with J. M. Sung and J. Reiger, SCM, 2009).

Brittany E. Wilson is assistant professor of New Testament at Duke University Divinity School in Durham, North Carolina. She is the author of *Unmanly Men: Refigurations of Masculinity in Luke-Acts* (Oxford University Press, 2015) and a number of popular and academic articles. Her research focuses on constructions of gender and the body in the New Testament, and she serves on the steering committees for the SBL Gospel of Luke and Book of Acts sections.

Christopher B. Zeichmann teaches at Emmanuel College in the University of Toronto. He received his PhD from the University of St Michael's College and specializes in the Roman military in the Gospels in addition to the racial politics of contemporary North America. He is author of the forthcoming book *A Guide to the Military and the New Testament* and his work has been published in *New Testament Studies, Catholic Biblical Quarterly*, among other biblical studies journals.

SERIES PREFACE: TEXTS IN/AT LIFE CONTEXTS

Myth cannot be defined but as an empty screen, a structure … . A myth is but an empty screen for transference.

Mieke Bal (1993)

Shiv'im Panim l'Torah (שִׁבְעִים פָּנִים לְתוֹרָה)

('The Torah has seventy faces')[1]

The discipline of biblical studies emerged from a particular cultural context; it is profoundly influenced by the assumptions and values of the Western European and North Atlantic, male-dominated, and largely Protestant environment in which it was born. Yet like the religions with which it is involved, the critical study of the Bible has travelled beyond its original context. Its presence in a diversity of academic settings around the globe has been experienced as both liberative and imperialist, sometimes simultaneously. Like many travellers, biblical scholars become aware of their own cultural rootedness only in contact with, and through the eyes of, people in other cultures.

The way any one of us closes a door seems in Philadelphia nothing at all remarkable, but in Chiang Mai, it seems overly loud and emphatic – so very typically American. In the same way, Western biblical interpretation did not seem tied to any specific context when only Westerners were reading and writing it. Since so much economic, military, and consequently cultural power has been vested in the West, the West has had the privilege of maintaining this cultural closure for two centuries. Those who engaged in biblical studies – even when they were women or men from Africa, Asia, and Latin America – nevertheless had to take on the Western context along with the discipline.

But much of recent Bible scholarship has moved towards the recognition that considerations of not only the contexts of assumed, or implied, biblical authors but also the contexts of the interpreters are valid and legitimate in an inquiry into biblical literature. We use 'contexts' here as an umbrella term covering a wide range of issues: on the one hand, social factors (such as location, economic situation, gender, age,

---

1. This saying indicates, through its usage of the stereotypic number seventy, that the Torah – and, by extension, the whole Bible – intrinsically has many meanings. It is therefore often used to indicate the multivalence and variability of biblical interpretation, and does not appear in this formulation in traditional Jewish biblical interpretation before the middle of the first millennium CE. Its most known appearances are in the medieval commentator Ibn Ezra's introduction to his commentary on the Torah, towards the introduction's end (as in printed versions), in Midrash Numbers Rabbah (13.15-16), and in later Jewish mystical literature.

class, ethnicity, colour, and things pertaining to personal biography) and, on the other hand, ideological factors (such as faith, beliefs, practised norms, and personal politics).

Contextual readings of the Bible are an attempt to redress the previous long-standing and grave imbalance that says that there is a kind of 'plain' unaligned biblical criticism that is somehow 'normative', and that there is another, distinct kind of biblical criticism aligned with some social location: the writing of Latina/o scholars advocating liberation, the writing of feminist scholars emphasizing gender as a cultural factor, the writings of African scholars pointing out the text's and the readers' imperialism, the writing of Jews and Muslims, and so on. The project of recognizing and emphasizing the role of context in reading freely admits that we all come from somewhere: no one is native to the biblical text, no one reads only in the interests of the text itself. North Atlantic and Western European scholarship has focused on the Bible's characters as individuals, has read past its miracles and stories of spiritual manifestations, or 'translated' them into other categories. These results of Euro-American contextual reading would be no problem if they were seen as such; but they have become a chain to be broken when they have been held up as the one and only 'objective', plain truth of the text itself.

The biblical text, as we have come to understand in the postmodern world and as pre-Enlightenment interpreters perhaps understood more clearly, does not speak in its own voice. It cannot read itself. We must read it, and in reading it, we must acknowledge that our own voice's particular pitch and timbre and inflection affect the meaning that emerges. Biblical scholars usually read the text in the voice of a Western Protestant male. When interpreters in the Southern Hemisphere and in Asia have assumed ownership of the Bible, it has meant a recognition that this Euro-American male voice is not the voice of the text itself; it is only one reader's voice, or rather, the voice of one context – however familiar and authoritative it may seem to all who have been affected by Western political and economic power. Needless to say, it is not a voice suited to bring out the best meaning for every reading community. Indeed, as biblical studies tended for so long to speak in this one particular voice, it may be the case that that voice has outlived its meaning – producing usefulness: we may have heard all that this voice has to say, at least for now. Nevertheless we have included that voice in this series, in part in an effort to hear it as emerging from its specific context, in order to put that previously authoritative voice quite literally in its place.

The trend of acknowledging readers' contexts as meaningful is already, inter alia, recognizable in the pioneering volumes of *Reading from This Place* (Segovia and Tolbert 1995, 2000, 2004), which indeed move from the centre to the margins and back and from the United States to the rest of the world. More recent publications along this line also include *Her Master's Tools?* (Vander Stichele and Penner 2005), *From Every People and Nation: The Book of Revelation in Intercultural Perspective* (Rhoads et al. 2005), *From Every People and Nation: A Biblical Theology of Race* (Hays and Carson 2003), and the *Global Bible Commentary* (GBC; Patte 2004).

The editors of the GBC have gone a long way towards this shift by soliciting and admitting contributions from so-called Third, Fourth, and Fifth World scholars alongside First and Second World scholars, thus attempting to usher the former and their perspectives into the centre of biblical discussion. Contributors to the GBC were asked to begin by clearly stating their context before proceeding. The result was a collection of short introductions to the books of the Bible (Hebrew Bible/Old Testament and New Testament), each introduction from one specific context and, perforce, limited in scope. At the SBL's annual meeting in Philadelphia in 2005, during the two GBC sessions and especially in the session devoted to pedagogical implications, it became clear that this project should be continued, albeit articulated further and redirected.

On methodological grounds, the paradox of a deliberately inclusive policy that foregrounds differences in the interpretation of the Bible could not be addressed in a single- or double-volume format because in most instances, those formats would allow for only one viewpoint for each biblical issue or passage (as in previous publications) or biblical book (as in the GBC) to be articulated. The acceptance of such a limit may indeed lead to a decentring of traditional scholarship but it would definitely not usher in multivocality on any single topic. It is true that, for pedagogical reasons, a teacher might achieve multivocality of scholarship by using various specialized scholarship types together; for instance, the GBC has been used side by side on a course with historical introductions to the Bible and other focused introductions, such as the *Women's Bible Commentary* (Newsom and Ringe 1998). But research and classes focused on a single biblical book or biblical corpus need another kind of resource: volumes exemplifying a broad multivocality in themselves, varied enough in contexts from various shades of the confessional to various degrees of the secular, especially since in most previous publications the contexts of communities of faith overrode all other contexts.

On the practical level, then, we found that we could address some of these methodological, pedagogical, and representational limitations evident in previous projects in contextual interpretation through a book series in which each volume introduces multiple contextual readings of the same biblical texts. This is what the SBL Contextual Biblical Interpretation Consultation has already been promoting since 2005 during the American Annual Meeting, and since 2011 also at the annual International SBL conference. The Consultation serves as a testing ground for a multiplicity of readings of the same biblical texts by scholars from different contexts.[2]

---

2. Since 2010, when this book series was started and the first volume published with this Preface, interest in contextual interpretation has grown considerably. Worth noting is the SBL Press series International Voices in Biblical Studies (IVBS). As can be seen from the website (http://www.sbl-site.org/publications/Books_IVBS.aspx), seven volumes have been published since 2010. However, the IVBS mission is different from ours, although two of the volumes (Vaka'uta 2011 on Ezra-Nehemiah 9-10 and Havea and Lau (eds) 2015 on Ruth) do discuss specific texts against contextual, geographical-cultural perspectives. Worth noting too in this connection is the SBL series Global Perspectives on Biblical Scholarship (https://www.sbl-site.org/publications/Books_GPBS.aspx), and especially the 2012 volume on postcolonial African interpretation, edited by Musa W. Dube, Andrew M. Mbuvi, and Dora R. Mbuwayesango.

These considerations led us to believe that a book series focusing specifically on contextual multiple readings for specific topics, of specific biblical books, would be timely. We decided to construct a series, including at least eight to ten volumes, divided between the Hebrew Bible (HB/OT) and the New Testament (NT). Each of the planned volumes would focus on one or two biblical books: Genesis, Exodus and Deuteronomy, Leviticus and Numbers, Joshua and Judges, the so-called history books and later books for the HB/OT; Mark, Luke-Acts, John, and Paul's letters for the NT. The general HB/OT editor is Athalya Brenner, with Archie Lee and Gale Yee as associate editors. The first general NT editor was Nicole Duran and is now James Grimshaw, with Daniel Patte and Teresa Okure as associate editors. Other colleagues have joined as editors for specific volumes.

Each volume focuses on clusters of contexts and of issues or themes, as determined by the editors in consultation with potential contributors. A combination of topics or themes, texts, and interpretive contexts seems better for our purpose than a text-only focus. In this way, more viewpoints on specific issues will be presented, with the hope of gaining a grid of interests and understanding. The interpreters' contexts will be allowed to play a central role in choosing a theme: we do not want to impose our choice of themes upon others, but as the contributions emerge, we will collect themes for each volume under several headings.

While we were soliciting articles for the first volumes (and continue to solicit contributions for future volumes), each contributor was and is asked to foreground her or his own multiple 'contexts' while presenting her or his interpretation of a given issue pertaining to the relevant biblical book(s). We asked that the interpretation be firmly grounded in those contexts and sharply focused on the specific theme, as well as in dialogue with 'classical' informed biblical scholarship. Finally, we asked for a concluding assessment of the significance of this interpretation for the contributor's contexts (whether secular or in the framework of a faith community).

Our main interest in this series is to examine how formulating the content-specific, ideological, and thematic questions from life contexts will focus the reading of the biblical texts. The result is a two-way process of reading that (1) considers the contemporary life context from the perspective of the chosen themes in the given biblical book as corrective lenses, pointing out specific problems and issues in that context as highlighted by the themes in the biblical book; and (2) conversely, considers the given biblical book and the chosen theme from the perspective of the life context.

The word 'contexts', like identity, is a blanket term covering many components. For some, their geographical context is uppermost; for others, the dominant factor may be gender, faith, membership in a certain community, class, and so forth. The balance is personal and not always conscious; it does, however, dictate choices of interpretation. One of our interests as editors is to present the personal beyond the autobiographical as pertinent to the wider scholarly endeavour, especially but not only when grids of consent emerge that supersede divergence. Consent is no guarantee of Truthspeak; neither does it necessarily point at a sure recognition of the biblical authors' elusive contexts and intentions. It does, however, have cultural and political implications.

Globalization promotes uniformity but also diversity, by shortening distances, enabling dissemination of information, and exchanging resources. This is an opportunity for modifying traditional power hierarchies and reallocating knowledge, for upsetting hegemonies, and for combining the old with the new, the familiar with the unknown – in short, for a fresh mutuality. This series, then, consciously promotes the revision of biblical myths into new reread and rewritten versions that hang on many threads of welcome transference. Our contributors were asked, decidedly, to be responsibly nonobjective and to represent only themselves on the biblical screen. Paradoxically, we hope, the readings here offered will form a new tapestry or, changing the metaphor, new metaphorical screens on which contemporary life contexts and the life of biblical texts in those contexts may be reflected and refracted.

The Editors

References

Bal, M. (1993), 'Myth a la Lettre: Freud, Mann, Genesis and Rembrandt, and the story of the son', repr. in A. Brenner (ed.), *A Feminist Companion to Genesis*, 343–78, Sheffield: Sheffield Academic Press. Originally in S. Rimon-Kenan, ed. (1987), *Discourse in Psychoanalysis and Literature*, 57–89, London: Methuen.

Dube, M. W., A. M. Mbuvi and D. R. Mbuwayesango, eds (2012), *Postcolonial Perspectives in African Biblical Interpretations*, Global Perspectives on Biblical Scholarship, 13; Atlanta: SBL Press.

Havea, J., and P. H. W. Lau, eds (2015), *Reading Ruth in Asia*, IVBS; Atlanta: SBL Press.

Hays, J., and D. Carson (2003), *From Every People and Nation: A Biblical Theology of Race*, Downers Grove: InterVarsity Press.

Newsom, C. A., and S. H. Ringe, eds (1992, 1998), *The Women's Bible Commentary*, Louisville, KY: Westminster/John Knox Press.

Patte, D. (2004), *The Global Bible Commentary*, Nashville: Abingdon Press.

Rhoads, D., ed. (2005), *From Every People and Nation: The Book of Revelation in Intercultural Perspective*, Minneapolis: Augsburg Fortress Press.

Segovia, F., and M. Tolbert, eds (1995), *Reading from This Place: Social Location and Biblical Interpretation in the United States*, Minneapolis: Fortress Press.

Segovia, F., and M. Tolbert, eds (2000), *Reading from This Place: Social Location and Biblical Interpretation in Global Perspective*, Minneapolis: Fortress Press.

Segovia, F., and M. Tolbert, eds (2004), *Teaching the Bible: The Discourses and Politics of Biblical Pedagogy*, repr., Eugene, OR: Wipf & Stock; originally published 1997.

Vaka'uta, N. (2011), *Reading Ezra 9–10 Tu'a-Wise: Rethinking Biblical Interpretation in Oceania*, IVBS; Atlanta: SBL Press.

Vander Stichele, C. and T. Penner, eds (2005), *Her Master's Tools?: Feminist and Postcolonial Engagements of Historical-Critical Discourse*, Atlanta: Society of Biblical Literature.

INTRODUCTION

James P. Grimshaw

This is the fourth New Testament book published in the Texts@Contexts series, following Mark, Matthew, and 1 and 2 Corinthians. The Luke-Acts volume, however, will be the first New Testament book published with Bloomsbury T&T Clark, the previous ones were with Fortress Press. As with the other volumes, this one features chapters where contributors intentionally analyse their own contemporary contexts as they interact with and interpret the biblical text.

The resulting critical conversations between context and text demonstrate, first, the intentionality and transparency of the interpretive process that is often hidden when readers do not reveal their interpretive choices. For example, in Chapter 5, Carter meticulously attends to his own Diaspora context and weaves this methodically into the Acts text in a way that makes very clear his interpretive choices. Second, these conversations uncover interpretations and highlight themes that often receive less attention in scholarship simply because this type of deliberate cross-cultural conversation can bring fresh insights to the text as well as to the contemporary context. In Chapter 4, Zeichmann's critique of queer-friendly interpretations of the Ethiopian eunuch and the centurion brings to light the complex nature of the characters' gender and sexuality and their oppressive political roles that are often overlooked. And, finally, when these conversations between contemporary context and biblical text are collected according to similar themes or approaches and put side by side in a volume like this, connections and comparisons emerge which then moves these academic conversations forward. For example, in Chapters 7 and 8, when Autero's and Gabaitse's two different chapters on readings with Pentecostal congregations are placed side by side, deeper understandings arise regarding the interpretive process.

The nine contributors of this volume are diverse. They live in Argentina, Botswana, Canada, the west and upper midwest and southeastern parts of the United States. And one contributor from Finland who currently resides in the United States is sharing the work he did while living in Bolivia. In addition to their geography, many different contexts foreground their work, including gender and sexuality, poverty and wealth, health and illness, children and families and marriage, politics and economics, race and ethnicity, and religion and humanism. Their contextual approaches vary as well: from exposing metanarratives to readings with ordinary readers; from examining the history of academic interpretations and their contexts to digging into popular cultural contexts.

The chapters in this volume are arranged in three parts. In Part I, Portraits of Jesus, three scholars paint depictions of Jesus as an 'only child', an unmanly and dependent figure, and an advocate for euthanasia. All three discuss, in different ways, the vulnerability of Jesus and those he interacts with – at the beginning of life, during times of suffering, or at the end of life. Jesus is sympathetic towards those who are dependent, especially through healing or the use of power.

Sharon Betsworth writes the first chapter and interprets three healing stories of only children (i.e. children without siblings) and then connects these stories to show how Luke depicts Jesus himself as an only child and one who cares for children (7.11-17; 8.40-56; 9.37-43). Betsworth uses a childist reading of Luke, which focuses on the agency, not the passiveness, of children in the biblical text. Her interest in children comes out of her academic work in feminist interpretation and also her care for children in the Midwestern United States as an elementary school teacher, youth minister, and camp counsellor. She has also worked at a summer literacy programme for underserved children in the state of Oklahoma, which is a state where many adults claim they are 'highly religious' while also ranking low regarding childhood health and well-being.

Several themes emerge out of the three healing stories. First, Jesus cares for the marginalized, which includes children and youth and especially only children. The possible loss of an only child would disproportionally affect the family who depended on them for future support. Second, Luke connects the healing of the only children to Jesus, and uses other redactions to further emphasize Jesus as an only child. Third, children in Luke are depicted as both valued and vulnerable. Betsworth further emphasizes this point as she documents her group readings with children in Oklahoma.

Brittany Wilson surveys the muscular Christianity movement in American Protestant culture and recent studies in Luke-Acts to raise questions about Jesus' masculinity and gender depictions. In the late nineteenth and twentieth centuries, American Protestants responded to the feminization of Protestant Christianity by depicting Jesus as rugged, heroic, and manly and also by birthing the YMCA and the Boy Scouts. Similarly, even recent studies in Luke-Acts depict Jesus as a noble man, rational, and in control. Wilson is particularly interested in how gender relations should function in our different contexts today regarding the proper use of power, especially in conversation with feminist, womanist, and Latina theologians.

Out of this contemporary context, Wilson examines the norms of ancient masculinity in the first-century Greco-Roman context and argues that Luke's Jesus does not represent elite masculinity. Jesus does not have elite status and he does not exercise power over others or control himself, especially in his expression of grief and his bodily invasion on the cross. Luke's depiction of Jesus as unmanly is also reflected more widely in how Luke portrays both men and women crying in Luke and Acts and the many accounts of men having their bodies invaded. Wilson sees Luke as reversing gender and power norms so that men are to be more dependent on God, like those on the margins – for it is God who is in control.

Finally, Jim Metzger considers whether Luke's Jesus might advocate for voluntary active euthanasia. Metzger, who is in remission from stage IV non-Hodgkin's lymphoma, has studied euthanasia from different religious and philosophical perspectives. Metzger now considers where Luke's Jesus might stand. Like Wilson's depiction of an unmanly Jesus, Metzger challenges pervasive Christian views. That is, while Christianity's historic stance has generally prohibited active euthanasia, and while it carries a stigma in the United States especially among Christians, might Luke's Jesus find it acceptable?

As he approaches the biblical text, Metzger draws from his own illness experience, disability studies, and philosophy. He also acknowledges that he reads the Bible as a humanist who finds the Bible insightful and deeply moving. Metzger notes that Luke never directly addresses active euthanasia and that Jesus appears to be able to cure any disease. But Metzger makes the assumption that Luke's Jesus is a highly skilled folk healer who may not be able to cure all diseases. He then surveys how Jesus sees the reality of the world, understands the human self, and depicts characters that experience chronic suffering. In that framework, Metzger finds evidence in Luke for a Jesus who has a high degree of compassion and sensitivity to those with chronic suffering and a sense of urgency in addressing their pain. Given those qualities, and Jesus' view that life in this world has little value, Metzger claims that Luke's Jesus would be hard-pressed to oppose active euthanasia to an individual who was truly suffering.

Authors in Part II, Negotiating Hegemony, examine how queer, African American, and Latin American readers can negotiate, without adopting, hegemonic influences that shape interpretations and life today. In light of the racist and colonialist rhetoric often used to support queer interpretations, Christopher Zeichmann is advocating for a more critical examination of the politics of queer readings as he focuses on the healing of the centurion's slave (Lk. 7.1-10) and the Ethiopian eunuch (Acts 8.26-40). For example, many queer-friendly interpretations of the centurion and eunuch idealize these characters and avoid confronting their use of or collaboration with state violence. Zeichmann compares this to similar problems in early feminist interpretations that saw Jesus as egalitarian over and against Jewish misogyny. He further argues that contemporary interpretations, as well as Luke's own redactions, promote respectability politics by reading the centurion as humble and the eunuch's connection with nobility, all of which prioritizes their respectable demeanour.

Zeichmann argues for an intersectional approach to gender politics in Luke-Acts that takes into account the links between race, gender, social class, and colonialism and that confronts colonial and racist interpretations. He is critical of queer biblical interpretations not to dismiss them but to make them better. By calling out the Lukan text, readers are better able to identify similar shortcomings in their own politics today. For example, he argues that contemporary political efforts to assimilate to dominant cultural standards (e.g. marriage equality valued more by the white middle-class LGBT community) is prioritized over efforts to address daily issues that recognize the intersectionality of sexuality with race (e.g. police harassment of queers of colour).

Identifying his position within Black America and the African Diaspora, Francis Carter challenges the privileging of dominant metanarratives in history and in biblical texts and offers a contextual reading of Acts with a diaspora-informed metanarrative. Along with his own experiences, Carter examines the stories of Crispus Attucks and Nathan Turner in US history to discuss the hegemonic and contextual nature of history writing (e.g. Was Turner dangerous and violent or sacrificial and fighting for justice?) and applies this to Acts.

The dominant metanarrative for Acts has a preference for binary pairs (e.g. Jew versus Gentile, appeasement of Rome but polemical against the Jews), a linear trajectory (e.g. from Jerusalem to the ends of the earth, from Jews to Gentiles), and homogeneity (e.g. divergent practices are inferior, Jewish identity is flat and negative). Carter's metanarrative, however, challenges simplistic binaries (e.g. instead of moving from Jews to Gentiles, the mixed community shows Gentiles as part of the Way and yet Jews have the leadership positions), sees Lukan themes as nonlinear (e.g. the Way is not the result of a linear progression but through adaptation, debate, and compromise as with the Hellenists and Hebrews) and uncovers heterogeneity (e.g. divergent practices are normal, Jewish identity is particular and diverse as Cyrenian or Asiatic). Carter recognizes the dominant metanarrative as one legitimate reading and is not replacing other metanarratives with his own, but argues that metanarratives are contextual and should be acknowledged as such. He finally suggests that he does not offer one particular interpretation of Acts but claims that his metanarrative allows for multiple readings.

In the final chapter of Part II, Néstor Míguez challenges readers to identify the global empire in the local (con)text through the use of two pericopes in Acts: the story of the slave girl exploited as a diviner in Philippi (Acts 16.16-24) and the harassment from local authorities against Paul's team in his missionary visit to Thessalonica (Acts 17.1-9). Born in Argentina, Míguez has taught and travelled in many different parts of the world, and he draws on his study of ancient and contemporary empires as well as his own experience of the imperial forces in Latin America. He highlights how global empires intervene in and dominate the local context through mechanisms such as economic exploitation, language dominance, power asymmetry, media, and religious justification.

In these two texts in Acts, the arbitrary nature of global political, economic, and religious powers are present and forceful in the local context as Paul and his companions face the anger of local authorities. As Paul dispossesses the slave in Philippi from her divination powers in Acts 16, he rids the master of his income and disrupts the flow of economic benefits from the vulnerable to the powerful and the accompanying political influence. Paul also challenges the use of popular religion by the slave girl that the empire tolerated as a conquering strategy. In the Thessalonian event in Acts 17, Paul and Silas and their host Jason are charged with bringing a global revolution to the local context (i.e. 'turning the world upside down') and challenging the Roman Empire (i.e. 'acting contrary to the decrees of the emperor'). Míguez argues that this approach helps readers recognize these texts as a critique of the imperial spirit yesterday and today, especially in regard to 'the overall search for profit, the sense of endless power that is divinely approved, the legitimacy of foreign rule, the lack of care towards the victims ... and the forced imposition of cultural standards' (see p. 118).

Reading with the church, the final part of the volume, features authors who claim close ties with a particular Christian tradition as they facilitate conversations between their traditions and Luke-Acts on one cultural theme. Autero and Gabaitse come out of the Pentecostal tradition and use the Contextual Bible Study approach to read with ordinary readers – Autero on the theme of wealth and Gabaitse on gender. Allen facilitates a different kind of conversation between the Evangelical Lutheran Church of America and Luke-Acts on marriage.

Esa Autero, a Finnish-American Pentecostal, spent eleven months in Bolivia using the Contextual Bible Study approach and empirical hermeneutics to read Lk. 12.22-34 with poor and wealthy Pentecostal communities. While Autero is middle class, he has worked with poor communities in Bolivia, India, and the United States. One church that he read with, from a socially and economically marginalized community, was part of a small independent Pentecostal denomination and was composed of about fifty members who were mostly manual labourers, small business owners, or unemployed. Interpreting Lk. 12.22-34, they understood God as one who provides for them and they identified their main worries as the basic necessities of food and clothing. They also emphasized solidarity with and generosity towards others.

The other church, from a wealthy upper middle-class community that met in a five-star hotel, was part of an independent neo-Pentecostal church with about 100 regular attendees who were affluent professionals. In their responses, they also saw God as one who provides but had a different set of worries they identified: children's birthday parties, finding a new rental apartment, losing a suitcase on a business trip. While both groups understood that one's actions brought certain consequences, this wealthy church emphasized financial gain as reward for their faithfulness, showing influences of the prosperity gospel. They also said very little about giving to the poor and spent more time on existential and spiritual concerns.

Rosinah Gabaitse, who identifies as a Motswana Pentecostal, draws from Gerald West's Contextual Bible Study approach to read selected texts from Luke-Acts with Pentecostal women in Botswana. Luke-Acts, with its focus on the Holy Spirit, has been an influential text for Pentecostal believers. While Pentecostalism has often been identified, by both believers and scholars, as a tradition that supports equality between men and women, recent studies in Africa and the West reveal that Pentecostalism is a space of both embrace and exclusion. Leadership models are often authoritarian and male supremacy is taught through biblical interpretation.

Gabaitse conducted research with fifty-one female members of the Pentecostal church (and three male pastors) ranging from 17 to 73 years old and living in urban, semi-urban, and rural areas. They read four texts, Lk. 4.1-19, Acts 2.1-47, Acts 6.1-7, and Acts 21.1-14, in which Gabaitse especially paid attention to interpretive strategies. One main group of interpretations affirmed patriarchy either through proof-texting or by selectively highlighting the spiritual aspects of the texts while ignoring social and political implications (similar to the wealthy congregation in Autero's study). These interpretations supported male leadership, the subjugation of women, and the prosperity gospel. A second group of interpretations subverted patriarchy either by readings that foregrounded the Holy Spirit and its power to transform relationships or through readings that underscored both the spiritual and social realms in the texts. These subversive interpretations resisted the traditional cultural ideologies and often critiqued the biblical text.

This Luke-Acts volume began with Betsworth's portrait of Jesus as an only child in his family and the view of children as valued and vulnerable. Returning to the family theme, the volume concludes with Amy Allen who opens up a conversation between Luke-Acts and the Evangelical Lutheran Church in America (ELCA) to examine its visions for the purpose and function of marriage. She has noticed significant social and economic shifts in her North American culture regarding marriage (e.g. LGBT and blended families, single parents, couples without children). While the ELCA has adapted its practices in some ways to address these shifts (e.g. a 2009 social statement, marriage liturgies), Allen argues that the denomination must develop a more coherent ideology to sustain better practices.

Although Luke-Acts is seldom consulted in biblical marriage debates, Allen finds Luke-Acts a good conversation partner for the ELCA. Luke-Acts moves away from first-century Greco-Roman views in seeing marriage as a focus on individual and household economics and social status. Rather, it identifies marriage as discipleship and economic redistribution to the larger community (against the example of Ananias and Sapphira) and emphasizes gender equality (as Aquila and Priscilla run a household together). Marriage also serves to embody the work of the spirit (as seen in Mary and Elizabeth's pregnancies and relationship) and protect the vulnerable (in the protection of widows by Jesus and the Acts community). Allen concludes that this is a vision that the ELCA should consider as it revises its ideology on marriage and family.

This volume could be used in a variety of ways in furthering academic research or in the classroom – and we hope it is! For the classroom setting, two or three chapters with a similar theme could be used together to show how context influences interpretation. For example, two chapters on Jesus or on hegemony or the first and last chapters on the theme of family. The volume could also be used to study interpretation, perhaps using the two chapters by Autero and Gabaitse on ordinary readers or other chapters on their different interpretive or contextual approaches. However it is used, the volume continues to make the case that the interpreter's context matters in interpretation.

Part I

PORTRAITS OF JESUS

Chapter 1

JESUS (AND) THE ONLY CHILD:
JESUS, CHILDREN, AND THE GOSPEL OF LUKE

Sharon Betsworth

The Gospel of Luke contains more material about children than the other canonical gospels do. The birth of both Jesus and John the Baptist is foretold and then recounted. Jesus' birth is narrated in more detail than in Matthew's Gospel. And Luke is the only Gospel in the New Testament that contains a story of Jesus' childhood. Jesus includes children in his parables and as metaphors in his teachings referring even to babies. But when it comes to the stories of the children whom Jesus heals, the author of the Gospel of Luke seems to have a soft place in his heart for the 'onlies', those children who have no siblings. Three stories in Luke contain an only child: (1) 7.11-17 tells of a widow whose son has died. The narrative does not specify if the son is an adult or a child, but several factors indicate that Luke may be describing at least an adolescent male and not an adult man; (2) 8.40-56 is the story of Jesus raising the daughter of Jairus; and (3) in 9.37-43, a father brings his son, who has an unclean spirit, to Jesus for healing. Even Jesus is depicted as one without siblings in Luke's Gospel.[1]

The context under consideration in this chapter is children in both the first-century world of Luke's Gospel and our twenty-first-century world. My discussion of these passages will engage in an emerging form of biblical interpretation that is referred to as a 'childist' reading. Kathleen Gallagher Elkins and Julie Faith Parker define the term 'childist' as

> interpretation that focuses on the agency and action of children and youth in the biblical text, instead of seeing them primarily as passive, victimized, or marginalized. Along with feminist and womanist approaches to the text, childist interpretation examines the construction and function of certain kinds of biblical characters while challenging traditional hegemonic assumptions. (Elkins and Parker 2016: 425; see also Parker 2013: 16–18)

---

1. I previously published portions of this chapter in *Children in Early Christian Narratives* (London: Bloomsbury/T&T Clark, 2015).

Uncovering the narratives and place of children in the biblical text is a natural extension of my work in feminist interpretation of the Bible, which as Elkins and Parker note shares many of the same concerns as childist interpretation. My interest in children is not just scholarly and theological. I have long been concerned with the welfare of children in our communities and world. I am a white Protestant woman, who grew up and lives in the midwestern region of the United States. I have spent many summers working with children at church and Girl Scout camps, and I have also been an elementary teacher and youth minister. I have also served on the board of a non-profit summer literacy programme for underserved children in Oklahoma. While the organization's central goal is to maintain or increase children's reading ability, it also addresses the urgent need of childhood hunger during the summer months when children are not in school. Oklahoma ranks low among the fifty states on a variety of indicators of childhood health and well-being including food insecurity, children without health insurance, child mortality, and teen pregnancy ('Kids Count Data Center' 2016). It is also a state with a high percentage of adults who consider themselves 'highly religious' (Lipka and Wormald 2016). In this context, what the Gospels say about children should matter a great deal.

To understand particularly what the Gospel of Luke has to say about children, this chapter will proceed as follows: I will discuss the three narratives in Luke's Gospel that have a child or youth as a main character. In the process of discussing each story, I will compare them to one another, demonstrating how the theme of the only child develops through the episodes. The story of Jesus as a boy in the Temple (Lk. 2.41-52) will also factor into the discussion as I compare the boy Jesus to the daughter of Jairus. I will argue that Luke also depicts Jesus as an only child and the resulting implication for the other only children in Luke's Gospel. This discussion will draw upon twenty-first-century understandings of the only child to more fully understand Luke's depiction of Jesus. In the last section of the is chapter, I will discuss several opportunities I have had to read Lk. 9.37-43 with child readers in Oklahoma. The goal here will be to see if these children, reading from their own context, draw similar conclusions about children in Luke as I did through my scholarly, exegetical process.

Jesus' Miracles Involving Only Children

After the infancy narratives and story of Jesus as a boy in Lk. 1–2, the first narrative containing a child or youth occurs in 7.11-17, where Jesus comes upon the funeral procession for a widow's only son. The episode closely resembles the narrative of the widow of Zarephath in 1 Kgs 17.17-24, that Jesus refers to earlier in his sermon at Nazareth (4.25-27). In both stories, a widow's son dies and the respective prophet restores the child to life. Like Elijah before him, Jesus comes into a town and meets a widow at the city gate (1 Kgs 17.10; Lk. 7.11). After Jesus resurrects the son of the widow of Nain, he gives him back to his mother (7.15). This is an explicit allusion to the Elijah narrative, which reports that the prophet does the same thing for the widow of Zarephath (1 Kgs 17.23) (Fitzmyer 1985: 656). However, while 1 Kgs 17.21-23 calls the widow of Zarephath's son a child, Luke does not specify the age of the son of the widow of Nain. Some English translations suggest the son was an adult man; for example, the New Revised Standard Version says, 'a man who had died was being carried out' (Lk. 7.12). However, the Greek simply uses a masculine singular participle, *tethnēkōs*, referring to a male person who has died. Later in the passage, Jesus calls that person *neaniske*, which means 'young man' or 'youth' (7.14). In Acts, Luke calls Eutychus both *neanias* (20.9), a related word which carries the same meaning, and *pais* (20.12), suggesting that at least for Luke the terms are interchangeable. Cornelia Horn and John Martens suggest that Eutychus may have been in his mid-teens (Horn and Martens 2009: 267). Like the two other children whom Jesus heals in Luke, the widow's son is also described with the adjective 'only'. There are several other links between the three healing stories as well, which I will discuss below. Thus, when hearing the account of the only son of the widow at Nain alongside the narratives of two other only children, it is reasonable to assume that Luke was making connections between the three stories, including that the widow's son was a non-adult child.

Jesus is compelled to act out of compassion for the widow (7.13). In the Ancient Near East, the phrase 'widow and orphan' was synonymous with those who were socially underprivileged. In the Hebrew Bible and the broader cultural context, the pair denoted the weak and vulnerable in the society: as a woman whose husband had died, a widow was without a male patron. Thus, the widow was vulnerable to economic, social, and legal difficulties (Galpaz-Feller 2008: 231). The loss of a son impacted a parent's financial future, but the situation was even more dire for a widow. All sons were called upon to care for their ageing parents, but the sons of widows were legally obligated to do so. For a widow to lose her only son would likely have meant the loss of economic security for her. She would be without the security of being a wife or mother (Ringe 1995: 101).

The text, however, does suggest that this widow may have had a support system. A large crowd, who consider it a work of mercy to help bury the dead, was with her (Vogels 1983: 274). Indeed, when Jesus approaches the town, Luke notes that there is both a large crowd with Jesus and a large crowd with the widow. A great number of people are present to witness this mighty act that is about to occur. Jesus meets the mother in the depth of her grief and compassionately bids her 'do not cry', recalling the Sermon on the Plain when Jesus declares that those who weep will laugh (6.21). As such, his words anticipate the boy's healing which is to come; though the mother weeps for her deceased son, soon she will have reason to laugh. This passage is also the first time since the birth narrative that Jesus is referred to as 'Lord'. In 2.11, the angel of the Lord calls Jesus 'the Messiah, the Lord'. In 7.13, the title prepares the audience for the miracle that will follow. Like God, who is also referred to as 'the Lord', Jesus 'will have power over life and death' (Ringe 1995: 101).

The cause of death is not disclosed, but the child is among the many children who died untimely deaths from disease, accidents, or a culture of violence. Yet what begins as a sad tale of death suddenly becomes a story of life (Ringe 1995: 101). When Jesus touches the bier, he issues a simple authoritative command, 'Young man, I say to you, rise!' (7.14). Luke uses forms of both *egeirō* and *anhistimi*, to mean 'raise, lift up' in the usual sense of getting up and going and also in the sense of raising from the dead. In this narrative, Jesus commands the boy to rise using an aorist passive imperative form of *egeirō*. Jesus will also refer to his own resurrection using an aorist passive form of *egeirō* (9.22). Thus, the raising of the young man from the dead anticipates Jesus' resurrection. The young man then sits up and begins to speak, demonstrating that he is alive. Jesus then gives 'him back to his mother' (7.15). While the mother's reaction is not described, the crowd has two reactions: they say, 'a great prophet has risen among us!' recalling the works of Elijah, and 'God has looked favorably on his people' (7.16). The latter are the same words that Zechariah proclaimed following the birth of John (1.68), suggesting a fulfilment of Zechariah's words. This first raising of the dead continues to build themes already established in the Gospel, especially Jesus' identity as a prophet and his ministry to the marginalized, among whom a widow and her son would be counted. It also introduces two themes that will reprise in the next child narrative, the raising of Jairus' daughter: the only child and resurrection.

Luke 8.40-56 narrates the intercalated stories of Jairus, a synagogue leader, coming to Jesus requesting healing for his daughter and a woman who has suffered a chronic medical condition for twelve years, also seeking healing from Jesus. Luke clearly follows Mark's version of the story (Mk 5.21-43), retaining Mark's overall flow and intercalation of the two stories. However, there are some significant differences in the Lukan version, most notably the length. In Luke, the introductory material is shorter, and Jairus does not have direct speech; rather the narrator describes his pleading. Thus, the reader moves quickly to the crux of the matter: Jairus' daughter is near death. Luke then brings the information about the age of the girl from the end of the story to the beginning of the story: she is twelve years old (8.42). In her first-century context, she is nearing womanhood, a girl for whom her parents might expect to arrange a marriage soon.[2] At the same time, Luke also discloses that this girl is her father's only daughter. The Greek does not imply that the man has sons as well, but that this daughter is truly his only child (Fitzmyer 1981: 745). Indeed, that Jairus comes to Jesus seeking healing for his daughter indicates the depth of both his despair and care for his daughter. A man of his status would normally go to an established medical centre or physician for help. Only those who were destitute or did not have the money or leisure to go to the medical centres would search out an itinerant healer for help (Ringe 1995: 123).

With the age of the girl at the beginning of the narrative, the audience may readily make a connection between the girl and the suffering woman: the girl has

---

2. The age was also traditionally associated with the onset of menstruation.

been alive as long as the woman has been ill (8.43). The woman is healed through her own initiative by touching Jesus. Jesus recognizes that someone touched him not so much because he feels the pressure of the touch, but rather because he felt that power had gone out from him (8.45-46).[3] Calling the woman 'daughter', Jesus announces that her faith has made her well, and he sends her on her way in peace. In that same moment, word comes that the younger daughter has died. Now Jesus admonishes Jairus, 'Do not fear, only believe'. While this is the same language that Mark uses, in the Lukan context it echoes the words of the angels in the birth narratives (1.13, 30; 2.10). The references to the infancy narratives in this passage and the story of the widow's son connect both children to the infant and child Jesus. In the next section, I will discuss why Luke ties together the narratives of the infant and child Jesus with the stories of these children whom Jesus heals.

Jesus enters Jairus's house with his disciples Peter, James, and John and the girl's father and mother (8.51). Although Luke does not state that there is a crowd at the house, v. 52 suggests that others are present as well. As with the widow in 7.13, Jesus admonishes them not to weep, for he knows what he is about to do. Jesus takes the daughter by the hand and says, 'Girl, get up!' The girl's breath returns, and the healing restores her to her family and her former life (Fitzmyer 1981: 744). Her parents are astounded at this miracle. Then Jesus tells the parents to give the girl something to eat and to tell no one of this event. As John Carroll remarks, Jesus's command jolts the parents out of their astonishment at the miracle and brings them back into the reality of providing for their daughter's everyday needs (Carroll 2008: 180).

A well-known literary technique that the author of Luke utilizes is pairing. Jerome Kodell describes three forms of what he calls 'exemplary pairs': (1) simple pairs, (2) parallels of people and narrative units, and (3) links between stories/parables and teachings (Kodell 1987: 417). One way in which Luke pairs people is to connect the narratives of male and female characters. Each character's story has a similar theme, and they function to reinforce Luke's central message and make the Gospel appeal to a wider audience. For example, Zechariah receives an announcement from the angel that his wife, who is too old to conceive, will have a child (1.5-20). Then an angel appears to Mary, announcing that she, who is a betrothed virgin, will also conceive (1.26-37). In each case, the story demonstrates the power of God and the faithful human response.

Another such male/female pairing is the narrative of the widow's son with the story of Jairus' daughter. The two stories are connected in several ways: both the son and the daughter are only children; both die and Jesus raises each one. Jesus' power to heal is exercised through his word using a direct address ('young man' and 'child' respectively) and an imperative form of the verb *egeirō* (7.15 and 8.53). Later, this verb also refers to Jesus' resurrection (24.6). Then the young man sits up and begins speaking, demonstrating that he is really alive; and Jesus commands the parents of the girl to give her something to eat, indicating that she is alive as well.

3. The same language is used in the Sermon on the Plain (6.19), which the first two child narratives also reference. This reinforces the connection between this woman and the children whom Jesus heals and Jesus's teachings in the Gospel.

The reaction of those present is awe or amazement. Together, the stories reinforce the life-giving power of Jesus, the power of his word, and his care for children and youth, especially those children who are the only ones in their respective families. They also anticipate Jesus' resurrection. These last two themes – the only child and resurrection – are strengthened through another pairing, which may not be quite as evident as some of the others.

Usually the stories that Luke pairs are in close proximity to one another. Although some material separates the widow's son from Jairus' daughter, the associations are still present. Another example of pairing, which is spread across a broader portion of the Gospel, is the pairing of Jairus' daughter and Jesus. There are several parallels between the two character's narratives evincing the pairing. First, while the story of the twelve-year-old girl is common to all three synoptic Gospels, the story of Jesus as a twelve-year-old boy is unique to the Gospel of Luke. Thus, only Luke contains narratives of both the twelve-year-old boy Jesus and the twelve-year-old daughter of Jairus. Second, Luke refers to both children with the word *pais*. Jesus is called *hō pais* (the boy, 2.43), and Jairus' daughter is called *hē pais* (the girl, 8.51, 54). Luke has redacted Mark's story of Jairus' daughter twice, substituting the neuter *to paidion* (Mk 5.40) with the feminine *hē pais* (Lk. 8.51) and also replacing *korasion* (Mk 5.41) with *hē pais* (Lk. 8.54).[4] These changes make the relationship between the twelve-year-old girl and the twelve-year-old Jesus clearer. Third, both children have a mother and father present in the narrative. While Joseph fades from the Lukan narrative after the episode in the Temple, at that point Jesus still has two living parents. Likewise, when Jesus heals the girl both of her parents are present. For a child to have both parents alive and still married was notable at that time (Betsworth 2015: 14–15). Finally, in both cases the reaction to the event of those present is amazement (2.47; 8.56). In addition, just as the boy Jesus at twelve clearly understands that he has a special relationship to God as his father, this twelve-year-old girl also has a special relationship with God through God's Son, Jesus.

The similarities between Jairus' daughter and Jesus are not limited to the story of Jesus' childhood. The girl is paired with the adult Jesus as well. Most obviously, both are raised from the dead, and the text uses forms of the same word *egeirō* (7.15; 8.53). As the girl is brought back to life, Luke reports, her spirit returned to her (8.55) which is echoed when Jesus gives up his spirit at this death (23.46). When the girl is resuscitated, Jesus commands her parents to give her something to eat (8.56). Likewise when Jesus is resurrected, he eats with his disciples (24.41-42). Finally, the parents' amazement at the miracle is echoed by the disciples' at Emmaus, who tell the stranger that 'some women of our group astounded [amazed] us' (24.22). Thus, the twelve-year-old girl uniquely ties the Gospel together, looking back to Jesus' childhood while looking towards to his death and resurrection.

---

4. Luke also omits a second use of *korasion* (Mk 5.42), using instead a feminine pronoun.

The final child narrative in Luke is the healing of the boy with the spirit in 9.37-43; it also draws upon the theme of the only child. As the scene opens, a crowd meets Jesus coming down from the mountain where he was transfigured before three of his disciples. A man in the crowds shouts to him, begging him to look at his son, his only son. Though Luke does not state the son's age, he refers to the son as *pais*, which is generally considered to be a prepubescent child, twelve or under. The man's plea for his only son is compounded when he describes the boy's affliction: a spirit attacks the child causing him to shriek, convulse, and foam at the mouth. At that time, to have one's only son afflicted by a life-threatening illness could lead to both day-to-day grief for his parents and could also affect their future. An illness like epilepsy with its associated seizures would not only cause distress for the parents concerning the child's well-being and safety. Such a condition could also be a source of shame. Parents might isolate themselves and their child to avoid the public display of a seizure (Neufeld 2014: 66). In the ancient world, a son often lived with or near his parents providing for them in their old age. If the man's son is destroyed by this ailment, the father's future may be at risk as well. Though the father begged the disciples to heal the boy, they were unable to. After expressing frustration at his disciple's faithlessness, Jesus heals the boy out of compassion for the father. The restoration of the boy contains three actions: first, Jesus' rebuke casts out the spirit; second, Jesus heals the boy; and third, he gives the boy back to his father. Following the healing, the reaction of those present is amazement.

This narrative is especially similar to the episode of the widow's son. First, both children are sons, and in general, boys were more valued than girls in the ancient world (Betsworth 2010: 56–9). Second, each boy has only one parent present; the first one has a mother and the second one has a father. This reflects the reality of many children at that time who may have lost a parent. Both of the parents are potentially in a marginalized position. The mother is alone, a widow with no husband and now no son to care for her. The father may feel shame due to his son's condition. Third, in both stories, Jesus gives the child back to the parent (7.15; 9.42). This action links Jesus to Elijah, who also gave a healed child back to his parent. Finally, the reaction of all those present is recorded (7.16; 9.43). Luke's careful and overlapping connections between these three stories reinforces the motif of the only child, which I will continue to explore below. Through these narratives, Luke presents a variety of family constellations – two parents with a son, two parents with a daughter, a widow with a son, a man whose marital status is unknown with a son. Thus the stories reflect the varied structures of families then and now.

Children in the ancient world were, to use Julie Faith Parker's phrase, 'valuable and vulnerable' (Parker 2013). They were valued by both society and their families (Betsworth 2015: 13), yet at the same time, they were vulnerable to abuse, disease, and death by various means. These children in Luke's Gospel clearly exhibit both qualities. They are cherished by their families as their parents' actions demonstrate, and their lives have been affected by disease and death. In the midst of their most vulnerable moments, Jesus comes to them, healing them of their afflictions and restoring them to their families. Together the stories reinforce Luke's message of

Jesus as a saviour of the lowly and marginalized. The question then is why does Luke depict these children as ones without siblings? Why is each child an only child, particularly when the word 'only' is clearly a Lukan addition to the story?

Jesus (and) the Only Child

Generally, commentators discussing these passages note the use of the word 'only' in each narrative. For example, Luke Timothy Johnson observes that 'only' links the three stories together (Johnson 1991: 141, 158). Joseph Fitzmyer states that in 7.12 'only' emphasizes the difficult situation in which the widow finds herself with her only son now dead (Fitzmyer 1981: 658). In the case of the other two narratives, however, Fitzmyer merely notes that Luke adds this element to Mark's version of the stories (Fitzmyer 1981: 743, 806). Neither, however, suggests a reason for the insertion or use of the word. When commenting upon the widow's son, Alan R. Culpepper states Luke does not use 'only son' in a Christological fashion (as John's Gospel does in 1.18) but rather to increase the tragedy of the death of the child (Culpepper 1995: 158). Yet he does not relate it to the other stories either. Carroll does connect the uses of 'only' in all of the stories; he recognizes that by making the children their parents' only child, Luke raises the stakes in each encounter, adding a poignancy to the cures and to the liberation that Jesus effects (Carroll 2009: 181). Indeed, in an era of high child mortality every surviving child was a blessing, but to have an only child survive a threatening illness or demon was perhaps understood as a double blessing.[5] But there is another reason why these children are only children, and it has to do with Luke's portrayal of Jesus.

While the Gospel of John is the only canonical Gospel that refers to Jesus directly as the only son (Jn 1.18), I argue that Luke is trying to make a similar point.[6] The author of the third gospel constructs his depiction of Jesus such that Jesus does not have siblings or rather despite the fact that Jesus has siblings, he is, in fact, portrayed as an only child.[7] To make this argument, I will first examine the birth narrative and Luke's use of the word 'firstborn'. Next, I will discuss the ways in which Luke redacts Mark's material that deals with Jesus' siblings. Finally,

5. See Tob. 8.17, in which Tobit gives thanks to God because Tobias and Sarah have survived a life-threatening situation, praying: 'Blessed are you because you had compassion on two only children'.

6. Technically, Jn 1.14, 18 does not include the word 'son' (*huios*) but it is implied by the use of 'only' (*monogenēs*). For a fuller discussion of this point see Betsworth 2015: 133.

7. I am not arguing that the historical Jesus had no siblings. Given the witness of Mark and Matthew, it is quite likely that Jesus had brothers and sisters. Rather, I am arguing that the author of the Gospel of Luke, for his own literary purposes, sought to depict Jesus as an only child. For a brief summary of the argument for the historical Jesus having siblings, see Dart 2002: 13–14.

I will draw upon present-day studies regarding only children to show that the depiction of Jesus in Luke's Gospel is consistent with the understanding today of only children.

When the third gospel narrates Jesus' birth, Luke describes him as Mary's firstborn (2.7), indicating there were no children born to Mary before Jesus, and thus under Mosaic law he would have the status of the firstborn (Exod. 13.2; Num. 3.12-13; 18.15-16; Deut. 21.15-17). The term also anticipates the dedication of the firstborn in 2.23, which places Jesus in the Temple as an infant where both Simeon and Anna encounter the child (Karris 1990: 683). The use of the word 'firstborn', however, raises a question. If Jesus is the firstborn, does that suggest there were other siblings of Jesus and children of Mary subsequent to Jesus' birth? Not necessarily. While 'firstborn' could imply there was a second born son, it does not require that Mary had more than one child (Johnson 1991: 50). Indeed, as Fitzmyer points out, it does not necessarily mean the firstborn of many. He then notes the use of 'firstborn' in the Psalm of Solomon 18.4 and 2 Esd. 6.58, which adds 'only' to make this point clear (Fitzmyer 1981: 407).

All of the Gospels, however, mention brothers of Jesus. In the synoptics, these brothers first appear in Mk 3.31-35 (Mt. 12.46-50; Lk. 8.19-21).[8] In both Mark and Matthew, Jesus is told that his mother and brothers are outside waiting for him. He responds with a rhetorical question that acknowledges the family members: 'Who are my mother and my brothers?' (Mk 3.33).[9] Jesus looks at those around him and declares that they are his mother and brothers. He then announces that those who do the will of God are his mother, brother, and sister. Luke's version of the episode is later in the narrative sequence than in Mark's Gospel, and it is located in between the raising of the widow's son and Jairus' daughter. Luke omits both Jesus' rhetorical question, 'Who are my mother and my brothers?' and his declaration that those around him are his mother and brothers. Rather, when the Lukan Jesus is told that his mother and brothers are outside, he does not acknowledge them at all. He simply announces, 'My mother and my brothers are those who hear the word of God and do it' (Lk. 8.19-21). In this way, Luke minimizes Jesus' attachment to any siblings.

A second episode in which Jesus' brothers are referred to, this time by name, occurs in Mk 6.3 and Mt. 13.55. In both gospels, Jesus is teaching in the synagogue, and the hometown people are questioning his source of power and wisdom. They are sceptical about him since they know who he is and who his family is. They know the names of his mother, Mary, and his brothers, James, Joses (called Joseph in Mt. 13.55), Judas, and Simon. Jesus' sisters are mentioned as well; however, they are not named in the text. Luke also recounts Jesus' preaching in his hometown synagogue. The people there too are initially amazed at his words. They also

---

8. The Gospel of John also mentions brothers in 2.12 and 7.3, 5, 10, but narratively, these are in a different context.

9. Matthew alters Mark's wording just slightly, 'Who is my mother and who are my brothers?' (Mt. 12.48).

question how this can be since they know him. In Luke, however, they only ask, 'Is not this Joseph's son?' (4.22). There is no reference to Mary or any brothers or sisters. In fact, Luke never names any brothers of Jesus. It seems then, that Luke has painted Jesus' siblings out of the picture or significantly minimized their presence, such that Jesus appears to be an only child.

Indeed, Luke's characterization of Jesus as a twelve-year-old boy in the Temple also points to his status as an only child. Not only are there no siblings mentioned, but the portrayal of Jesus in the Temple also leads to this conclusion. In this scene, Jesus seems to be the only child present, and he is engaging the teachers in discussion. He is depicted as a highly intelligent child, who is comfortable among the adults. He also interacts with his parents more on the level of a peer rather than as a child. When Mary questions Jesus about his actions, he answers in a rather unchild-like fashion, 'Why were you searching for me? Did you not know I must be about my father's affairs?' (2.49).[10] In these ways, his behaviour is consistent with findings today regarding children without siblings. Studies have found higher intellectual scores among children with no siblings than children with siblings. In addition, only children are more likely to be precocious as a result of increased time spent interacting with adults (Falbo 2012: 43). Only children themselves report that their relationship with their parents is similar to a friendship or is almost a peer-like relationship, rather than an authority-based relationship (Roberts and Blanton 2001: 131.) In a variety of ways, then, Luke's portrayal of Jesus in the Gospel is, among other things, as an only child.

Although Luke does not explicitly call Jesus God's *only* son as John does, through Luke's portrayal of Jesus as an only child, he makes a similar claim. Jesus is God's son (Lk. 1.32); God chooses to become incarnate as a human, but not just as an adult as in Mark's Gospel. God also manifests God's self as a child, an only child. In a similar fashion, the adult Jesus chooses to heal not just adults but also children. Like Jesus, each child he heals is an only child. As such, it is not just the child whom Jesus saves when he restores each one to health, but the whole family. The loss of an only child could leave the parent(s) in a more vulnerable position than the loss of one child among many would. These stories about the only child and Jesus then continue to expand the Gospel's interest in the vulnerable, marginal, and oppressed.

Real Children Read Lk. 9.37-43

I will now turn to present-day readers to illuminate this theme of Jesus and the only child further. As I worked on these passages in which Jesus is interacting with a child, I decided to read Lk. 9.37-43 with a variety of children and youth to gauge how those close in age to the boy might understand this story.[11] I worked with five separate groups. Three groups were from two middle to upper middle-class

---

10. My translation.

11. At the time I submitted this chapter, Melody Briggs's book *How Children Read Biblical Narrative: An Investigation of Children's Reading of the Gospel of Luke* was not available. Briggs presents an in-depth analysis of how children read the Bible.

United Methodist churches in the Oklahoma City metropolitan area.[12] The first group consisted of ten youth aged 11–13 years, evenly split between boys and girls, who were all Euro-American. The second group included eleven youth aged 11–14, with eight boys and three girls. One boy was bi-racial while the rest were Euro-American. The third group was a more diverse group in terms of age. There I had seven boys and one girl ranging in age from 5 to 12 years, one Afro-Caribbean boy and the rest Euro-American. The fourth group was at the Salem United Methodist Church in Drummond, Oklahoma, a small rural community with about 400 residents. The children who gathered had come to the church that evening for 'Family Fun Night', which was a community outreach event hosted by the church.[13] The group of eighteen 5–12-year-olds was evenly split between boys and girls, half of them were Euro-American and the other half were Hispanic. I also conducted the same lesson with a first-year liberal arts seminar at Oklahoma City University, in which we were studying children in the Gospels. The thirteen students were all first-semester college freshmen, 18–19-year-olds consisting of one African American male, and twelve females, including a Native American (Kiowa), an African American, and two who identified as bi-racial (African American and/or Native American and/or Euro-American), the others identified as Euro-American. Most of the students were from Oklahoma, though a few were from other western, midwestern, and northwestern states. As mentioned earlier, like many of the participants in the study groups, I am a Euro-American female from a middle-class midwestern background.

With each of these groups, we began the lesson viewing a painting by Harold Copping depicting the boy with the spirit. I asked the groups to describe what they saw and tell me what the story might be. A few of the children and youth knew what story the painting was depicting. Next, I asked one of the participants to read the story and another to summarize it. Then I led the groups through a series of questions about the story, the boy, the father, and Jesus. Finally, I asked the children and youth to use watercolours to paint the most important part of the story. I then asked them to tell me about their paintings.

In each group, some children immediately began interpreting the story from their own context and knowledge base. More than once when I asked what was wrong with the boy, I received the response that he had rabies, since he was foaming at the mouth.[14] One boy reacted to the Copping painting, which depicts most of the figures wearing robes that covered their heads, with the exclamation that 'they are wearing hoodies'. That particular Sunday at his church everyone was invited to

---

12. They were St. Stephen's United Methodist Church in Norman, Oklahoma, and Epworth United Methodist Church in Oklahoma City. I thank Krista Ford Ohne, Hannah Frye, and Trina Bose North for facilitating these gatherings.

13. I thank Shannon Rodenberg for allowing me to join this event.

14. I wondered if there had been a recent increase in rabies in Oklahoma that the kids were reacting to, but that did not seem to be the case.

wear hooded sweatshirts to protest proposed legislation in the state which would have made wearing the hood up on a sweatshirt illegal in some instances.

The children in rural Oklahoma similarly drew upon their own context when hearing this story. The whole lesson was a bit chaotic, since there were eighteen children in a very small room and several of the children had never previously been to the church. But they were all eager to participate, especially when it came time to paint. Most of the group did not paint the story per se, but did in effect re-contextualize it in their own way. I visited the church in late August at the end of a very hot and dry summer in Oklahoma. The church had prayed for rain for weeks (maybe months). Not surprisingly, perhaps, many of the children painted rain and rainbows. They did not need Jesus for physical healing, but they did need Jesus to bring rain. One girl, however, painted a whole line of girls, because she felt that the story of the boy with the spirit needed some girls in it.

Then there was Hannah's picture, which was quite different from the rest. At that time, Hannah was seven years old, and when I asked who in the group was an only child, she immediately raised her hand (several of the other kids claimed to be only children as well, but apparently this was just for the attention value). In keeping with the discussion earlier about only children, Hannah was more verbal than most of the other children in the room. Of course, being seven and processing the Bible primarily on a literal level, when I asked the group why the boy in the story might have called an 'only' son, Hannah offered, 'Because he is!' Her painting though was very interesting. She depicted the moment in the story just as Jesus heals the boy. In the lower right-hand corner was a yellowish blob. When I asked her to tell me about her picture, she confirmed that it was just after Jesus healed the boy. The yellow mass in the corner of the picture, she said, was the demon that had come out of the boy.

An interest in the demon/spirit or the supernatural element in the story was also a theme with the other groups. A younger boy at St. Stephens depicted the demon as an object in his painting similar to Hannah's. One of the girls depicted the spirit as a red flowing line coming out of the boy, and the boy exclaiming, 'Holy Gosh! I'm not epileptic anymore. Wow!' Another girl wrote the verse 'Jesus rebuked the unclean spirit, healed the boy and gave him back to his father' at the top of the page because she felt that was the most important part of the story. She then drew Jesus and the boy with a yellow flash between them labelled 'saving power'. Yet another boy included an abstract blob of colour in between Jesus and the boy, which he labelled as 'Jesus Magic'.[15] He could not fully articulate why that stood out to him or why he had labelled it 'Jesus Magic'.

There was clearly a developmental difference between the younger participants who painted a concrete depiction of the demon and the youth who were becoming

---

15. These four examples occurred in two separate groups, so it was not just a case of the kids copying from one another. That said, there did seem to be a liberal sharing of ideas among the kids in any particular group. For example, in one group of eight children, three painted crosses to depict Jesus.

more abstract in their thinking (i.e. 'saving power' and 'Jesus magic'). Yet even these youth could still participate in or appreciate the cosmic world depicted in the Gospels that includes angels and demons, while many adults in my cultural context often want to explain away these aspects of the stories. Some of the youth, however, had already progressed to a higher level of abstract thinking and were less willing to take the story at face value. In one group, when I asked what was wrong with the boy in the story, a girl appropriately responded, 'He has a spirit'. To that, one of the boys interjected, indignantly, 'He had epilepsy!' I told him that Luke does not call it that, though Matthew's Gospel does. 'Well thank you, Matthew, for being a realist!' he declared.

I shared with one group from St. Stephen's my theory that Luke depicts Jesus as an only child in his Gospel. I also asked both St. Stephen's youth groups why they thought Luke specifically describes the child in each story as an only child. In each group, one youth suggested that Luke was an only child, and that is why he depicted the children in Luke's Gospel as only children. A girl then very thoughtfully added that perhaps Luke portrayed Jesus as an only child so that he (Jesus) could relate better to the children who are only children. She felt there was a deeper connection between Jesus and each child because they were both only children.[16]

This theme of a connection between the children and Jesus was also raised among the college freshmen. They too felt that as an only child Jesus would be able to relate more to the only children. One young woman remarked that the children became his brothers and sisters (cf. Lk. 8.19-21). They had also read the story of the widow's son at the same time as they read the story of the boy with the spirit. As first-year college students, they may have been around the same age as the young man who had died. They thought that perhaps Jesus could relate more to the plight of the widow, since his own mother seems to be widowed by the time Jesus was an adult. Luke mentions Joseph only once after the infancy narrative, and it is as a means to identify Jesus (4.22). The scenes in which Jesus' mother and brothers are calling for him does not mention a father.[17]

---

16. One aspect I wish I would have explored more with the kids was what they thought the boy felt and experienced. I could have asked what they imagine his life was like before and after his encounter with Jesus. This may have yielded further insights about the story and especially the nature of Jesus's interactions with children. I did realize during the lessons that most of the children and youth knew the stories of Jesus in a broad, general sense. However, few knew the stories of Jesus and children beyond the scenes of Jesus blessing the children in the synoptic Gospels (Mt. 19.13-15; Mk 10.13-16; Lk. 18.15-17). I do not fault the children and youth for their limited knowledge. As I have been writing and teaching about children in the Gospels for the past few years, I have discovered that few adults are aware of these narratives.

17. The other gospels seem to corroborate this point; Joseph is not mentioned at all in Mark and is not mentioned in Matthew beyond the infancy narrative.

Conclusion

Reading Luke's stories of children in the context of both the first century and the twenty-first century reveals that these ancient stories may be re-contextualized for present-day readers. Children and youth in the ancient world and today are valued by their families but are also vulnerable to vicissitudes of life. The constellations of families are similar now as they were in the ancient world – some children have both parents living with them, while others have only one parent. Likewise, some parents have several children or only a single child. Luke seems particularly concerned with the families who have only one child. For the parents, especially for the widow, the loss of an only child potentially impacted their future, leaving them in a vulnerable position in their elder years. Jesus, as his mother's only child and God's only son, reaches out to these families and children. As he heals the children, he gathers them into his family as his brothers and sisters. The raising of the widow's son and Jairus' daughter also anticipates the death and resurrection of God's own child, Jesus. Luke's narrative of Jesus as a child also reminds us that God chose to become human not just as an adult but also as a child embracing the low status and powerlessness of children. The children and youth with whom I read these stories made similar connections, demonstrating that young people can draw meaningful conclusions about the biblical text based upon their own experiences and when they are creatively guided through the narrative. The children in Luke are one among the many groups of marginalized persons whom Jesus encounters in the Gospel, but their stories often remain unknown to readers today. Yet like all persons on the margins, then and now, these children also deserve to be seen and heard.

Chapter 2

MASCULINITY IN LUKE-ACTS: THE LUKAN JESUS AND MUSCULAR CHRISTIANITY

Brittany E. Wilson

During the late nineteenth century, a movement known as muscular Christianity found its way into American Protestant popular culture. First propagated by novelists such as Thomas Hughes in Victorian England, muscular Christianity arose in reaction to what some men perceived as the 'feminization' of Protestant Christianity (Hall 1994; Kimmel and Aronson 2004: 557–8). Such men responded to this perceived crisis by valourizing strength and self-control as core values for Christian men and holding up Jesus as the epitome of manly ruggedness. As historian Stephen Prothero relates, muscular Christians maintained that Jesus was not a 'sissified … young man with flabby forearms and a sad expression', but a strong carpenter with 'muscles hard as iron' and 'steel-like nerves' (Prothero 2003: 101–2). Jesus' defining story was not his shameful death on a cross, but his 'heroic' actions of overturning the money tables and conquering his opponents. Books such as Robert Warren Conant's *The Virility of Christ* (1915) and Jason Noble Pierce's *The Masculine Power of Christ, or Christ Measured as a Man* (1912) urged Christian males to 'man up' and be like Jesus (Prothero 2003: 87–123). Like Jesus, Christian men needed to cultivate their physical strength, display their power, and exert their control in the world around them.

Such exhortations for Christian men to be manly are by no means remnants of a bygone era. Muscular Christianity gave birth to Christian athletic and civic organizations that continue to this day, such as the Young Men's Christian Association and the Boy Scouts of America (Macleod 1983). During the latter half of the twentieth century, a resurgence of muscular Christianity manifested itself in associations such as the Fellowship of Christian Athletes and evangelical men's groups such as the Promise Keepers (Ladd and Mathisen 1999; Bartkowski 2004). While predominantly white, evangelical groups like the Promise Keepers were influenced by the secular mythopoetic men's movement, especially the 1990 book *Iron John* by Robert Bly, they retained muscular Christianity's emphasis on Jesus' strength and stoicism. During the twenty-first century, these emphases continued to be disseminated by popular evangelical preachers and writers. Mark

Driscoll, for instance, the former pastor of the Seattle megachurch Mars Hill, was a very public proponent of muscular Christianity until his forced resignation in 2014. Prior to Driscoll, evangelical author John Eldredge promoted a Bly-inspired, adventure-seeking view of Christian manhood in his 2001 bestseller *Wild at Heart*, a book that is now considered a 'classic' by many Christians today (Hall 2016: 53–4). According to Driscoll, Eldredge, and others who perpetuate the tenets of muscular Christianity, the 'real Jesus' is not effeminate or weak or emotional, but a man among men; Jesus is the very embodiment of manliness itself.

In the field of biblical studies, muscular versions of Jesus have also emerged, a not surprising trend, perhaps, given that American New Testament scholars have overwhelmingly been white Protestant males. In scholarship on Luke-Acts, for instance, Jesus and his disciples are often termed 'heroes'; they emerge as triumphant defenders of the faith who perform mighty feats and miraculous deeds (Gaventa 2004: 43–4). Jesus is also specifically portrayed as a 'noble man' who stoically embraces death and triumphantly exerts control during his crucifixion. Jerome Neyrey, for example, writes: 'Jesus … is not a victim, out of control, subject to irrational passion; on the contrary, he is portrayed as practicing virtue … and being *manfully* obedient to God' (Neyrey 1980: 171, emphasis added). Jesus especially evinces such manliness in Luke's Gospel, scholars maintain, for Luke is the most elite of all the evangelists and the one who is most interested in defending Jesus' shameful death before an elite, Gentile audience.

Although many scholars assume that Jesus is an exemplar of an implied manliness, a handful of scholars have turned their attention more specifically to Jesus' masculinity vis-à-vis ancient masculine norms (Moore 2003: 1–22). Such scholars explicitly situate Jesus within his ancient context and ask whether he looks like a manly man or not. In effect, they ask whether Jesus perpetuates ancient – as well as modern – manifestations of muscular Christianity. For some of these scholars, the Lukan Jesus particularly fits the profile of a manly man. Mary Rose D'Angelo and Colleen Conway, for instance, argue that Luke presents Jesus' masculinity in a manner that is comprehensible – and often agreeable – to an elite imperial public (D'Angelo 2002: 44–69; Conway 2008). Despite what would appear to be a growing consensus, however, other scholars, myself included, maintain that the Lukan Jesus in fact problematizes ancient constructions of masculinity (Wilson 2015; 2016: 24–35). The present chapter continues in this vein by nuancing claims that the Lukan Jesus is a manly man according to ancient and modern standards.

To be clear, Luke identifies Jesus as the most important 'man' in his gospel. Like the other evangelists, Luke likens Jesus to masculine forerunners such as Moses, David, and Elijah, and he bestows Jesus with a myriad of masculine titles, such as messiah, prophet, king, saviour, Son of God, Son of Man, and Lord. Like John, Luke also applies the gendered term *anēr* – or 'man' – to Jesus (Lk. 24.19; Jn 1.30; Acts 2.22; 17.31; cf. Eph. 4.13) (D'Angelo 2002: 58–60). Luke further clarifies that Jesus was circumcised, thus clearing up any anatomical questions (Lk. 2.21). Yet while Jesus may be a specifically sexed 'man' in Luke, he often does not adhere to elite representations of masculinity in the Greco-Roman world. Jesus may have the biological markers of manhood, but his life and death do not always fit the markers of elite manhood. In other words, this chapter maintains that Luke does not provide a very 'muscular' looking Jesus.

To unpack this argument, I begin by providing a brief overview of the Lukan Jesus in relation to ancient masculine norms. I then focus more specifically on Jesus' violation of two key masculine markers: his expression of grief and his bodily invasion on the cross. Many ancients thought that tears were the purview of women, and even today there are gendered stereotypes that insist 'real' men don't cry. Many ancients also thought that men were supposed to protect their bodily boundaries, and, once again, the stereotype of the self-controlled, inviolate man still persists to this day. Indeed, both of these stereotypes often find expression in modern manifestations of muscular Christianity. Finally, after discussing Jesus' transgression of these two tenets concerning manly self-control, I reflect on how this transgression may expand our understanding of men and women in Luke-Acts as a whole. Throughout the chapter, I take it for granted that Luke writes from an androcentric perspective. Furthermore, I take it for granted that Luke presents 'man' as the implicit norm throughout his two volumes. I am interested, though, in how Luke presents this norm vis-à-vis his likewise androcentrically oriented contemporaries. Such a question may provide a more fully developed picture of Jesus' masculinity in Luke, as well as gender in Luke-Acts more broadly speaking.

Overview: The Lukan Jesus and Elite Masculinity

In the ancient world, manly men – at least according to elite standards – had to meet two main criteria (Wilson 2015: 39–75). First, 'true' men had to be elite. Status was key in ancient representations of masculinity, and one's relationship to Roman imperial power was also crucial. Slaves, conquered peoples, and so-called barbarians, for instance, automatically failed to qualify as manly men. Second, men had to exercise control over both themselves and others. Maintaining one's manliness meant exercising power, especially with respect to sexual power, paternal power, political power, and military power. In this regard, men were defined in opposition to their ostensible antithesis: namely, women. Women were not typically afforded the overlapping rights of sexual, paternal, political, or military power, and they were often characterized as being – not self-controlled – but out of control. Women could not even control themselves, so elite males wrote, and thus the prerogative of control fell to men, both in terms of self-control and controlling others.

Yet when we compare the Lukan Jesus to these 'manly' markers, it quickly becomes clear that he falls short (Wilson 2015: 192–201, 248–54). First, Jesus is not an elite. Jesus is instead born into a low-status Jewish family, and he is raised in the small village of Nazareth without access to wealth, prestige, or a formal education. Jesus primarily converts low-status Jews living in Galilee and Judea, and he clashes with the religious and political elite throughout his ministry. Jesus is also emphatically a Jew, a member of a conquered people living in the Greek East (Lopez 2008: 26–118). Jesus, as noted earlier, is even circumcised (Lk. 2.21), a unique

Lukan detail that would have been synonymous with castration to many non-Jewish elites (Abusch 2003: 75–86). To Luke's Jewish hearers, Jesus' circumcision would have confirmed his status as a male member of God's covenantal people. But to Luke's Gentile hearers, Jesus' circumcision may have held very different (and unmanly) connotations.

Second, Jesus does not exercise sexual, paternal, political, or military power, at least as conventionally conceived. Jesus himself is not married, and scholars have detected hints of sexual asceticism in Luke's narrative (Allison 1998: 172–216; Seim 1999: 115–25; 2002: 89–105). His own human father, Joseph, is a largely ancillary character who plays no role in physically conceiving Jesus (e.g. Lk. 1.34-35; 3.23). During his ministry, Jesus does not exercise or promote paternal power. Jesus instead leaves behind the traditional household and adopts a life of itinerancy; he is someone who has 'no place to lay his head' (9.58) (Moxnes 2003: 46–71). Jesus also proclaims a different sort of household, known as the fictive family of God (Martin 2006: 106–9). Jesus identifies God as the 'father' of this fictive family, and he defines his fellow family members as those who 'hear and do the word of God' (8.19-21; cf. 11.27-28). Jesus brings division among biological family members (12.51-53), and he instructs his disciples to leave behind – and even 'hate' – their own spouses and families in order to follow him (9.57-62; 14.26).

With respect to political and military power, Jesus is clearly the Davidic Messiah according to Luke (e.g. Lk. 1.32). Jesus, however, is not a Messiah who expels the Romans with military might (Collins 2010: 215–37); Jesus does not conquer the Romans, but instead dies at the hands of the Romans. Furthermore, Jesus does not promote the use of military might or violence. He rebukes the disciple who cuts off the ear of the high priest's slave on the Mount of Olives (22.51), and he reiterates that faithfulness may in fact commit followers to becoming *targets* of violence (e.g. 12.4-12; 21.10-19). According to Luke, followers of Jesus should not exercise violence against others, but they may become the recipients of violence by the political and military powers-that-be.

In sum, Jesus is not a purveyor of masculine power in its traditional forms. All the same, the following question still remains: Does Jesus exercise power over himself? In other words, does Jesus embody manly self-control? Of the synoptics, the Lukan Jesus is most frequently identified as being self-controlled; he is a stoic martyr who dies a heroic death with equanimity.[1] Unlike the Markan Jesus and the Matthean Jesus, the Lukan Jesus masters his emotions and does not endure the same degree of bodily infliction. Jesus does not convey distress on the Mount of Olives (cf. Mk 14.33-35; Mt. 26.37-39), nor does he utter the cry of dereliction on the cross (cf. Mk 15.34; Mt. 27.46). To be sure, Luke presents a more self-controlled Jesus than either Mark or Matthew. At the same time, Luke's presentation of Jesus' control still does not meet the standards of elite masculinity. Let us now examine this

---

1. For an overview of this scholarly trend in studies on the Lukan passion narrative, as well as scepticism towards this trend, see Willert (2011: 17–23).

claim more closely by specifically focusing first on the Lukan Jesus' emotions and second on his bodily violation during his passion.[2]

Tears and Bodily Violation: The Lukan Jesus and Self-Control

According to many elite males in the ancient world, controlling the emotions – or the passions – was an integral part of being manly. The Stoic tradition in particular stressed this need, arguing that men had to exert reason over the soft, 'womanish' emotions in order to achieve the virtuous life (Aune 2007: 48–66; Nussbaum 1994). Cicero, for example, assigns weeping to 'women's nature' (*Tusc.* 2.21.50), and Marcus Aurelius writes that 'anger is as much a mark of weakness as is grief; in both of them men receive a wound, and submit to a defeat' (*Med.* 11.10).

On the one hand, the Lukan Jesus is more emotionally restrained than either of his synoptic counterparts. Luke omits instances of Jesus' love, anger, and grief found in Mark, and he lessens Jesus's distress during the passion narrative (Wilson 2015: 216–8). On the other hand, Luke still describes Jesus embracing a range of emotions throughout his ministry, including compassion, amazement, and exceeding gladness (Lk. 7.9, 13; 10.21). In 12.50, Jesus is also 'distressed', or 'hard pressed' (*sunechomai*), about his forthcoming death. During the Last Supper, Jesus even expresses the cardinal passion of desire. Here Jesus pronounces: 'I have desired with desire [*epithumia epethumēsa*] to eat this Passover with you before I suffer' (22.15). With repetition reminiscent of the Septuagint, Luke emphasizes Jesus' cardinal passion of 'desire' (*epithumia*) and highlights the necessity of Jesus 'to suffer' or *pathein*, a cognate of the word 'emotion', or 'passion' (*pathos*), itself (9.22; 17.25; 22.15; 24.26, 46; Olbricht 1964: 9:904–39).

Jesus' most evocative display of emotion, however, occurs when he first arrives in Jerusalem, the city where he will be crucified. In 19.41, Luke uniquely records that Jesus begins his final days in Jerusalem by weeping. With a brevity akin to Jn 11.35, the only other New Testament reference to Jesus' tears, Luke states that '[Jesus] wept [*eklausen*]' (Lk. 19.41). Unlike John, though, Luke uses the verb *klaiō*, a word that connotes both tears and audible cries (BDAG: 545; Matthews 2013: 384–5). After this audible weeping, Jesus goes on to speak words of lament in the vein of Israel's prophets, especially Jeremiah, the 'weeping prophet' (Fisk 2008: 147–78). Such clear allusions to the Jewish prophetic tradition of lament problematize Shelly Matthews' argument that Jesus' weeping in Lk. 19.41 evokes the manly weeping of Roman generals and other 'great men' (Matthews 2013: 381–403). Here Jesus does not weep as a general over a subjugated city, but as a prophet alongside a subjugated people who lament the loss of their most holy city. Luke even indicates Jesus' sorrowful state by the disjointed, opening words

---

2. For a more in-depth discussion of Jesus' emotions and bodily violation in the Lukan passion narrative, see Wilson (2015: 190–242).

of Jesus' lament: 'If you had known on this day – even you – the things of peace! But now they are hidden from your eyes' (19.42). Jesus' broken syntax very likely reflects the use of aposiopesis, or a breaking off of speech due to strong emotion (Voorwinde 2011: 149–50). Indeed, as Jesus weeps over Jerusalem, he is so upset that he can barely get the words out.

Just as Jesus does not always exercise emotional control, he also does not always exercise corporeal control. Instead, Jesus violates a cardinal rule of ancient masculinity: he fails to protect his bodily boundaries from outside invasion. In the ancient world, only elite males were able to invade the bodies of others, whether they be women, slaves, or non-citizens (Walters 1999: 29–43). Elite males were likewise the only ones legally able to defend their own bodies from invasive assaults, such as being blinded, beaten, and sexually penetrated. True men were 'impenetrable penetrators', to use classicist Jonathan Walter's turn of phrase (Walters 1999: 29–43), and they were supposed to remain in control of their bodies. During his passion, however, Jesus allows his body to be invaded by others. Granted, Jesus is in control of the situation since he goes willingly to his death and permits his crucifixion to occur. But his bodily invasion, according to Luke, becomes the means through which liberation occurs. Luke may not depict Jesus' bodily invasion in the same way as Mark and Matthew, but he still dwells on this invasion during the passion narrative and its divine necessity (Lk. 24.26; Wilson 2015: 227–35).

Near the outset of the passion narrative, Luke uniquely records that 'the men' (*hoi andres*) who hold Jesus in custody are the first to inflict physical and verbal attacks on him. In staccato-like fashion, Luke rattles off the abuse they heap on Jesus: they mock, beat, blindfold, strike, and blaspheme him (Lk. 22.63-65). Of all this abuse, Jesus' beating and blindfolding in particular mark him as unmanly. Beating was a punishment reserved for slaves and other so-called non-men who were characterized by their corporeal vulnerability (Glancy 2010: 24–47). The Roman playwright Plautus indicates that one can recognize a slave by his scarred back (*Amph.* 446), and Luke himself associates beating with slaves earlier in his gospel (Lk. 12.47, 48; 20.10, 11) and with the disciples and other believers later in Acts (Acts 5.40; 16.37; 22.19). Temporarily blindfolding Jesus also robs him of his sight or power 'to gaze', a power that men were assumed to possess in the ancient world (Wilson 2015: 162–71). Sight itself was considered the most powerful, active, and 'masculine' of the senses, yet Jesus' male attackers deprive him of his ability to see. Only three verses earlier, Jesus' piercing stare caused Peter to recall 'the word of the Lord' concerning his betrayal (Lk. 22.61), yet now Jesus' powerful gaze is covered up, thus rendering him powerless (22.64; cf. Mk 14.72).

In addition to physical abuse, Luke also subjects Jesus to the voyeuristic gaze. More than any of the other gospels, Luke positions Jesus as the object of sight. Indeed, in the passion narrative, Jesus' naked body hangs on display as a mark of public shame. Victims of crucifixion were often stripped naked in public before being crucified, and Jesus himself is presumably stripped at some point since Luke, like the other evangelists, depicts Jesus' clothing being divided by lot casting

(Lk. 23.34). What is more, Luke, contra the other evangelists, immediately follows this reference to the division of clothes with the following statement: 'And the people stood watching [*theōrōn*]' (23.35). Such a detail heightens the public nature of Jesus' shame since 'the people' (*ho laos*) stand gazing at his naked body hung high for all to see. Even Jesus' followers and acquaintances stand at a distance 'to see [*horōsai*] these things' (23.49), and Luke terms Jesus' entire crucifixion a 'viewing', or 'spectacle [*theōrian*]' (23.48). Whereas Jesus' gaze earlier caused Peter to dissolve into tears (22.61-62), Jesus is now the object of other people's sight. Not only did Jesus lose his ability to see by being blindfolded (22.64), now he is the spectacle itself.

Finally, Luke indicates that Jesus' bodily boundaries are broken by being nailed to the cross. Victims of crucifixion were either tied or nailed to crosses in the ancient world (e.g. Pliny, *Nat.* 28.11.46), and Luke – along with John – suggests that Jesus was affixed to the cross by nails. Luke and John reveal this detail after the crucifixion in an encounter between the resurrected Jesus and his disciples (Lk. 24.36-43; Jn 20.19-29). In Luke, Jesus commands his disciples to 'look at my hands and my feet', and he then shows them his hands and feet (Lk. 24.39-40). Such a display suggests that his hands and feet were pierced during the crucifixion and that the marks of the nails are still visible. While Jesus hangs on the cross for all to see, phallic-like objects penetrate his flesh, thus mirroring the symbolic penetration of his bodily boundaries throughout the passion narrative.

Overall, Jesus does not conform to the protocols of elite masculinity. Jesus is born into a low-status family, and he advocates unconventional 'family values'. Jesus is conceived without male penetrative power, and, as a sexual ascetic, he does not exercise his own penetrative power. Jesus mainly associates with Jewish peasants, and he criticizes the religious and political powers-that-be. He reneges violence and warns followers that they, like him, may experience violence. He at times evinces strong emotions, such as weeping, and he allows his body to be beaten, blindfolded, stripped, gazed upon, and penetrated with nails. In Luke's Gospel, both male and female followers are called to follow Jesus, but Jesus himself does not follow the parameters of elite masculinity.

Men and Women in Luke-Acts: The Lukan Jesus and Gender

Luke's picture of an 'unmanly' Jesus has ramifications for his depiction of men and women in his larger narrative. In regard to weeping, Luke does not criticize tears elsewhere in his gospel, even though Stoic philosophers and other elites often cautioned men not to succumb to the emotion of grief (e.g. Diogenes Laertius, 7.111-112; Cicero, *Tusc.* 3.7.14; 12.27; 4.6.14; Philo, *Spec.* 2.30, 157; Plutarch, *Mor.* 101F–122A; Seneca, *Ep.* 63.13; Sir. 30.21, 23; 38.18). Instead, Luke depicts weeping – by both men and women – as an appropriate response to tragic situations, especially death.

In addition to Jesus, those who weep in Luke include the widow of Nain who weeps over the death of her only son (Lk. 7.11-17), the so-called sinful woman who bathes Jesus' feet with her tears (7.36-50), a crowd that weeps over the synagogue leader Jairus' only daughter (8.49-56), Peter who cries bitterly after he denies Jesus (22.54-62), and the weeping 'daughters of Jerusalem' (23.27-31). With respect to the sinful woman, or the woman who 'loved much' as Jesus calls her, Jesus commends her actions, including her tears, and holds her tears up as an exemplar to the male Pharisee Simon (7.44). With respect to those weeping over the death of an only child, Jesus tells them *not* to weep before he raises the child from the dead (7.13; 8.52). Jesus' words here, however, do not function to critique the act of weeping, but to signal that their tears are no longer necessary. Weeping is an appropriate response to death, but Jesus is about to raise the children from the dead. Jesus' words to the widow of Nain are specifically motivated by his compassion (7.13), and they recall his earlier words during the sermon on the plain: 'Blessed are those who weep now, for you will laugh', but 'woe to you who are laughing now, for you will mourn and weep' (6.25; cf. 8.52-53). (Indeed, 'weeping', along with 'gnashing of teeth', characterizes those thrown out of God's kingdom in 13.28.)

Yet in addition to the loving woman, grieving widow, and crying crowd, Luke also depicts Peter – Jesus' most prominent male disciple – as weeping. Aside from Peter's appearance in the textually disputed 24.12 and an indirect reference to him in 24.34, the last we see of Peter in Luke's Gospel is in Chapter 22, when he exits the scene 'weeping bitterly' (22.62). Peter denies knowing Jesus three times (22.56-60), and Jesus' piercing stare causes Peter to remember that Jesus foretold this denial, a remembrance that incites his onslaught of tears (22.61-62).

Of all the tears shed in Luke, though, Jesus' tears most parallel the tears shed by the weeping daughters of Jerusalem in Luke 23. Here Jesus addresses a group of women who follow behind him on the way to the cross, beating their breasts and wailing for him (23.27). Jesus turns to them and says:

Daughters of Jerusalem, do not weep [*klaiete*] for me, but weep [*klaiete*] for yourselves and your children, because, behold, the days are coming in which they will say 'Blessed are the barren and the wombs that have not given birth and the breasts that have not given suck.' (23.28-29)

Jesus' directive echoes his own weeping over Jerusalem in Chapter 19, when he foretold the coming destruction of the city and her children using the same verb *klaiein* 'to weep' (19.41, 44). According to Luke, the women are not to weep for Jesus, but to join Jesus in his weeping for the inhabitants of Jerusalem; they are to emulate Jesus' own earlier weeping (Spencer 2004: 129–35; Wilson 2015: 223–4).

In sum, both women *and* men weep in Luke. Luke does not portray male weeping as an act that impinges on a man's manhood, and he often depicts weeping in terms of gendered parallels. The loving woman's tears parallel Simon the Pharisee's lack of tears, the widow of Nain's grief over her only son parallels the grief over Jairus and his wife's only daughter, and the daughters' of Jerusalem weeping parallels Jesus' weeping lament over Jerusalem. Controlling the emotions – especially the emotion of grief – was a frequent mandate among elite males (especially in philosophical discourse), but Luke does not appear to have this mandate in view. Instead, Luke falls within a tradition of depicting male and female tears as an appropriate response to death and other lamentable events (see Fögen 2009).

Both women and men cry in Luke, and in Acts, men cry more so than women. In Acts, widows weep over the death of the disciple Tabitha (Acts 9.39), but 'devout men' make 'loud lamentation' over the martyr Stephen when they bury him (8.2). Furthermore, Paul himself twice recalls his tears in his farewell discourse to the Ephesian elders (20.19, 31), and this discourse concludes with collective male weeping, grieving, embracing, and kissing (20.37-38). The only potentially critical account of tears occurs in Acts 21.13, when Paul chastises those in Philip's home – presumably both men and women – for weeping. Paul rebukes those weeping, however, because their crying is 'breaking his heart' and he does not want to be deterred from his journey to Jerusalem, a journey that Paul knows will most likely end in his death (21.13). Yet aside from this unspecified group who are breaking Paul's heart and the weeping widows, men are the ones who predominantly shed tears in Acts.

In regard to bodily penetration, Luke, of course, does not narrate the bodily penetration of any other character – male or female – to the degree he narrates Jesus' passion and crucifixion. At the same time, it is striking that those whose bodies are inflicted by an outside source in Luke are almost univocally *men*. For example, a male slave has his ear cut off on the Mount of Olives (Lk. 22.50), and two male criminals – literally 'evildoers' – are crucified on Jesus' left and right (23.33). Jesus' parables also feature males who experience bodily infliction. In the parable of the good Samaritan, for example, a man is stripped, beaten, and abandoned half dead (10.30). In the parable of the wicked tenants, the tenants beat the vineyard owner's two slaves and kill his son (the latter a clear allusion to Jesus) (20.9-19).

To be clear, men are not the only ones to experience bodily vulnerability in Luke. In a series of sayings about watchful slaves in Luke 12, Jesus mentions a slave who beats his fellow slaves, including both male and female slaves (Lk. 12.45). Jesus also talks about the destruction of cities such as Jerusalem and the residents therein – residents that include women, as his words to the daughters of Jerusalem indicate (23.28-31; cf. 10.11-16; 13.1-5, 31-35; 17.20-37; 19.41-44; 21.5-38). Moreover, Jesus speaks about future persecution (12.57-59; 21.12-19), and we see in Acts that this persecution includes women since Paul – also known as Saul – drags off 'both men and women' to prison (Acts 8.3; 9.2; 22.4).

At the same time, Luke more frequently portrays the invasion of male bodies in his narrative. In Acts, men are the ones who typically have their bodies invaded via beatings and death. Stephen, for example, becomes the first Christian to be killed (Acts 7.54-8.1), and James the brother of John is killed with the sword (12.2). Paul's travelling companions are dragged into a theatre (19.29), and Paul himself repeatedly suffers corporeal violation through being stripped, stoned, beaten, and imprisoned (14.19; 16.22-24; 21.27–28.31) (Wilson 2016: 141–53).

Luke especially portrays such male corporeal violation through the inclusion of punitive miracles, an inclusion that is unique among the four evangelists (Wilson 2015: 79–112, 154–89). Luke in fact begins his gospel with a punitive miracle in the story of Zechariah, the father of John the Baptist. In a surprising turn of events, Zechariah – a seemingly praiseworthy male – is silenced by the angel Gabriel (Lk. 1.5-23). Gabriel takes away Zechariah's ability to speak (a male prerogative in the ancient world), and Zechariah does not regain his ability to speak until he demonstrates his dependence on God.

Zechariah's silencing is the first of seven punitive miracles that Luke records in his two volumes, the other six all occurring in Acts. In Acts, the recipients of these punitive miracles are almost always men: Ananias and Sapphira mysteriously drop dead after withholding a portion of their land sale (Acts 5.1-11), Paul is blinded by Jesus on the way to Damascus (9.1-9), Herod is struck down by an angel of the Lord (12.20-23), Bar-Jesus is blinded by 'the Lord' via Paul (13.4-12), and the sons of Sceva are physically overpowered by a demon (19.11-20). Of this group, of course, the one woman who receives a punitive miracle is Sapphira. Yet Sapphira arguably receives this fate for consenting to Ananias's leadership (5.1-2). In Acts 5.3-4, Peter addresses Ananias alone, but in Acts 5.8-9, he consistently addresses Sapphira in relation to her husband. Sapphira, then, does not appear to exert her own initiative, but follows her husband's initiative regarding the land sale and its proceeds. Ananias – who is apparently someone of means since he has property to distribute – finds good company with the other powerful men who receive divine infliction, for the other men are either political and religious leaders or magicians who wield their own brand of power. All of these men attempt to encroach on God's power (Lk. 1.20; Acts 5.3-4; 9.4-5; 12.21-23; 13.6-11; 19.13-16) and are thus 'taken down' as a result.

On the one hand, Luke's predominant focus on male bodily violation may simply be indicative of his overall androcentric orientation. But on the other hand, Luke's focus may also suggest that men are the ones who most need to renege the traditional trappings of power. In both the ancient world and today, men are the assumed purveyors of power, at least in relation to women. But in Luke, men are the ones who repeatedly encounter God's power by losing their own assumptions of power. Punitive miracles are directed towards men such as Paul and Herod because such men are the ones who need to be reminded of their place in the cosmic hierarchy. Persecution, then, may be experienced more so by men because the loss of male bodily control signifies a reversal of gender norms and thus a reversal of power norms. Such a reversal would not necessarily be communicated if the subjects were women; instead, women and others on the margins of traditional power often exemplify the dependence on God that Luke deems faithful. Luke, for example, lifts up Jesus' mother Mary as an exemplary believer (e.g. Lk. 1.38, 42-45), and Luke situates servant-like behaviour as the model of discipleship (e.g. 22.24-27). Overall, men (or at least men with power) are called to be more like those on the margins and to follow in the footsteps of Jesus, who is himself the epitome of powerless power. According to Luke, Jesus is not manly, but a servant who reigns; he is a 'man' crucified on a cross; he is a paradox of lowly power.

Conclusion: The Lukan Jesus and Muscular Christianity

In conclusion, looking at Luke through the lens of ancient masculinity can produce potentially far-reaching results. Such a focus situates Jesus with respect to ancient gender norms and illuminates portrayals of both women and men in Luke-Acts. This depiction in turn can enable us to question how gender relations should function in our different contexts today. In this brief survey, we have seen that the Lukan Jesus looks remarkably unmanly when compared to ancient elite constructions of masculinity, constructions that find many parallels in modern-day expressions of muscular Christianity. Although Luke is arguably the most elite of all the canonical gospels, the Lukan Jesus does not easily align with elite masculine norms. Indeed, both women and men are called to emulate Jesus, but manliness is not the ideal towards which they are to aspire.

First, we have seen that Luke does not perpetuate elite rhetoric that identifies weeping as a womanish failure. Luke instead presents weeping as a valid, scriptural expression of grief that connects one to Jesus. Ancient and modern assumptions that men should not cry find no place in Luke-Acts. Jesus himself weeps loudly in Luke, and both men and women follow in his footsteps. Second, we have seen that Luke more frequently depicts men losing bodily control. Such loss of control intersects with Luke's understanding of discipleship and of Jesus' paradoxical power. In Luke, neither men nor women are called to be manly, but men are specifically called to be lowly. In our own context, Luke's male-oriented directive to renege power in fact finds good company with a long-standing feminist – as well as womanist and Latina – refrain. Feminist, womanist, and Latina theologians, among others, have emphasized that the call to 'carry one's cross' should be directed more towards those who are typically in positions of power: namely, men.[3] Cross-carrying, so the argument goes, has tended to fall along gendered lines, with women bearing the brunt of the heavy lifting. Instead of sacralizing women's bodily violations, whether it be in situations of domestic violence or systemic injustice, the ones who need to renege power are those who actually have power to renege. With Luke's narration of men whose bodies are violated in ways often restricted to women, twentieth- and twenty-first-century arguments regarding gender and power find surprising points of correspondence.

Overall, attending to masculinity in Luke helps us to unravel Luke's configuration of gender more broadly. For Luke, men are not to exert control over themselves and others, but to recognize that God is ultimately in control. The disposition of discipleship is not manly self-control, but the so-called feminine posture of dependence on the divine. Men are to emulate the weeping, cross-bearing Jesus who is the embodiment of God's powerless power. According to Luke, a 'muscular Christianity' is in fact antithetical to the gospel. Indeed, according to Luke, Jesus himself shows strength in weakness, power in powerlessness, and triumph in defeat.

---

3. See, for example, the classic article by Saiving (1960: 100–12). See also Reid (2007) and Terrell (2006: 19–49).

Chapter 3

VOLUNTARY ACTIVE EUTHANASIA AND THE LUKAN JESUS

James A. Metzger

Although I have recently been treated for stage IV non-Hodgkin's lymphoma, early scans suggest that I am in remission. However, because the disease may recur at any time, and because the cell-type with which I was diagnosed is uncommonly aggressive, developing a tentative ethical response and concrete plan of action remains a matter of some urgency. While I turned first to academic literature on euthanasia for insight as to how to formulate such a response, my scope soon broadened to include journalistic essays, illness narratives, documentary films, and even fictional characters. This chapter constitutes part of my larger project to prepare a morally sound course of action should the cancer return, and I do so by posing a rather straightforward question: Might Luke's protagonist allow for voluntary active euthanasia[1] in extremis, or might he endorse Christianity's traditional stance, which (generally) has been to prohibit suicide under any circumstances, no matter how much pain an individual may be in? The results proved surprising: theologians and ecclesiastical authorities, I suggest, would be hard-pressed to claim the Lukan Jesus as yet one more staunch advocate for the church's historic position on elective death. Given the depth of compassion that the protagonist shows for the chronically ill and disabled, it is hard to imagine that he would ask them to endure intractable pain and/or loss of bodily integrity

---

1. By voluntary active euthanasia, I mean a 'case in which a competent patient makes a fully voluntary and persistent request for aid in dying' (Brock 1992: 10–22), generally as a consequence of unbearable and irremediable suffering. One might classify it as a type of 'instrumental suicide' (Wood 1980: 151–60) by which someone aims to shorten the duration of his or her suffering and/or to avoid an unacceptable loss of autonomy or bodily integrity. Some philosophers and physicians have challenged the distinction between active and passive euthanasia, and although I find their criticisms persuasive on the whole, I will continue to use the traditional distinction in this chapter so as not to overcomplicate matters. For the most widely anthologized challenge to this distinction, see James Rachels's 'Active and Passive Euthanasia' (1975: 78–80).

until certain disease processes should run their full course and bring all neural and physiological function to an end.

Contributors to this volume take for granted that the search for objectivity in biblical interpretation is now over. Hermeneutics is invariably shaped by contextual factors such as family of origin, educational background, socio-economic status, race, gender, sexual orientation, religious affiliation (or lack thereof), and so on. The so-called postmodern turn has shifted our focus from text to reader, from artefact to subject. The long-standing, venerable distinction in biblical studies between exegesis and eisegesis, as Fernando Segovia has observed, has 'altogether collapsed', so that one might even go so far as to say that 'exegesis [is] ultimately eisegesis' (2000: 152).

Given our commitment not merely to acknowledging but to *embracing* the role of context in interpretation, I begin by introducing (1) a recent encounter with a potentially fatal disease that ultimately led to the selection of this particular topic; (2) my current ethical response to a possible relapse as well as the theoretical approach upon which it is based; and (3) the hermeneutical vantage point from which I interpret the biblical writings generally. In the second section of the chapter, I turn to the Gospel itself in search of clues that might help us draw a well-informed conjecture about how the Lukan Jesus might respond to someone whose suffering has become grievous and irremediable. In particular, I explore Jesus' overall world view, his understanding of the human self, as well as the feelings he seems to have for those who suffer from chronic illnesses and/or disability. I will suggest that these three features, when taken as a whole, may put Jesus at odds with the church's historic stance against active euthanasia. I conclude by addressing what the results of this study have contributed to my own emerging perspective on euthanasia, although especially within the context of terminal illness coupled with the prospect of a rapidly diminishing quality of life.

Context: Diagnosis, Ethical Response, and Hermeneutical Vantage Point

Non-Hodgkin's Lymphoma and Its Aftermath

Two years ago, during halftime of the Carolina-Duke basketball game, the upper abdominal pain I had been experiencing for about two months abruptly surpassed what I was able to tolerate. So, off to the emergency room we went. After what seemed an interminable amount of gratuitous poking and pressing upon a very tender and distended abdomen, the physician assigned to my case finally ordered a CT scan, which revealed numerous lesions in the liver. I was written prescriptions for oxycodone and tramadol, then instructed to follow up with my primary care doctor as soon as possible.

The following week, results from a liver biopsy and several imaging tests offered a clear reason for the pain: non-Hodgkin's lymphoma. Since the diagnosis, I've completed a standard course of chemotherapy (commonly known by the acronym R-CHOP), and the most recent PET/CT scan suggests that I am in remission.

Given how far the cancer had spread – once it reaches a major organ like the liver, physicians automatically classify NHL as 'stage IV' disease – I consider myself lucky to be alive.

Since completing R-CHOP, however, I've been trying to resolve complications both from the lymphoma and the chemotherapy. Treatment for a pre-existing autoimmune illness known as ankylosing spondylitis (AS)[2] has resumed, albeit in abridged form (and that only after a little pleading on my part), so at least my rheumatic symptoms are stable once again.[3] But chronic abdominal pain, distension, and lymphedema persist, presumably because of long-term damage to the liver and lymphatic system. A recent liver biopsy has showed 'extensive fibrosis, necrosis, and scattered inflammation', and scans have consistently shown evidence of ascites, but thankfully no signs of relapse. After more than a year of searching for ways to resolve pain in the upper abdomen, I've finally conceded that this, too, will probably be a lasting, perhaps even permanent, part of my life. Some days bring intense pain, and it's not clear to me why this is so, or whether there may be triggers over which I might exercise at least some control. My physicians have given me a number of medications to experiment with, and they do help. But they offer only a temporary reprieve that allows me to take in a full meal, and therefore to maintain a normal BMI. They do not alter any fundamental anatomical or biochemical changes resulting from the cancer or chemotherapy. Regeneration of the liver will take time, and whether this regenerative process ultimately will help diminish the pain and distension to a satisfactory level is hard to say. With a little luck, maybe it will, and life won't feel so much like a duty, or even a sentence.

Formulating a Tentative Response: A Utilitarian Approach to Elective Death

In addition to addressing complications from the chemotherapy, I've spent a fair amount of time considering what I might do if the cancer should return. At the moment, I am strongly disinclined to pursuing what are commonly called 'salvage therapies', high-dose chemotherapy regimens followed by autologous stem cell transplants. As with R-CHOP, cure remains the aim, but it is a far less likely outcome, and the side effects are much worse. A large majority who pursue these therapies end up merely extending their lives, sometimes by many years, but not without exacting a rather high toll. Eventually, the disease wins.

I am not persuaded that salvage therapy would yield both a cure *and* a satisfactory quality of life afterwards. I have always been temperamentally inclined to following

---

2. AS is an autoimmune disease that causes inflammation to the spine and one or (more often) several joints. For many, however, various soft tissues – the eyes or gastrointestinal tract, for example – may be involved as well.

3. It is possible that the TNF blocker I was on for AS contributed to my developing lymphoma, so my rheumatologist was reticent to restart the medication when pain and swelling reappeared just a few weeks after completing chemotherapy. We tried other options first, but none seemed to have much of an effect on my symptoms.

probability rather than to 'beating the odds', and probability in this case strongly suggests that I will not be the one of, say, seven or eight who try it and manage to achieve both aims. Chances are that even if I do obtain a cure on a second attempt, I will be in far worse shape afterwards than I am now, and that is not a life I want. As it is, I spend far too much time managing pain, far too little time actually living.

My desire, then, should the cancer return, would be to opt for palliative or single-agent chemotherapy that helps reduce tumour burden, or even just slow tumour growth, and to continue pursuing this option as long as the side effects do not outweigh the benefits. Once the side effects exceed the benefits, I would begin making preparations to actively end my life, most likely through a combination of self-starvation (VSED)[4] and a high dose of opioids. But this is merely *my* wish, and because I happen to be a utilitarian, it is imperative that I take into account others' needs and preferences as well, especially when making a decision of this magnitude.

Although utilitarian philosophers have developed an array of attractive models, the approach towards which I gravitate is based on two fundamental principles. First, I take for granted that each individual generally ought to be free to satisfy her own preferences, so long as she does not harm or unduly impede others in pursuing their own preferences. This conviction is based both on Kantian respect – people ought to be treated as ends in themselves and never only as a means – and the assumption that greater autonomy generally yields greater well-being. Second, with John Stuart Mill, I hold that government ought not to prohibit or overregulate self-regarding behaviours that do little or no harm to others, even when many might consider these behaviours to be self-destructive, or at least not in a person's best interests. Government certainly may tax self-destructive or risky behaviours for which we all pay (consumption of nicotine or alcohol, for instance), but an individual ought nevertheless be free to engage in self-harm, so as long as others' basic rights are not unduly impeded in the process. The latter is sometimes referred to as the 'harm principle', which Mill himself put in the following way:

> The only purpose for which power can be rightfully exercised over any member of a civilized community, against his will, is to prevent harm from others. His own good, either physical or moral, is not sufficient warrant. … The only part of the conduct of anyone for which he is amenable to society is that which concerns others. In the part which merely concerns himself, his independence is, of right, absolute. Over himself, over his own body and mind, the individual is sovereign. (qtd. in Groll 2014: 198)[5]

---

4. The acronym stands for 'Voluntary Stopping of Eating and Drinking', and is recommended by several reputable organizations (e.g. Compassion & Choices) to terminally ill individuals who do not have access to physician-assisted suicide. It is advised, however, that the process be undertaken in consultation with a physician while under hospice care.

5. The utilitarian approach to which I generally subscribe is a form of 'preference utilitarianism', and therefore similar in kind to that employed by Peter Singer in his article on voluntary euthanasia (2003: 526–41).

How might these two principles shape my stance towards voluntary active euthanasia? Put simply, when faced with a case of irremediable and unbearable suffering, an individual generally ought to have the freedom to determine the time, means, and circumstances of her death, so long as others are not unduly harmed or thwarted in pursuing their own aims as a result. I therefore see elective death as a natural right[6] that ought to be readily available to all competent adults who have tried to resolve or acclimate themselves to their pain but still find it intolerable.[7]

Ideally, though, we ought to press beyond this minimum criterion and do whatever we can to maximize the well-being of any who may be affected by our actions. The right to terminate one's life is constrained in particular by weighing how one's decision is likely to affect those to whom one is obligated in the most significant ways. For me, this happens to include both my spouse and son. Because my death would have the greatest impact upon their future well-being, their needs and preferences remain paramount. While my friends, siblings, mother, and colleagues would be saddened by my passing, at the moment an early exit would not so significantly diminish the quality or course of their lives that I should be required to relinquish my right to a peaceful and dignified death. I would not expect any of them to endure unreasonably burdensome treatments merely on my account, and my hunch is that they would not expect that of me either. As a general rule, I think it's fair to say that transient sadness *alone* does not offer sufficient justification to curtail or withdraw any terminally ill individual's right to active euthanasia.

With my immediate family, however, the consequences of an early departure would far exceed short-lived melancholy. Just as I depend upon each of them in innumerable ways, they, too, depend upon me. For instance, I currently provide about half of our family's income, and I offer both a degree and kind of companionship that would not easily be replaced by someone else. This is not to say that they would fail to adjust successfully to my absence over time and go on to lead productive, rewarding, and happy lives. I'm quite confident they would. But because the contractual and covenantal obligations I currently hold towards them far outweigh any obligations I maintain towards other individuals

---

6. When we decide to call something a natural right rather than a mere liberty right, we are also saying that society has an obligation to create opportunities for citizens to exercise this right. For a concise discussion of the differences between these two types of rights, see Battin (1995: 180–97).

7. Practically speaking, this minimally would entail making available the means to a peaceful and dignified death, ideally in the form of a drug that acts quickly and reliably without causing pain. Physician-assisted suicide of the kind now available in a few states offers one reasonable option of providing access to such means, although I would gladly endorse far more permissive varieties of euthanasia legislation such as the Dutch law, which includes no requirement that one have a terminal illness and allows for unbearable suffering that is primarily physical, emotional, or even existential in nature.

or organizations, it is these obligations that concern me most. My death would affect them in significant ways that would alter the course and quality of their lives.

What criteria, then, might I need to meet before pursuing the option of elective death? I think it would depend chiefly upon whether (1) I have met, or could continue to meet, obligations that I still reasonably can be expected to fulfil given certain limitations brought on by the illness; (2) my wife should choose to release me from, or to hold me accountable to, any of these outstanding obligations; (3) I am able to retain enough normal neural function and equanimity to remain the unique person my wife and son have come to know and value; and (4) some very great harm might still be averted by enduring a level of suffering I find unacceptable (say, because a life insurance company has threatened to withhold a payout).

Because my son is still too young to fully grasp the circumstances of what is at stake here, I would need my wife's consent in particular in order to move forward with palliative treatment and altogether jettison low-yield salvage therapies. At some point, she would willingly have to set me free from any further duties that I might reasonably be able to fulfil. If she is unable to do so, then a decision for palliative chemotherapy, at least when considered within a utilitarian framework, is much harder to justify. But we have been married sixteen years now, so I have a strong feeling that she would respect my wishes. I might also add that my wife happens to have an optimistic temperament, a strong network of healthy relationships, and extensive training in psychology and counselling. Should I reach a point where I develop a desire to bring about a permanent end to consciousness and choose to act upon that desire, I find it highly unlikely that she would subsequently fall into an irremediable clinical depression that would prohibit her from fulfilling her parental and professional duties. Admittedly, it is difficult to gauge the effect of a father's premature death on a young child, but our son at the moment happens to be emotionally healthy and resilient, the beneficiary of several close friendships, and involved in several extracurricular activities. The likelihood that he would suffer some utterly catastrophic or debilitating psychological trauma as a consequence of my early departure that would forever derail his chances at happiness is, at least in my view, quite low.

Divorce, which has become an acceptable (if sometimes still unfortunate) option for most Americans, offers a fitting parallel here. Consider, for instance, the effects of a separation on a young child in which the father elects (or perhaps is forced) to play a very minor or even nonexistent role in the child's future. While the consequences would vary widely and depend upon an array of complex psychosocial factors, the father's future absence would not *inevitably* lead to a diminished quality of life for the child. Many children who have experienced the loss of a father through a divorce in which the father severs virtually all ties to his former family have gone on to lead very rewarding lives. I am not convinced that a father's death is necessarily more traumatic than a divorce of this kind. In fact, divorce introduces a whole new set of logistical and psychosocial challenges that death does not, especially in cases where the parents live far apart and whose dysfunctional relationship continues to adversely affect the child's emotional well-being.

Although space does not permit a full treatment of the impact of the cost of pursuing salvage therapy, I do wish to point out that it must be taken into account when employing any utilitarian approach, in spite of most American physicians' reluctance to do so. Among all alternatives, salvage therapy is far and away the most likely option to adversely affect the family's future financial well-being. No salvage therapy is likely to work, and even if it should manage to forestall death for many months or years, chances are that it will (1) not lead to a cure; and/or (2) leave the patient with additional, and perhaps disabling, complications that only further diminish his well-being. In certain cases, salvage therapy may leave the patient so incapacitated that he ends up consuming far more of the family's resources than he is able to bring in. Although matters related to cost are often sidestepped in the United States, partly because most citizens (at least profess to) believe that every human life possesses inestimable value and is therefore worth our every effort to save it, from a utilitarian perspective, these matters must be given serious consideration.

I have included this lengthy section because I think it is only fair that the reader know where I currently stand on active euthanasia and how I arrived at this position. Nevertheless, as noted above, this stance remains tentative. I am always looking for additional interlocutors who may offer further insight.

Hermeneutical Vantage Point: Reading the Bible as a Humanist

Although five states now grant physicians the right to assist the terminally ill in dying with dignity, voluntary active euthanasia still bears a heavy stigma in the United States. It is generally viewed as an option pursued only by the faint of heart, the lonely or depressed, or those sadly misguided humanists who believe they have every right to dispose of their lives as they see fit, so long as they bring no significant harm upon others. While recent polls attest to rapid disaffiliation from traditional religious communities, especially among the so-called Millennials,[8] religious language to a great degree still determines how we think and speak about euthanasia.

For instance, many American Christian communities often claim that human beings are unique among Earth's inhabitants in having been created in God's likeness and endowed with souls capable of surviving the death of the body. As the apple of God's eye, the crown of all creation (Gen. 1.26-31), there is not one among us who hasn't been assigned a special place and purpose in this world, not one whose every hair has not been numbered (Mt. 10.30; Lk. 12.7). Because we have been fashioned lovingly in the womb by a deity who promises to watch

---

8. Nearly 23 per cent of Americans now report being unaffiliated with any religious tradition. See, for instance, the results of the recent – and now widely cited – poll conducted by the Pew Research Center (Religion & Public Life). Their written report, titled 'America's Changing Religious Landscape', was first released on 12 May 2015, and may be viewed online at: http://www.pewforum.org/2015/05/12/americas-changing-religious-landscape/

over and guide us every step of the way, human life is especially sacred, a gift for which we ought to be supremely grateful, and which we are obliged to use as our creator intended. Some also claim that because we ultimately belong to God, self-annihilation would infringe upon his exclusive right to determine the proper course and duration of a human life. To take our own lives would be to usurp God's authority, to dispose of something that does not rightfully belong to us.

But the Christian narrative no longer commands automatic respect or allegiance. I happen to be among those for whom recent narratives in the social and natural sciences have displaced the Christian understanding of the nature of reality, humanity's place in the cosmos, and what sorts of values, behaviours, and social institutions are most beneficial for our species. Today, I see no reason to appeal to an unseen realm or a supernatural being to explain the origin of the universe, the evolution of life, consciousness, moral sensibilities, altruism, or even love. In fact, introducing unseen agents like gods, angels, demons, or ancestors into the mix only seems to create more intellectual trouble than they're worth. As Richard Dawkins and other outspoken atheists have pointed out time and again, even the rather simple suggestion that a supremely intelligent artificer or prime mover created the universe does nothing whatsoever to terminate the causal chain that would eventually give rise to *Homo sapiens*. The so-called 'God hypothesis' merely raises the question of where the artificer himself came from. Furthermore, our best scientific theories for the origin and nature of the cosmos come with plenty of empirical evidence. Religious cosmogonies or cosmologies, on the other hand, rarely (if ever) come with this intellectually satisfying advantage. More often than not, religious adherents are exhorted simply to 'have faith' in the words of long-deceased visionaries or prophets who claimed to have communicated directly with a supernatural being, and not to concern themselves too much with whether certain claims can be verified by evidence that may be subject to peer review.

When reading the Bible, then, I do so not as a religious adherent but as a humanist, as someone who treats the biblical writings no differently than one might treat any other literary corpus. Although I happen to believe that the Bible preserves the words of writers endowed with keen insight and the ability to move us deeply, it holds no special authority for me. Rather, what I find in the Jewish and Christian canons is a magnificent array of highly intelligent and imaginative interlocutors with whom I might converse but to whom I award no final say either in the way in which I construct reality or in how I choose to conduct my life.

As a humanist, I also view the self as a construction of culture and accumulated experience that has no stable, unchanging, durable 'core' that might be capable of surviving the death of the body. When neural activity ceases, so do we. We are but a transitory and ever-evolving assemblage of atoms and molecules that begins an irreversible process of disintegration and dispersal once the heart, lungs, and brain cease to function. Needless to say, then, given what we now know about human biology, particularly the brain and how it works, I take for granted that any traditional dualistic model that presumes the existence of an immaterial soul or spirit[9] has now been rendered obsolete. The evidence to date strongly suggests that we *are* our bodies. Even renowned Christian philosophers and theologians like Richard Swinburne (1997) and John Hick (1994) have conceded that the church now has little choice but to revert to some notion of bodily resurrection or replication. The cognitive sciences have made it clear that without our brains and sense organs in particular, there simply is no 'us', for without them we lose nearly all of the ordinary human capabilities and experiences that we value.

Death, then, is in all probability what John Martin Fischer (1993: 14–29) calls an 'experiential blank', and therefore cannot be construed as a loss or harm for the one who chooses to end her life. Without a subject, there is no one – no locus of consciousness or sentience – to experience regret, deprivation, or injury. As Epicurus concluded, merely being aware that death can do no harm to the deceased should offer us some comfort, both when we contemplate our own deaths, and even when someone we love passes away. Because postmortem nonexistence experientially is no different than prenatal nonbeing, death ought not to be feared. Like prenatal nonexistence, death is an 'experiential blank', a total – and permanent – loss of consciousness.

Might the Lukan Jesus Allow for Voluntary Active Euthanasia?

As noted above, although I have already begun forming a position on euthanasia in the event that the cancer should return, my current stance remains provisional. I remain open to hearing from new conversation partners who might help me better formulate a response that has my family's best interests in mind. And so it is with this desire for further insight – for yet one more conversation partner, yet one more perspective – that I turn to the Lukan Jesus. Of course, as is true for same-sex relations, abortion, animal welfare, and so many other moral issues of pressing concern to Americans today, Jesus never *directly* addresses active euthanasia, which means that we as readers are left to draw inferences the best we can. Nevertheless, we have before us much to work with, and I'm confident that a well-informed conjecture might be drawn.

I will argue that based on how the Lukan Jesus constructs reality and the human self, and based on how he customarily treats people who are chronically ill and/ or disabled, there is little reason to believe that he would prohibit voluntary active euthanasia, *but only if he were also convinced that an individual truly is in unbearable and irremediable pain*. To be sure, the narrator of Luke-Acts presents readers with a mythic figure of extraordinary power who seems capable of curing any malady, whether by ridding an individual of a malevolent spirit responsible for a given

---

9. Eastern traditions often refer to this immaterial animating force as *ātman* or *jīva*, which differ from the Western understanding of a soul chiefly in that neither has a beginning or end.

illness, or by altering underlying biologic processes or anatomical abnormalities that would ordinarily require surgical or pharmaceutical intervention today. The narrator even goes so far as to claim that the protagonist can revive those who have recently died – that is, reverse the process of decomposition and restore an individual's prior unique molecular arrangement, although presumably one that antedates the somatic dysfunction that led to his or her death in the first place.

As a humanist, I cannot accept such claims without at least some empirical evidence, especially when we are also told that they are the product of supernatural agency. Humanists defer to recent work in the sciences for their chief source of information about our world, and so far as we know, no folk healer or exorcist is – or ever has been – capable of some of the most extraordinary feats attributed to Jesus: regeneration of damaged spinal cords (Lk. 5.17-26) or atrophied limbs (6.6-11), instantaneous cure of profound and disabling psychological illness (8.26-39; 9.37-43), or immediate and total remediation of major organ or lymphatic system dysfunction that manifests itself in severe oedema (14.1-6). Folk healers may be able to address certain psychosomatic disorders, help people better cope with pain or illness, or achieve successful social reintegration, but they cannot repair serious anatomical injury or anomaly, nor can they alter the vast majority of underlying biochemical processes that cause us so much suffering.

So, in order to seriously engage the Lukan Jesus on the matter of euthanasia, we have to imagine that he is willing to acknowledge that certain diseases and impairments prove resistant to his healing methods. To be sure, the narrator offers no indication that he would be inclined to acknowledge such limitations, but neither, importantly, does the narrator explicitly inform us that every one of his attempts to heal or cure was entirely successful. For instance, no mention is made of any effort to follow up with Jesus' 'patients' at various intervals – say, every six months over the course of several years. Access to such information would be required to assess the efficacy of his techniques. On the one hand, then, I think it's entirely fair to continue to view the Lukan Jesus as a highly skilled folk healer who, in some cases, truly is capable of diminishing human suffering, or even of curing certain psychosomatic or conversion disorders (Capps 2008). But for the conversation to go anywhere, we also need to envision an individual who is willing to concede the obvious: there are, in fact, diseases that cannot be cured and impairments that cannot be 'fixed', and because this is so, there are those who really do experience grievous and irremediable suffering.

I wish to add one final point before turning to the Gospel itself. I have been referring to the Lukan Jesus thus far in order to indicate that I am addressing – and will continue to address – a character in a narrative rather than the historical figure as such. Because continued use of the qualifier would likely weary the reader, for the remainder of the chapter I will simply refer to this figure as 'Jesus'. Luke's protagonist, however, does not emerge in a historical vacuum. The Gospel's author based him on a real Jewish folk healer, exorcist, and teacher who was executed by Roman authorities in Jerusalem ca. 30 CE, presumably because both his message and movement posed a threat to imperial power. Furthermore, the author's narrative-world is derived in large part from the social and political climate in which the

historical figure lived, and therefore quite naturally takes for granted a wide array
of institutions, beliefs, and practices rooted in that environment. Because this is so,
I think it is entirely appropriate to access any relevant scholarship on early Roman
Palestine that might assist us in situating this character within the thought-world
of the Gospel. So, while all further references to Jesus presume *Luke's* Jesus – the
story's protagonist rather than some ad hoc reconstruction of the historical figure –
I will not hesitate to set his teachings and deeds against the backdrop of what little
we do know about life during the time period within which the story is set.

My aim in this section is to highlight certain views and qualities of Jesus that are
especially relevant for inferring how he might respond to someone who is suffering
both grievously and irremediably and who expresses a desire to terminate her life.
Among them are his (1) construction of reality as a whole; (2) view of the human
self; and (3) characteristic treatment of the chronically ill and disabled.

Jesus' Construction of Reality

In Luke, Jesus constructs a world that is hardly optimal for human flourishing. For
a large majority of the people in early Roman Palestine with whom he chooses to
spend most of his time – 'the poor ... captives ... blind ... [and] oppressed' (4.18) –
life is extraordinarily difficult, a 'vale of tears' from which death might prove a
welcome release, especially if they happen to be among those who have already
embraced Jesus' message and therefore have good reason to believe that they will
enter 'paradise' (*paradeisos*) when neural function ceases (16.19-31; 20.43).

On the one hand, the physical and emotional challenges first-century Palestinian
Jews face are due in part to having little understanding or control over natural
processes that would have adversely affected virtually all ancient peoples. Without
the advances in science, technology, and medicine that we enjoy today, they
would have been far more susceptible to disease, accident, impairment, premature
death, drought, flood, and so on. And that's precisely what we find in Luke: many
struggle to secure basic provisions such as food and clothing (11.3, 5-8; 12.22-31),
suffer from painful and debilitating illnesses of body and mind (5.17-26; 8.26-
39, 43-48; 9.37-43; 13.10-17; 14.1-6), watch helplessly as their sons and daughters
die prematurely (7.11-17; 8.40-42, 49-56), and find themselves within (or near)
architecturally primitive and structurally unsound edifices that collapse without
warning, claiming the lives of many innocent people (13.4). Furthermore, without
a sophisticated judicial system and a well-trained police force, the few possessions
one does have – cooking utensils, farming equipment, livestock – are especially
vulnerable to theft, and nearly everything one has is subject to breakage or
decay (12.33).

Prior to the emergence of the natural and social sciences, one way to explain the
cause of at least some of the hardships above is by appealing to an unseen world
populated by demonic forces whose chief aim is to thwart human well-being. Like
others of his era, this is precisely what Jesus does. For him, the world is flush with
opportunistic malevolent spirits, eager to take up residence in a human host upon
whom they might bring misfortune or utter ruin. Jesus presumably has the ability

to displace these spirits temporarily, but he can't kill them, as some other *shamans* (both past and present) have claimed, so one therefore must remain vigilant even after a successful exorcism has been performed (11.24-26).

Put simply, early Roman Palestine's poor live in an insecure, unpredictable world not always amenable to human well-being, and most work long hours just to make ends meet, hoping that weather patterns allow for a bountiful harvest, that their children manage to avoid serious illness or accident and survive into adulthood, that mothers and mothers-to-be do not die in childbirth, and that they do not lose what little they have to theft, rot, or the whim of unscrupulous local elites. Wealth may have diminished one's vulnerability to at least some of these natural and moral evils, but not nearly to the extent that it would today. Even the elite were still subject to high infant mortality, acute and chronic illnesses that we can easily treat or cure, as well as to loss of private property. The walls around their estates and the locks on their doors afforded only so much protection from banditry, ordinary theft, and ever-shifting political alliances in which their ancestry or social rank ceased to offer any protection.

Compounding the suffering of most ordinary Palestinian Jews was the presence of a foreign imperial power that either introduced or helped sustain oppressive social, economic, and religious institutions. These institutions heavily favoured the elite at the expense of independent farmers, sharecroppers, merchants, artisans, labourers, slaves, and people whose impairments or 'impurity' (say, from a chronic skin condition (5.12-16) or bleeding disorder (8.43-48)) prohibited them from participating in the workforce and/or in religious rituals at Yahweh's temple in Jerusalem. In fact, some scholars estimate that taxation alone may have deprived an ordinary farming family of roughly 25–45 per cent of the annual yield,[10] the proceeds of which were ordinarily funnelled towards urban areas, where they were used to fund the projects and lifestyles of the elite (Hanson and Oakman 1998: 116, 128; Harland 2002: 515; Oakman 1986: 78, 211). Many ended up incurring extraordinary debt, and they eventually had little choice but to surrender their small ancestral plots to salvage their freedom. Some farmers chose to stay put and rent the land they once owned, but others either abandoned their homes altogether for menial work in a nearby city, allied themselves with bandits who raided caravans and wealthy estates, or simply resorted to begging. Jesus himself also alludes to egregious abuses of political power in which people are tortured or even killed (13.1), as well as to corrupt judicial systems that failed to distribute justice to society's most vulnerable members (18.2-5). On one occasion, Jesus suggests that the political situation in early Roman Palestine will eventually become so unstable and hostile to Jewish interests that many will desire death as a release from their suffering (23.30). Indeed, he is persuaded that at some point in the near future, life will become so unbearable that it would be wise for families to quit bringing children into the world altogether (23.28-29).

---

10. For the many types of direct and indirect taxes imposed by civic and religious elites, see Hamel (1989: 144–9), Pastor (1997: 138–9), and Oakman (1986: 66–7).

In the event that one choses to become a committed follower of Jesus' nascent movement, which involves leaving behind biological kin, homes, vocations, and possessions for an itinerant life of preaching and healing (9.1-6, 57-62; 12.33; 14.25-33; 18.18-30), he or she can expect even greater hardship. Jesus tells them that they should anticipate being insulted, reviled, betrayed by family members and friends, interrogated by religious authorities, imprisoned, and even executed (12.49-53; 21.12-18).

It is important to acknowledge here that Jesus' pessimism is not a comprehensive antinatalism of the kind we might find in, say, Qohelet or Schopenhauer. His negative view of the world is due not to an indifferent or inherently flawed cosmos that would discourage or prohibit the realization of human well-being on a broad scale. In fact, along with both the Yahwist and the Priestly Writer, he seems to take for granted that God initially created a magnificent and well-ordered world of abundance specifically tailored to human happiness (Gen. 1–3). Jesus merely happens to have been born into a highly unstable and oppressive political environment in which most social, economic, and religious institutions were 'rigged' to promote the welfare of the elite at the expense of most ordinary Jewish Palestinians. He also happens to have been born during an era when Satan and his legions had been granted enormous power to thwart human interests. For him, in fact, most so-called natural evils such as illness are due not to Yahweh's indifference, incompetence, or malfeasance, as some of his contemporaries appear to believe (11.5-13; 18.1-8),[11] but rather to Satanic influence.

For Jesus, then, once imperial rule comes to an end, Satan and his cohorts are sent back 'into the abyss' (8.31), and all who stubbornly refuse to follow God's will and acknowledge Jesus' authority are either thrown into *Gehenna* (12.5) or 'slaughtered' (19.27), a peaceful and enjoyable existence will be available again. For the moment, though, most ordinary people are only able to find a true and lasting happiness of the kind God originally intended for our species in 'paradise' (23.43; cf. 16.19-31).[12]

11. Elsewhere, I argue that in both parables Jesus is contesting the (apparently) widespread belief that Yahweh is *not* invested in Israel's welfare, at least to the extent that certain religious authorities think he is (2010a: 33–47). To many of the ordinary people of Roman Palestine who have experienced misfortune, their suffering suggests to them that God is either angry, indifferent, or even amoral. Jesus acknowledges the legitimacy of this construction of Israel's deity, but argues that the god he has come to know personally actually cares quite deeply about them, in spite of what the evidence might suggest.

12. In Luke, although those whom Yahweh favours enter paradise immediately upon death, there are several hints that a final resurrection and judgement are imminent as well (11.30-32; 14.14; 20.35-36). After this event, it appears that 'the righteous' will resume lives similar to those they led before, although Yahweh, Jesus, and the twelve apostles will reign supreme (10.22; 22.28-30, 69), no one will go hungry, justice will prevail, and nothing – including, presumably, human bodies (18.30; 20.36) – will be subject to decay. Admittedly, it is unclear precisely *where* this utopian realm shall be. Are we to imagine that it is located

Jesus' View of the Self

Given how Jesus constructs the world in which he and his contemporaries find themselves, it should come as no surprise that his view of the human self *in its present condition* is generally unfavourable as well. Once again, his perspective is shaped to a great degree both by the unpredictable and unforgiving political climate in which he was raised and by the many anxieties and travails ancient peoples had to face in the absence of modern technology and medicine. As noted above, high social standing may have served as a minor buffer, but even the rich remained vulnerable to a variety of illnesses we have either eliminated or can cure, to sudden changes in their natural environment, as well as to unforeseen shifts in power relations in which their lineage and wealth failed to safeguard them.

The metaphors that Jesus uses to characterize even those for whom Yahweh shows special favour, which would include both his most committed followers and Roman Palestine's 'poor … captives … blind … [and] oppressed' in general (4.18), are especially revealing. While technologically advanced societies of the global North tend to view human beings as rational and moral agents of 'intrinsic worth' who are endowed at birth with 'natural' or 'inalienable rights', Jesus and his Jewish contemporaries did not. For instance, Jesus most often likens even his own followers to slaves (12.35-48; 14.15-24; 15.29; 17.7-10; 19.11-27), animals (12.32; 15.3-7), and children (18.15-17; 20.36). Notably, all three are held as property by someone else of superior rank and told what to do. None have inherent worth, and none are granted inalienable rights or the generous measure of autonomy many of us enjoy today. On one occasion, Jesus refers to his disciples not merely as slaves but as '*worthless* (*achreioi*) slaves', and here the adjective is applied to those who are actually doing what Jesus asks of them (17.7-10). Any disciple who fails to heed his commands, even if acting prudently and with good intent, is deemed a '*wicked* (*ponēre*) slave' and subsequently stripped of her responsibilities and privileges in the community (19.22-26). On another occasion, Jesus drops the metaphorical language altogether and simply calls his disciples 'evil' (*ponēroi*) – not, importantly, because they are guilty of having committed some horrendous crime such as murder or rape, but rather because they are just so inclined by nature (11.13).

When Jesus compares his followers to animals, he most often likens them to 'sheep', then widely known for their docility and lack of intelligence (12.32; 15.3-7). In early Roman Palestine, they generally were raised not to serve as companions (as a dog or cat might today), but rather to be *used* by human beings, either for their wool, hides, or meat, or even as a sacrificial offering to Yahweh. Sheep, in other words, were raised as *commodities* to be bought and sold in the marketplace. They were not viewed as sentient beings of intrinsic worth that ought to be treated with dignity and respect, as many progressive philosophers

in an otherworldly realm, or perhaps even here on a (recreated) Earth? Jesus simply doesn't offer readers enough information.

and theologians may view them today. Many animal welfare activists would press even further and extend certain nonhuman species 'rights' with which they are endowed at birth.[13] As far as we know, such notions were foreign to Jewish thinkers of the first century.

Jesus compares his disciples to birds as well, but not in a particularly flattering manner. His closest companions are not held to be of 'inestimable value' but merely '*of more value* than the birds' – or, more precisely, 'of more value than many sparrows', which are sold in the *agora* for a mere 'two copper coins' (*duo assariōn*; 12.6-7, 24). As with 'sheep', disciples are again likened to a commodity, in this case one probably consumed as food by the poor (Fitzmyer 1985: II, 960). Jesus does not make it clear how many sparrows might approximate the value of a human being. Shall we assume, say, fifteen, twenty, or even thirty? Or, shall we be more generous and say that each of us is worth several hundred sparrows? But doesn't 'several hundred' stretch the ordinary meaning of 'many' (*pollōn*) a bit too far? The point, in any case, is that no person is of *inestimable* value – or, as Kant would put it, 'above all price' and therefore of 'unconditional worth' (1990: esp. 29–53).

In addition to comparing disciples to slaves, children, and animals, all of which are at least sentient beings, he also likens them to inanimate objects. Perhaps most unsettling is Jesus' willingness to view followers who are unable to maintain the rigorous ascetic and itinerant lifestyle he requires of them, or who simply lose their zeal for proclaiming the gospel, to 'salt' ('*alas*), which, once it loses its potency, is 'suitable neither for the soil nor for the manure pile', and therefore simply thrown out into the street, presumably to be trampled underfoot (14.34-35). Although pure sodium chloride is a stable compound that cannot lose its taste or potency, it would seem that Jesus has in view a complex rock or sea salt native to the region whose other ingredients – gypsum, phosphate, or ammonia, for instance – may have masked the taste of sodium chloride over time, diminished its ability to fertilize the soil or kill weeds, or weakened its capacity to slow fermentation of the manure heap located just outside town.[14] In any case, any disciple who 'puts a hand to the plow and looks back' (9.62) by, say, returning to her biological kin or failing to part with *all* of her possessions (14.25-33), is compared to an inert substance, one that is discarded immediately once it loses its usefulness or potency.

So far, I have introduced metaphors that Jesus applies primarily to people whom Yahweh favours. Those who have placed themselves outside Yahweh's social contract altogether, either by rejecting the gospel, by accepting it with enthusiasm but later severing ties to the movement, or by refusing to acknowledge Jesus' authority, are generally cast as 'enemies' (*echthroi*) whose ultimate fate is either to be 'slaughtered' (*catasphaxate*) in Jesus' presence (19.27) or to be tossed into the

---

13. For one of the most widely anthologized and accessible arguments, see Regan (1985: 466–74).

14. For me, the most helpful discussions of this perplexing passage may be found in Deatrick (1962: 41–8), Marshall (1983: 595–7), Shillington (2001: 120–1), Garlington (2011: 743), Green (1997: 567–8), and Fitzmyer (1985: II, 1067–70).

unquenchable fire of *Hades/Gehenna* (10.15; 12.5; 16.22). Indeed, for any town that does not warmly welcome early Christian missionaries and embrace their message, Jesus vows that 'it will be more tolerable for Sodom' than for members of this community when God's kingdom finally arrives (10.12). In view of Sodom's sudden and horrifying end, it is difficult to imagine a worse fate (17.29; cf. Gen. 19.12-29). According to Jesus, then, anyone who refuses to accept his message, or to acknowledge his authority when finally enthroned at Yahweh's right hand (10.22; 22.69), faces either utter annihilation (19.27) or unbearable postmortem agony (13.28; 16.19-31).

There is one final and particularly unnerving passage worth mentioning here that helps strengthen my contention that Jesus views the earthly self as having little value. In a (somewhat) thematically arbitrary assemblage of teachings offered late in Luke's travel narrative, Jesus warns his followers not to create impediments or snares (*skandala*) for 'one of these little ones' (*tōn mikrōn toutōn 'ena*; 17.1-2), a *hapax legomenon* in the Gospel (Marshall 1983: 640–1) variously understood as new converts, as longtime members struggling to maintain their allegiance to the movement (Fitzmyer 1985: II, 1138), or even as the poor, ill, and disabled featured in the co-text (Green 1997: 612). Occasions for tripping up these 'little ones' are bound to come, concedes Jesus, but anyone through whom a *skandalon* is introduced can expect to be punished with the greatest severity. In fact, Jesus regards misleading 'one of these little ones' as such a serious infraction that he suggests one is far better off having a millstone tied around one's neck and hurled into the sea (17.2).

Because the scenario in 17.1-2 is sketched so thinly, it is difficult for readers to envision precisely what Jesus has in mind here. Are we, for instance, to imagine that someone is being punished by execution for some egregious transgression, or are we to imagine the voluntary suicide of someone who hasn't (yet) done anything wrong? If we are to envision a suicide, I think we have to assume that the individual is receiving some assistance, given that the Greek text literally reads, 'It is better for him if a millstone is tied (*perikeitai*) around his neck and [that] he has been tossed (*erriptai*) into the sea than that he should cause one of these little ones to stumble' (17.2). Many of the millstones we have unearthed are quite large (Culpepper 1995: 321), especially those designed to have been turned by a donkey (cf. Mk 9.42; Mt. 18.6), so if we are to envision a suicide, it is understandable that an individual seeking to end her life in this manner would request help. Most ordinary people would not be able to pull off a drowning of this nature without assistance.

Because no mention is made of the individual having already committed some serious infraction worthy of execution, I am inclined to assume that Jesus is recommending a kind of 'religious suicide' by which one aims to avoid an act of disobedience that might result in exclusion from paradise. Such 'prophylactic' suicides are well-attested in other religious traditions across time and culture (Wasserman and Wasserman 2009: esp. 19–76), and given Jesus' unwavering conviction in Yahweh's absolute power to decide one's postmortem fate, it is not unreasonable to imagine that he might advise at least those few followers who may exhibit a predisposition for creating impediments for other members of the community to opt for an early exit. A premature death, he might say, is a far better option than suffering (eternally?) in *Gehenna*.

The logion above is especially important for my argument, for if Jesus would recommend suicide over a rather banal transgression that certainly need not cause irreparable harm, and from which one could later make amends and be forgiven, I fail to see why euthanasia could not become an option for someone who is suffering unbearably and irremediably. At some point in one's life, one invariably will 'trip up' others, whether intentionally or not. 'Misleading' and 'being misled' are unavoidable aspects of being human. If we happen to have misled someone, and we arrive at the realization that we've done so, the proper thing to do is to approach the individual whom we've wronged, apologize, and, if at all possible, make things right. I have a hard time imagining any Christian today would actually recommend suicide to a fellow adherent precisely so that she might avoid the possibility of causing another member of the community to stumble. It is equally difficult to imagine that any sane and even moderately sympathetic adherent who may have been misled by another would wish that the offender had taken her life prior to having introduced a *skandalon*, even if this individual did so knowingly and with ill intent.

From Jesus' perspective, then, even human beings at their best are deemed 'worthless' (*achreioi*; 17.10) and inclined to 'evil' (*ponēroi*; 11.13), and like slaves, children, sheep, sparrows, coins, and salt that has lost its potency, certainly none, as Kant would have it, are held to be 'above all price'. Thankfully, at least some followers can take comfort from the fact that their 'names have been written in heaven' (10.20), and that at death they will enter paradise, where they may claim their 'unfailing treasure' (12.33) and be endowed with bodies that 'can no longer die' (20.36). But while still on Earth, even Yahweh's most favoured are valued largely by how *useful* they can be within the divine economy. None possess intrinsic value or unconditional worth. For those who fail to prove useful to Yahweh, or for those who refuse to acknowledge Jesus' authority upon his return, there is little hope. They shall be tossed into *Gehenna*, where they shall suffer unbearable agony, or they shall be executed in Jesus' presence.

Jesus' Customary Response to Chronic Illness and Disability

One of the most striking characteristics of Jesus is his depth of compassion for anyone who is suffering from chronic illness, pain, and/or disability. Although readers are presented with just a handful of exemplary healings and exorcisms, the narrator makes it clear on more than one occasion that Jesus spends many long hours easing the suffering of people in pain or whose impairment(s) may have prevented them from participating fully in communal life (4.40-41; 6.17-19).

His uncommon sensitivity to chronic pain and/or disability is most evident during those episodes when he heals on the Sabbath and is challenged by religious leaders for doing so (6.6-11; 13.10-17; 14.1-6). It appears that a number of Jewish leaders and scholars of the first century held that healing constituted a form of work, and therefore ought to be postponed until the Sabbath was over (Johnson 1991: 212). Their reasoning, at least in the case of a chronic condition, for postponement would have been rather straightforward: if an individual had been suffering for many months or years, it is far more prudent to wait a few hours than to risk violating the Mosaic law – and, in this case, not just any law, but one of the Ten Commandments.

Jesus, however, seems to view long-standing suffering with a sense of urgency.[15] The closely situated and structurally similar stories of Jesus healing a woman whose spine was badly misshapen (13.10-17) and a man with severe oedema (14.1-6) together offer a fine illustration. We might describe the woman's illness today as a form of spondylitis, a rheumatic disease of the spine and peripheral joint(s), or perhaps an advanced case of osteoarthritis (Fitzmyer 1985: II, 1012; cf. Wilkinson 1977: 195–205). For the man suffering from oedema, the excessive accumulation of fluid might suggest major organ dysfunction such as kidney disease, congestive heart failure, or cirrhosis of the liver (Fitzmyer 1985: II, 1041; Green 1997: 546), or even a disorder of the lymphatic system. If the swelling were severe enough, it would not only cause pain, burning, and stiffness, but also put one at increased risk for ulceration and infection. Without the assistance of modern surgical techniques, medications, and compression garments, both conditions minimally would involve chronic pain and loss of mobility.

When confronted by religious authorities for proceeding to heal these two people on the Sabbath, Jesus responds by likening their experience of chronic illness to that of an animal or child who longs for immediate relief from distress or deprivation (13.15; 14.5). While the religious authorities blithely presume that waiting another day ought to pose them no problem whatsoever, Jesus reasons quite differently: precisely because these two individuals have suffered far too long as it is, healing ought not to be postponed even one more hour. If relief or remediation is readily available *now*, why wait?

Jesus' sympathy, however, typically extends beyond mere physical pain and limitation to include the emotional distress brought on by social isolation (5.12-16; 8.43-48), exclusion from the labour force (5.17-26; 14.1-6), and cognitive impairment or imbalance (8.26-39; 9.37-43). For him, social reintegration and emotional well-being appear to be just as important as analgesia and restoration of physical function. Certain illnesses such as psoriasis (5.12-16) or chronic haemorrhage outside ordinary menstrual flow (8.43-48) would have rendered an

---

15. Elsewhere, I have argued that this particular inclination of his, along with other evidence both from within the narrative itself (e.g. 4.23) and from other Christian communities' willingness to view him through the lens of the fourth 'Servant Song' of Isaiah, suggests that the historical figure upon which the author of Luke-Acts constructed his protagonist may have had intimate, firsthand knowledge of chronic illness and/or disability (2010: 12 n.12). The claim in part would help to explain why he feels so strongly drawn to the ill and disabled, and why he is willing to devote so much of his time to relieving their suffering.

individual 'unclean' or 'impure' (Lev. 13.3; 15.25-27), which, wherever Levitical laws were still observed in early Roman Palestine (Avalos 1999: 66–71), may have resulted not only in a diminution of social status, but also in exclusion from important religious rituals, especially those performed at the temple in Jerusalem (Olyan 2008: 26–46). Although Jesus could not have cured psoriasis or a chronic haemorrhage, it is conceivable that he found creative ways of removing the stigma associated with these illnesses, or of encouraging communities to reintegrate those who had been isolated or even been asked to leave their household because they had been declared 'unclean'. Either achievement itself might have significantly diminished an individual's suffering, even if he or she continued to feel pain or cope with physical limitations.

I would like to conclude this section by identifying two features of Jesus' healings and exorcisms that may prove problematic for some readers. First, in certain cases, Jesus proceeds to heal, exorcize, or raise the dead without asking the ill or deceased *what their preferences actually are*. Too often, they remain voiceless and anonymous throughout the episodes in which they briefly appear, then are casually dismissed once healed or restored to life. In fact, it's difficult not to feel as if the author has deployed them as mere 'props' to highlight Jesus' extraordinary curative abilities, wisdom, and rhetorical prowess. None of them are ever really 'brought to life' as unique and interesting characters in their own right.

In the event that an explicit request is made, it often originates with family members or friends, who may or may not represent the preferences of the ill or recently deceased. By acting without ill individuals' free consent, Jesus fails to grant them autonomy as rational and moral agents worthy of respect. A few examples include Jesus' (1) restoration of a man's ability to walk, which he performs chiefly for the purpose of showing religious authorities that 'the Son of Man has authority on Earth to forgive sins' (5.17-26); (2) healing on the Sabbath of a man's atrophied hand, a woman's badly misshapen spine, as well as a man's severe oedema (6.6-11; 13.10-17; 14.16); (3) revitalization of a dying slave at the behest of his wealthy master (7.1-10); (4) revivification of a recently deceased girl at the request of her father (8.40-42, 49-56); and (5) resurrection of a young man out of sympathy for his widowed mother (7.11-17). But contemporary readers who value the right to self-determination may wonder: if already in paradise, can we be sure that the recently deceased girl and young man actually *want* to return to Earth? Or, can we be sure that the expiring slave doesn't view his illness as a great boon that would forever release him from bondage? Might the man with the atrophied limb have finally come to 'own' his impairment, to view it not as some freakish anomaly but merely as somatic variation, and see no need whatsoever to have it restored or 'normalized'?

Second, although the following observation is closely related and probably evident to most readers at this point, I nevertheless think that it's important to make it explicit. On occasion, Jesus heals or restores someone to life chiefly for the benefit of someone *other* than the person who is ill or who has recently died. Many Americans today would find this practice unacceptable. Generally, we hold that adult patients of sound mind have the final say not only as to what kinds of treatment they might be willing to receive, but also as to whether they will accept any treatment at all. Once again, I'll offer a few examples, a few of which overlap with those already listed above. Jesus (1) revives a slave belonging to a Roman centurion exclusively on the grounds that he had proven himself especially 'valuable' (*entimos*) to his master (7.1-10); (2) resurrects a widow's only son, presumably because his absence would have left her vulnerable in the profoundly patriarchal society of first-century Roman Palestine; (3) revivifies what appears to be the only child (here, a daughter) of a highly esteemed synagogue leader, whose subsequent childlessness may have resulted in stigmatization or loss of honour in his local community (8.40-42, 49-56); and (4) performs an exorcism on a man's only son, whose erratic and (self-)destructive behaviour not only would have brought shame on the father's family, but probably also rendered his son unfit for marriage, childrearing, and/or maintaining a stable occupation (9.37-43). In each of these episodes, Jesus heals, exorcizes, or revives not primarily for the benefit of the ill or deceased, but rather so that their closest associates (among them a wealthy Roman slave owner!) will not be inconvenienced, shamed, or required to seek assistance from other members of the community.

So, while Jesus' sympathy for people in pain is one of his most attractive qualities, the episodes in which he tries to ease or even eliminate their suffering are not entirely unproblematic. In some cases, it appears that he defers to the wishes of family member or friends rather than to the preferences of the ill, and on occasion he performs a healing ritual not primarily to relieve pain or restore physical function for the ill themselves, but rather for a relative or close associate who would stand to benefit if an ill or recently deceased individual were able to resume their prior duties.

Summation, Analysis, and Reflections

To begin, I think it's important to acknowledge the obvious: from Jesus' perspective, my refusal to recognize his authority, or even my mere inability to believe that the Jewish god created and presides over the cosmos, automatically excludes me from Yahweh's favour. My postmortem fate is sealed: either (eternal?) agony in *Gehenna* or utter annihilation. If the latter should prove to be part of God's plan, then active euthanasia may be an attractive option. But if some version of a self is to persist beyond the grave, and I am to end up in *Gehenna*, then I may want to cling to life here as long as possible, so long as I do not bring undue harm upon my wife and son in the process. After all, the imagery Jesus offers as to what life will be like in *Gehenna* is truly horrifying (13.28; 16.19-31).

But let's assume for a moment that someone whom Yahweh actually favours is suffering unbearably and irremediably and wishes to opt out early. Better yet, let's assume that Yahweh has a change of heart and decides to include within his social contract any who do what they can to treat others with dignity and respect – or, to draw upon Jesus' own language, make an effort to love their neighbours as themselves (10.27) – and either (1) find themselves unable to subscribe to Jesus' construction of the sacred after a thorough and honest examination of the evidence; (2) were never presented with the Christian gospel at any point in their lives; (3) were only presented with a version of the gospel that many would find morally problematic because of, say, its devaluation of women, gays and lesbians, people of other faiths, or even of nonhuman species; or (4) never thought to take a careful look at Christianity because the tradition to which they presently subscribe seems to be enhancing their overall well-being. According to the Jewish and Christian scriptures, Yahweh has altered his intentions before – often as a result of human persuasion (Gen. 18.22-33; Exod. 32.11-14; Num. 14.13-25), but occasionally after he himself arrived at the realization that he had behaved in an unusually cruel or capricious manner (Gen. 8.20-22; Job 42.7-17) – so there is biblical precedent to think he may do so again.

So, for the sake of argument, we will assume that we are presented with a person whom Yahweh *now* favours, whether she is a baptized and active member of a Christian community or not, but one whose pain is irremediable and has rendered life a burden overall. For this person, the costs of pressing on no longer justify the few meagre scraps of pleasure that occasionally come her way, and her strong preference is to opt out before the pain utterly overwhelms her or she succumbs to an unacceptable loss of dignity. Might Jesus, in such a case, allow for active euthanasia? The answer, I would suggest, is 'Yes', but only if we bear in mind the one very important caveat introduced at the beginning of this chapter: he must be willing to acknowledge that his healing methods cannot address all maladies, and that some people really do endure grievous pain or an unacceptable loss of bodily integrity without any realistic chance for improvement.

I have defended this conclusion by appealing to three features of Luke's protagonist. Most importantly, we meet a character who is uncommonly sympathetic to people who are subject to chronic illness, pain, and/or disability. In fact, he seems to view any kind of chronic suffering, whether primarily physical or psychological, with a sense of urgency. This sense of urgency, I noted, is most evident in stories in which he cures on the Sabbath and is subsequently confronted for doing so by religious leaders who view healing as a form of labour. Where the religious authorities reason, 'If the chronically ill have endured for this long, surely they can hold tight for one more day', Jesus takes a different tack altogether: 'Precisely because these individuals have suffered so long already, we should not wait even one more minute, especially when I may be able to assist them now'.

I have also argued that Jesus constructs the world in which he and other ordinary Palestinian Jews find themselves in profoundly negative terms. Life proves incredibly difficult for a large majority of those with whom he spends most of his time: they struggle just to make ends meet, suffer from innumerable disorders they neither understand well nor have much control over, and endure grave injustices under an imperial regime. To make matters worse, Jesus and his contemporaries happen to have been born during an era when Satan and his legions have been awarded extraordinary latitude to thwart human flourishing. Opportunistic malevolent spirits seem to lurk about everywhere, eager to bring misfortune or utter ruin upon the unwary. In Jesus' world, chances of stumbling into an enduring happiness of the kind Yahweh initially intended for our species are non-existent.

Shaped to a large degree by his construction of reality, Jesus' view of the earthly human self is equally pessimistic. Even those whom Yahweh presently favours and are responsibly carrying out their assigned tasks are deemed 'evil' (Lk. 11.13) and 'worthless' (17.10). Like slaves, children, sheep, sparrows, salt, and coins, none are 'above all price' or possess 'unconditional worth'. They are valued precisely for what service they can render within the divine economy, and not, as Kant would have it, treated as 'ends in themselves'. If, at any point, they fail to carry out their obligations, lose their zeal, or refuse to acknowledge Jesus' authority, they are either discarded like salt that has lost its potency, tossed into *Hades*, or annihilated. Simply put, no earthly self, whether favoured by Yahweh or not, has *intrinsic* worth, and certainly none have been awarded anything like an 'inalienable right' to the pursuit of 'life, liberty, and happiness'.

What, then, might all of this mean for someone who wishes to exercise the option of active euthanasia? Because Jesus is uncommonly sensitive to chronic suffering, and because he places so little value on *life in this world*, I have a hard time believing he would oppose active euthanasia when presented with an individual whose suffering truly is grievous and irremediable. Earthly life is just not worth deploying extraordinary measures 'to save' (*sōsai*; 9.24) or 'to make secure' (*peripoiēsasthai*; 17.33), and the self with which one is presently endowed, even at its best, is inclined to 'evil' (*ponēroi*; 11.13) anyhow. Well-being of the sort originally intended for our species is currently available only in paradise. If, therefore, pain or debility has rendered life a burden overall, and if one can no longer be of service within the new community Jesus has established, what is left to prevent one from exchanging this body for another that 'can no longer die' (20.36) and claiming one's 'unfailing treasure' in heaven (12.33)?[16] 'Better to depart and continue one's service in paradise', he might say, 'than to suffer unbearably here and do nothing at all'.

I tend to share Jesus' overall pessimism towards the often cruel and unforgiving world in which we find ourselves. The variety and magnitude of both natural and moral evil is simply astounding. To some degree, I even identify with his construction of an earthly self that has little enduring or significant value, although not because it is intrinsically 'worthless' or inclined to 'evil', but rather because of the apparent meaninglessness of our lives when considered within the grand scheme of cosmic history. If there is some important or even essential role that we and other species on Earth currently are fulfilling in the unfolding (and final collapse?) of our universe, there is no clear indication as to what that might be.

However, just because our lives may have no *ultimate* significance, that certainly does not mean we are 'worthless'. There may be no creator to value or love us for

---

16. Jesus has little if any regard for obligations one may have had to biological kin. It is one's *fictive kin* and the role one has been assigned within this new group that matter now (8.19-21; 9.57-62; 11.28; 14.25-33; 18.28-30).

the unique and beautiful people we are (or are capable of becoming), but we and others certainly do, and that, I think, is sufficient. Indeed, even if much of what we accomplish will not last or be remembered by future generations, and even if our species were eventually to go extinct, as nearly all of Earth's species already have, it would not negate the fact that we and the gifts we offer matter to others *right now*. We are hardly 'worthless'. Quite the contrary: we are valued, often deeply, both by others and by ourselves.

Furthermore, although we are clearly capable of horrendous evil, I think one would be hard-pressed to say that our species is inclined to 'evil' by nature. Given favourable living conditions, and given a certain set of cultural inheritances, *Homo sapiens* is equally disposed to doing 'good' – to treating others with respect, to showing compassion, even to altruism. I am therefore more than happy to continue thinking of ourselves as, say, having 'unconditional worth' (Kant) or naturally disposed to feeling sympathy for others in distress (Mencius), so long as we are also willing to concede that both notions are not necessarily true in some deep, 'objective', or comprehensive sense. For, outside the sacred canopy, *we* are the ones who choose to see ourselves as having 'unconditional worth'. Mere worth or value alone, whether conditional or not, is not something intrinsic to our species, as many of our philosophical and religious forbearers claimed, but rather something we acquire only by virtue of actually being valued. From a humanist perspective, all value is extrinsic: it does not exist 'in itself' apart from actual valuers. And, whether one is inclined to sympathy depends upon a wide array of factors, including one's unique genetic endowment, family of origin, psychosocial history, cultural traditions, current political landscape, and so on. If pressed, then, we would have to acknowledge that both of these ways of speaking about the self are fictions. Nevertheless, they are 'noble fictions' that have contributed to the development of far more fair and humane societies that offer greater opportunities for human flourishing, and because this is so, I think it would be imprudent to discard them, just as it would be unwise to dispense with equally venerable and beneficial fictions like 'inalienable rights' or 'free will'.

In view of Jesus' harsh living conditions and cultural inheritances, his unflattering characterization of the earthly self is certainly understandable – and, as I noted above– does retain a measure of truth that resonates with me. But continuing to think of the self predominantly as 'worthless' and disposed to 'evil' isn't going to prove very helpful for us in the long run. As a utilitarian, my overarching aim is to maximize happiness and minimize suffering, and it would seem that the Kantian and Confucian understandings of the self better lend themselves to the realization of this aim. So, while I do, then, resonate with Jesus' construction of reality and the self to some degree, neither notion, if adopted on a broad scale, is likely to assist our species in creating conditions conducive to human happiness.

I do, however, differ markedly from Jesus on two very important points. First, while he seems to have no trouble whatsoever acting in what he believes is in the best interests of another without first consulting this person directly, I place a premium on individual autonomy, which requires that we both inquire into and respect a person's preferences[17] – so long, of course, as it appears as if this individual's choices would neither impede the exercise of others' rights nor bring undue harm upon others. Second, while Jesus takes for granted the existence of a densely populated sacred order, and views the self chiefly in relation to our obligations within that order, I maintain no belief in a transcendent realm whatsoever, and therefore view the self primarily in relation to those earthly others with whom we interact regularly and to whom we have made important promises. My value, then, is not determined by how useful I might (or might not) be within a divine economy managed by Yahweh, but rather by the unique person I am as I relate to numerous others *here and now* – to family, friends, co-workers, and even to certain nonhuman species. My value is also derived from what little I may be able to offer others of this and future generations through, say, my writing, teaching, or parenting.

I would like to close by acknowledging one disposition we both share: sympathy for people in pain. Importantly, this is not a trait for which I, at least, deserve credit. It grew naturally out of my own pain, of having endured nine years of an incurable autoimmune illness and a gruelling treatment regimen for stage IV NHL, not from having deliberately set out to become more compassionate. It arose much in the same way that most of our beliefs do – effortlessly, without any planning or force of will. In Luke, Jesus' exceptional sensitivity to pain is among his most prominent and attractive character traits, and I would like to believe that his depth of compassion would trump any other (religious) reason he might have for discouraging voluntary active euthanasia when confronted with an individual who is suffering grievously and without hope for relief. To be sure, while he would not vote 'yes' on a referendum for Dutch- or Belgium-style euthanasia legislation, there is little evidence to suggest he would demand that such an individual hang on to the bitter end, no matter how bad things might become. I would like to think he'd say, 'You are hurting, and there is nothing more we can do to relieve your pain. If you wish to go, you have my blessing. When you are ready, let's arrange for a way so that you can exit quickly, peacefully, and with dignity.'

---

17. Daniel Groll concludes – rightly, I think – that 'when clinicians act on the *beneficence principle* to the exclusion of the *autonomy principle*, they act paternalistically' (italics his; 2014: 195). This is precisely the problem of applying Jesus' 'Golden Rule' (6.31) indiscriminately and uncritically. We are far better off *asking* someone how they would like to be treated rather than simply assuming they hold the same values and preferences that we do.

Part II

Negotiating Hegemony

Chapter 4

GENDER MINORITIES IN AND UNDER ROMAN POWER: RACE AND RESPECTABILITY POLITICS IN LUKE-ACTS

Christopher B. Zeichmann

For most of the twentieth century, it was a truism among biblical scholars that there was little that might support queer political projects – biblical texts condemned or at best ignored the issue. In 1974, for instance, queer theologian Tom Horner (1974: 92) felt able to unequivocally state, 'Jesus Christ never said anything about homosexuality – one way or the other.' But this consensus has become contested with the slow introduction of queer theory and LGBT interests into the study of the New Testament. Exegetes have proposed that there are a handful of pericopae in the Gospels that address same-sex intercourse or gender non-conformists with varying directness: Mt. 19.12 on eunuchs, homoeroticism in Secret Mark, John's beloved disciple, and so on. Such interpretations originated as attempts by LGBT Christians to excavate favourable readings from a document that had long been associated with hostility towards their sexual practices. These concerns emerged due to the increased presence of queer populations within Christian social life in the 1970s, a presence that warranted biblical justification, since such sexual and gender practices were commonly described as sinful. This visibility within Christianity corresponds to a broader prominence that came about with the Stonewall Riot of 1969, a series of events that catalysed queers as a viable political movement across the United States. These readings in part served defensive purposes of justifying their practices to critics, but queer Christians also endeavoured to find similar figures in the Bible, especially via models of queer discipleship, biblically endorsed same-sex relationships, and alternate gender practices. Despite the proliferation of queer readings, few such interpretations have achieved acceptance outside of popular LGBT venues and academics interested in queer interpretation. Two particular pericopae, however, have found more success in mainstream New Testament scholarship: a number of scholars contend that the Healing of the Centurion's Slave (Lk. 7.1-10) may suggest Jesus approved of a sexual relationship between two men and that the Ethiopian eunuch (Acts 8.26-40) may be understood as a gender non-conforming man who became an exemplary Christian.

The Healing of the Centurion's Slave is attested in Lk. 7.1-10. Among scholars accepting the two-source hypothesis, it is agreed that the pericope derives from the Sayings Gospel Q, given its parallel in Mt. 8.5-13. Luke narrates the story of a centurion located in the Galilean village of Capernaum whose slave became ill. The centurion, seeking aid for his slave boy, requested that local Jewish authorities contact Jesus that he might heal the slave. Jesus did so with enthusiasm, as the centurion displayed a greater degree of faith than Jesus had encountered among his fellow Jews. One encounters the Ethiopian eunuch in the second volume of Luke's Christian epic. The eunuch is a royal official whom the apostle Philip meets in Acts 8.26-40. Philip found the eunuch reading the book of Isaiah on a chariot and helped elucidate an obscure text for him. Philip then propounded a Christological sermon to the eunuch and eventually baptized him, whereupon Philip was instantaneously transported from Gaza to Azotus.

At first glance, there appears to be little to justify a supposition of queer subtexts in either story: there is no explicit discussion of romance, sex, gender norms, or anything else of the sort. It may be helpful to walk through standard arguments for the LGBT interpretation regarding each pericope. To start with the Healing of the Centurion's Slave, the centurion's dialogue uses two distinct Greek words for 'slave': *doulos* is employed in reference to slaves in general (Lk. 7.8; cf. Lk. 7.2, 3, 8, 10, which are not direct discourse), but the word *pais* is found when the centurion refers to the slave boy who is ill (Lk. 7.7). The term *pais* not only referred to children and young slaves in Greek, but also to junior partners in male-male sexual relationships. This vocabulary in itself does not necessitate one to prefer the homoerotic sense of the word *pais*, but Lk. 7.2 further refers to the slave as *entimos*, meaning something like 'dear' or 'honored'. This description could express the usefulness of the slave to his master, but may also imply an emotional bond. Finally, sex between men and slaves was prevalent in Hellenistic and Roman armies. While no one of these points requires contemporary readers to suppose the centurion was involved in same-sex intercourse, some interpreters contend that the whole is greater than the sum of its parts and so cumulatively indicate a sexual relationship between the centurion and his slave. The fact that Jesus says nothing about same-sex intercourse may imply his tacit acceptance of the practice.

The argument for the Ethiopian eunuch is much more straightforward. The term 'eunuch' (*eunouchos*) was ambiguous in antiquity: though it often denoted eunuch as a title in a royal court (e.g. LXX Dan. 1.3, 2 Kgs 25.19), those holding that status were often castrated. The frequency of castration among eunuchs varied from kingdom to kingdom, and still remains debated among scholars. The anthropology of most ancient civilizations closely linked genitalia with gender, consequently positioning castrated men as gender-deviant. Masculinity was usually connected with the testes throughout most of the ancient world, evident in the Roman Empire by the requirement that all soldiers have both testicles. This has led some interpreters to characterize eunuchs as precursors to modern-day transgender women (i.e. people designated male at birth but come to identify as female).[1] Many transgender women undergo surgery that entails modification of their genitals, a process that many have identified as similar to the eunuch's own surgery. Moreover, eunuchs occasionally engaged in sexual intercourse with male elites; because eunuchs were understood to be deficient in their masculinity, penetrative intercourse was not believed to violate their bodies in the way it did most other men.

Both of these figures are celebrated as archetypes of queer discipleship. The centurion risked humiliation by contacting Jesus – who was a potentially hostile Jewish local – on behalf of his lover, only to be commended for the excellence of his faith, and the Ethiopian eunuch became a noble Christian while flouting the prevailing gender norms. But for all the enthusiasm the queer readings of the Healing of the Centurion's Slave and the Ethiopian eunuch have generated among sympathetic laity, scholarly support remains marginal.[2] Tom Hanks (2000: 195) attributes academic neglect to 'heterosexist male advocacy scholarship', but Theodore Jennings and Tat-Siong Benny Liew (2004: 473 n. 16) also observe that queer issues have only recently taken hold in related fields such as classics. Regardless, these readings have little impact on mainstream New Testament scholarship; no serialized commentaries even address queer interpretation of the centurion's slave and Jennings and Liew's article in the *Journal of Biblical Literature* remains the only work in a major biblical studies journal to advocate the LGBT reading of the Healing of the Centurion's Slave.[3] Academic treatment of the Ethiopian eunuch is similarly hesitant to go as far as popular publications: Sean Burke's volume *Queering the Ethiopian Eunuch* discusses the topic extensively, but explicitly avoids imposing contemporary identity categories, such as 'transgender', onto ancient gender practices (2013: 118–9).

But rather than belabouring the historical plausibility of queer interpretations, I would like to attend to their politics in light of intersectional approaches to

---

1. Though some commentators refer to eunuchs of antiquity as transgender or even a third gender (e.g. Jennings 2003: 155–6; Ringrose 2003), this seems to be an act of misgendering: eunuchs seem to be consistently referred to with male pronouns in ancient literature, but more tellingly participate in *masculine* competitions for social power. Though eunuchs certainly did not perform normative masculinity and are often referred to as 'unmanned', these should be understood *rhetorically* and not as an index of eunuch identity claims. As a parallel, the word 'queen' was a common slur against effeminate gay men decades ago, but it certainly does not indicate that such gay men identified as female. To rephrase, my choice of the male pronoun to describe the eunuch should not be understood as an act of intentional misgendering, but the rectification of such.

2. Only a few scholarly publications whose primary end is not elaborating a normative vision of contemporary sexuality (i.e. 'activist interpretation') seriously entertain the LGBT reading of the Healing of the Centurion's Slave (Gowler 2003: 118; Jennings and Liew 2004; Valantasis 2005: 82–3; Velunta 2000). Such interpretations of the Ethiopian eunuch are more common.

3. But see the critical rejoinder also published in Saddington (2006).

gender and sexuality. Recent work on gender and sexuality has drawn attention to the tendency of queer-friendly discourse to utilize racist and colonialist rhetoric to advance their interests. These are often characterized as saviour discourses – colonial 'civilizing' missions. Gayatri Chakravorty Spivak has offered a particularly famous condemnation of feminist saviour discourse, declaring it 'white men saving brown women from brown men' (1988: 296). This style of queer-friendly and woman-friendly rhetoric has seen significant use in justifying the war on terror, for instance. One thinks of Laura Bush's national address shortly after 11 September, claiming that 'the brutal oppression of women is a central goal of the terrorists', as part of her husband's campaign to initiate the attacks on Iraq (2001). Or the recent campaign by the Obama administration to shore up support for the war in Afghanistan among German and French nationals by emphasizing the plight of Afghan women.[4] It is also worth noting that saviour discourses also encourage us to disregard *our* role in the perpetration of sexual crimes in occupied zones as citizens of the United States, such as the sexualized tortures at Abu Ghraib and the Mahmudiyah rape and killings. To this effect, George W. Bush insisted that none of these horrific actions represented American values, while nevertheless suggesting that the invaded countries were fundamentally misogynist.

I find myself interpreting the New Testament in this complex context. In the United States and Canada, we are at once experiencing increasing visibility and legal rights for queer folk, simultaneously using these achievements as indices of our own progress over and against geopolitical foes (thereby authorizing military action against them). I also find it difficult to willingly comply with the cultural imperative to revel in these moments of purported progress, moments that render invisible those who may feel little compulsion to celebrate – queers identifying marriage as an apparatus of the capitalist economic system, communities of colour who experience police violence, trans women of colour who are murdered at astonishing rates, among many others. I thus find myself frustrated with mainstream queer political projects, where assimilation to normative cultural standards (marriage, class ascendancy, respectability politics, etc.) is typically a higher priority than ensuring the livelihood of marginalized queers. This is troubling and, as will become clear, this complicity should not be a necessary part of queer political projects.

In this chapter I would like to explore the use of similar discourse and tropes in the interpretation of Luke-Acts. I will devote particular attention to three problems with prevailing queer interpretations of the pericopae. (1) The propensity to contrast images of sexually liberated colonizers with the perverse and sexually backwards colonized, a contrast that typically racializes these populations. (2) A reliance upon respectability politics to advance the social interests of present-day sexual minorities. (3) The failure to account for the role of the centurion as

---

4. Various news sources reported on the leaked 2010 cable named 'Afghanistan: Sustaining West European Support for the NATO-led Mission – Why Counting on Apathy Might Not Be Enough'.

a perpetrator of state violence and the eunuch as a collaborator thereof. I will suggest that an emphatically *intersectional* approach to gender politics in Luke-Acts attends better to social shifts regarding modern-day queers from their initial articulation in the 1980s and 1990s. This approach highlights links between race, gender, social class, and settler colonialism. The intersectional approach adopted here has the benefit of disavowing colonial and racist exegetical methods that treat Jews as a foil for more enlightened Christians, while calling to account the often-problematic politics one encounters in Luke-Acts. Foregrounded in the proposed method of interpretation is a call to multifaceted accountability: for the interpreter's politics, for the contemporary context's politics, for the politics of characters in the narrative, and for the politics of the biblical text itself.

This chapter will be critical of queer biblical interpretation, but the intended implication is *not* that queer biblical interpretation should not be practised. Rather, this chapter should be understood foremost as the suggestion that its social history *can be done better.*

Colonial Christian Elites

Many queer interpretations of these pericopae are caught up in a schema that purports prevalent Jewish hostility to practitioners of same-sex intercourse and gender non-conformists. Consider, for instance, the comments of Jeffrey John on Jesus's discussion with the centurion about his slave:

> The probability that the relationship was homosexual would not have escaped Jesus, Matthew or Luke, and in view of Jesus' systematic inclusion of so many other categories of person who were declared to be 'unclean' or 'abominable' under the levitical rules, it is a real question whether we are meant to see Jesus as deliberately 'including' homosexuals here as another category of the despised. Certainly there is no sign of anything but approval on Jesus' part for the centurion and his remarkable faith, nor any hint of 'Go, and sin no more' after his servant is restored to him. (2001: 158)

In discussions of the eunuch, the ostensive exclusion of testicle-less men among Jews is similarly contrasted with Gentile and Christian respect for such individuals – this very pericope indicates they sometimes held elite positions in Ethiopian administration and were accepted among Christians.[5] The point of mentioning these examples is not to insinuate that these commentators have a hidden motive, but to call to mind some problematic assumptions that undergird their interpretation. Setting aside the historical inaccuracy of the depiction of

---

5. For example Mona West (2006) contrasts the unequivocal rejection of eunuchs in Deut. 23.2 with the 'highly revered' status the Ethiopian eunuch held in his homeland as a royal adviser.

Judaism as inherently and completely homophobic,[6] there are serious problems with their arguments. One particular issue is that the depiction of Judaism often includes ethnic generalizations. This occurs through the near-equivocation of 'Judaism' with 'closed-minded fundamentalism' or a similar concept. In drawing out the implications of the text for modern readers, this reading adopts a sort of ethical supersessionism that is commonplace among New Testament interpreters. That is, the closed-minded and provincial ethics of Judaism pale in comparison with the ethical cosmopolitanism of Jesus (and thus Christians as well). Jesus is lauded for recognizing the inconsequentiality of sexual practices in contrast with strict Jewish norms that ostensibly condemned same-sex intercourse.

Gender theorist Jasbir Puar is particularly critical of the way in which queerness has come to support American military endeavours, particularly insofar as it serves to authorize saviour imperial missions in the manner used by Laura Bush and Barack Obama above. Puar situates this activity within a multifaceted concept she terms 'homonationalism' (see Puar 2005, 2007; Puar and Rai 2002). Central to this concept is the perception that certain (usually Western) nation-states are distinguished by their secular tolerance of queers, whereas terror-states are inherently hostile to its queer denizens. The homonational western state finds its inverse in the violently homophobic fundamentalist residing in terror-states. The fundamentalist is not only marked racially, but he is also distinguished sexually by his perverse masculinity, religiously by his refusal to comply with liberal democratic norms of cultural pluralism as manifest in his intolerance of queer sexualities, and mortally by his inevitable death. Moreover, queer secularity locates transgressiveness as a site of proper agency, thus finding those who adhere to 'religious' sexual norms as deficient. Praise of sexual transgression thus becomes implicated in American nationalism, as it delimits the parameters of the exceptional and unexceptional. Homonational discourse is particularly troubling insofar as (a) the perceived tolerance of LGBT populations is an increasingly significant component of American foreign policy, (b) nations supporting LGBT rights tend to be most supportive of Western military policies, and (c) those countries with few measures protecting LGBT populations tend to be already framed as hostile to Western political aims, thereby driving a wedge between ethnic and LGBT populations in a manner conducive to imperialistic and globalized capitalism.

6. There is modest evidence of Jewish men practising same-sex intercourse during the early Roman period. 1) Josephus insinuates that Herod the Great (*Ant.* 16.230) and his son Alexander (*Ant.* 16.418; *War* 1.489) both had sexual relations with royal eunuchs (cf. *Ant.* 17.309; *War* 1.511); 2) Rabbi Judah ben Pazzi reportedly witnessed a pair of men midst intercourse (*y.Sanh.* 6.3, 23b-c); 3) Martial accused a Jewish poet of stealing a male youth's affections from him – a charge laden with sexual wordplay (*Epigrams* 11.94; cf. 7.35, 7.55, 7.82); 4) the Warren Cup, depicting two male pairs midst intercourse. A member of Herod's court may have owned this cup, as it dates to the turn of the era and was probably found in Bethar. There are numerous other instances that might be cited, but are of less historical value due to polemical qualities (e.g. Tacitus *Hist.* 5.5; Josephus *War* 4.560-563).

To use the language of Sara Ahmed (2004a), the proximity of discourses on sexual liberality, Christian supersessionism, and race generates a shared 'stickiness' between ancient Judaism and modern ethnic groups that entails an exchange of attributes. Ahmed also notes that intolerance is depicted differently with regard to minority groups, most especially Islam: 'Homophobia [is] viewed as *intrinsic* to Islam, as a cultural attribute, but homophobia in the West [is] viewed as *extrinsic*, as an individual attribute' (2011: 126). A similarly hostile posture towards same-sex intercourse is assumed as intrinsic to ancient Jewish culture, further evincing their affective proximity. This anti-Judaism is not merely hypothetical, as Marianne Bjelland Kartzow shows how the Ethiopian eunuch proved to be significant in the development of patristic anti-Jewish polemic (2012: 46–58). Such readings of Luke-Acts not only naturalize the assumption that racialized minority groups are inherently hostile to gender and sexual minorities, they also grant such a position authority by rooting it in a text as culturally significant as the Bible.

Respectability Politics

The racialization of these figures extends beyond an East-West divide, also being caught up in racial issues within North America. Some problems relating to queer interpretation are also evident in the emphasis many interpreters put on the social status of the centurion and the eunuch. Jeff Miner and John Tyler Connoley note the following about the Healing of the Centurion's Slave:

> The actions described are made even more remarkable by the fact that this was a proud Roman centurion who was humbling himself and pleading with a Jewish Rabbi to heal his slave. The extraordinary length to which this man went to seek healing for his slave is much more understandable, from a psychological perspective, if the slave was his beloved companion. (2002: 49)

Central to the argument about same-sex intercourse is the value of the centurion's dignity in light of his prestige in the Roman military. Others comment on the nobility of the Ethiopian eunuch as a court adviser of the queen. This line of interpretation sometimes takes on the troubling quality known in activist circles as 'respectability politics'.

Respectability politics refers to rhetorics that locate the resolution of injustices against a dispossessed group in their adherence to dominant social norms; those who fail to adhere to respectable norms are thus responsible for any injustices they experience. Modern examples are numerous, but memorable instances in the recent past include media outlets' contrast between the ostensibly more 'respectable' protests of Martin Luther King Jr with the protests of the urban poor: King's clothing choice of suits is contrasted with that of the more recent urban wear ('pull up your pants', as the saying goes), King's diction is contrasted with African American Vernacular English, King's strict adherence to non-violence is contrasted with recent confrontations with state authorities, and so on. These differences between respectable and unrespectable practices are not only used to explain the unrespectable's experience of injustice, but to also discredit their protests and efforts at rectification: the implication is that protesters who do not dress and speak properly are not worth taking seriously. Respectability politics are particularly frustrating in activist circles because they tend to ride on classist assumptions dictating that the achievement of such decency should govern activist concerns more than rectification of injustice (see the classic discussion of respectability politics in Young 1990: 137–48). Any metaphorical dirt can be sufficient reason for respectability politicians to distract from socio-structural causes of injustice in favour of individual blame for their circumstances. In addition to its attempt to delegitimize activist efforts, this approach overlooks how 'decency' is produced differently within various subcultures and fluctuates greatly even within small geographic areas.

But how does all of this relate to Luke-Acts, a document quite distant from twenty-first-century activist contexts? I would like to suggest that not only does a similar rhetoric underlie many interpretations of these pericopae as described above, but that politics of respectability in Luke-Acts itself is central to these pericopae as well. Observe that the text is interested in characters that are explicitly wealthy and respected in both instances. In the case of the centurion, Luke redacts his source to not only make him considerably wealthier (Lk. 7.3-5), but to give him prestige within the community. Luke depicts Jesus as fascinated with the centurion and only interested in his slave insofar as his master cares for him. The Ethiopian eunuch may be even more egregious; Richard Pervo (2009: 217–29) notes that this pericope is typical of Lukan chauvinism: Philip ignores less prestigious characters (e.g. the chariot driver goes unmentioned even by the narrator) to focus on the man who advises the Ethiopian queen.

Luke's elitism in these cases runs parallel with concerns that queers of colour have voiced about the monopolization of queer political discourse by middle-class white, gender-conforming queers – for instance, the emphasis on the legalization of gay marriage in the United States has frustrated many activists because it occurs at the expense of other, less-glamorous concerns that affect queers of colour, such as protections for sex workers and freedom from police harassment. Luke-Acts evidences an editorial tendency to locate Christians and their sympathizers at the high levels of Mediterranean society as a way of asserting the new religion's credibility. Steven Friesen, for instance, notes the significant discrepancy between the socio-economic status of Pauline congregations when contrasting the uncontested epistles as opposed to their depiction in Acts (2010). Friesen observes a tendency to render Pauline Christians wealthier in Acts, a tendency complemented by the disproportion of attention devoted to the stories of those Christians. Luke thus foregrounds high-status individuals that he believes will placate imperial elites in his own context, likely untrustworthy of the new Christian religion – that is, Luke-Acts functions as *apologia pro imperio* (Harrill 2012: 97–101; Vaage 2006: 257–9; Walaskay 1983). This concerted effort in showing Christianity not only to be harmless to the Roman state, but actively support its imperial measures, as we will now see.

Collaboration with State Violence

A third problem in many queer interpretations of these pericopae is the inattention to the centurion and eunuch as collaborators with state violence. Rather than simply depicting early Christians as docile within the context of the Roman Empire, Luke-Acts idealizes individuals who perpetrated violence of the Roman state. The case of the centurion is fairly obvious: centurions played large roles in local military functions throughout the empire and there is no reason to assume Herod Antipas' Galilee was any different. The duties of centurions included protection of local elites and state-employees and overseeing the ruler's construction projects. Beyond this, we have a papyrus indicating a centurion extorted money from local Judaean farmers through loan-sharking at exorbitant interest rates for his personal profit (*P. Yadin* 11; see Lewis 1989: 41; Oudshoorn 2007: 160); other examples of centurions extorting money from civilians are known elsewhere in the empire. This is not to mention their role in pacifying native denizens. Unifying centurions' duties in frontier regions such as Galilee was the imperative to integrate the territory into the empire, economically, geographically, socially, and ideologically. This process was not a neutral one, but served elite interests at the direct expense of the peasantry. The centurion's post seems to serve precisely these functions in Luke-Acts; Capernaum was located at the Galilean border of the principalities with Batanaea on regional trade routes, where the centurion could ensure the protection of state functionaries, such as toll collectors, who operated from the village (Lk. 5.27-32; cf. Mk 2.13-17). In attempting to redeem the centurion for modern readers, some have speculated that the centurion must have manumitted his slave (e.g. Miller 2014: 186), though there is no textual basis for this claim.

The eunuch's participation in state violence is less obvious than a military officer who served a client king dependent upon the Roman Empire. The duties of those holding the office of eunuch varied from kingdom to kingdom, but it typically entailed a role as adviser regarding military – well evidenced in the Babylonian Empire – or economic matters (Kedar-Kopfstein 1999: 346–50F). Insofar as eunuchs often advised on military matters, they had a direct hand in perpetuating violence in their state. Acts describes the Ethiopian eunuch as head of the royal treasury (8.27), indicating that at the very least he held authority in economic matters; economic concerns were impossible to separate from a kingdom's exploitation of its peasants, a pattern well attested throughout the Mediterranean world and the Ancient Near East. The monies collected did little to serve the interests of the populace themselves, but funded those things that interested elites and would contribute to further income. Ethiopia's primary sources of international income were luxury goods and such monies funded the military ventures into adjacent territories, for which the Ethiopian warrior queens were known among Roman writers (Bunson 2002). Thus, even if the eunuch's duties did not include military planning specifically, the imperial aspirations of the Ethiopian kingdom were unimaginable without the economic support and planning such advisers provided.

Exemplary Queers?

To what extent are these two figures viable as exemplars or prototypes of queer discipleship today? It is clear that Luke regards them as living lives worthy of imitation: the centurion exhibits faith unlike that which Jesus found among his fellow Jews (Lk. 7.9) and the eunuch seems to be the first African Christian in Acts' narrative; Luke does not draw attention to any flaws they might have. But is Luke's commendation of these characters a sufficient basis for our own?

On the one hand, it is important to consider the underrepresentation of gender minorities in the canonical New Testament. As noted in the introduction, Jesus' allusion to eunuchs (Mt. 19.12) appears to be the only instance where a New Testament text explicitly praises gender non-conformists, aside from these pericopae. The general invisibility of gender and sexual minorities in the biblical tradition leaves these characters as perhaps the best available option as exemplars. Significantly, one of them is Ethiopian (*Aithiops*), too: the Greek term *Aithiops* is used twice in Acts 8.27 and serves two distinct functions. In the first instance it identifies him ethnically – the term was commonly used during the Roman period to describe dark-skinned Africans, regardless of their ethnic background or country of origin. In the second instance, it describes the dominion of the queen he serves, outside the direct influence of the Roman Empire but proximate to it. Thus, the eunuch is among the few Black figures in the New Testament, and an exemplary one at that. The eunuch is thus appealing insofar as he represents the sort of intersectionality this chapter has attempted to foreground.

On the other hand, these characters are implicated within the problematic politics described above: Luke foregrounds these particular characters because they present a friendly face to the Roman Empire, requiring us to either ignore or explain away questions about why they were appealing to imperial elites. The centurion and the eunuch participated in and enabled state violence, practices that an intersectional approach would condemn for their effect on the dispossessed. Moreover, Luke depicts the centurion as a beneficiary of settler colonialism: a Gentile who apparently did not originally hail from Capernaum, has settled in Galilee to oversee local military operations. The process of settler colonialism in Capernaum is not entirely clear, but archaeologists' failure to discern a burn layer from the Jewish War – which would indicate significant combat and destruction – suggests that its inhabitants remained loyal to Rome; by the reign of Hadrian, a permanent garrison was established in Capernaum having the comforts befitting Roman soldiers, such as a bath house. Moreover, the centurion's patronage of the local synagogue (Lk. 7.3-5) does little to justify his ownership of a slave who was probably Jewish – given the propensity of Roman officers to capture local youth for enslavement (Mattingly 2011: 94–121; Saddington 2006; Zeichmann 2015: 48–50). One should not forget that 'consent' was not part of a slave's vocabulary when discussing the possibility of a sexual relationship between the centurion and his human property.

At the very least, a variety of complicated issues are at play. How should one go about discussing passages that have figured into queer and Black biblical interpretation, but at the same time appear to be 'texts of terror'? I would like to suggest that this tension is perhaps best left unresolved and may be instructive as such. The activist impulse to 'call out' and demand accountability seems warranted in this case.

Luke-Acts' importance is inextricable from North American social life, especially among Christians. As many feminist interpreters have observed, it is impossible to simply excise harmful passages from the Bible, as one would be left with a book resembling bad Swiss cheese. Moreover, merely rejecting problematic passages from one's canon-within-a-canon can obscure the ways in which the politics of the passage are pernicious and appear in more subtle forms elsewhere. This is certainly the case with Luke's respectability politics and cosy relationship with elites – especially elites representing Roman interests. One would be mistaken if one were to suppose that the omission of a few pericopae would erase all traces of Luke's difficulties. By calling Luke to accountability, one is positioned to not only name those problematic aspects, but also to critically engage them by understanding their function within the author's broader politics of early Christianity. In this case, one is encouraged to understand Luke's interest in the expansion of the Gospel beyond Jews to the Gentiles and the function of both the eunuch's and the centurion's ethnicity in advancing this narrative goal. A final reason it is unproductive to disavow the sections of Luke-Acts that one dislikes is that Luke's authority and the prevailing interpretations of it remain uncontested. Such a move would thus allow dominant readings to prevail with less resistance, and thus retain their importance as not only the 'correct' reading of Luke, but also ethically unproblematic interpretations.

Reflexive Calls to Accountability

The call to accountability can also function helpfully as a reflexive hermeneutic as well. That is, drawing attention to the shortcomings of characters in Luke-Acts can highlight analogous problems today. That is, discussion of problematic politics often ends up locating the source of the issue 'over there', implicitly freeing the accuser of participation (Ahmed 2004b, 2011). However, calling out a text to which we are socially, culturally, and theologically proximate, we are better positioned to identify similar shortcomings in our own politics. These problematic politics might be examined on both the literary and scholarly levels.

In the preceding discussion, I have tried to draw attention to the often-overlooked issues of complicity and class ascendancy in queer interpretation of the Bible. At the literary level, identifying these problems in the Bible can facilitate recognition of similar practices it is taken to authorize, namely our own respectability politics and complicity with state violence. Consider, for instance, the discourse on Proposition 8 – a ballot initiative to ban same-sex marriage in the state of California during the 2008 election cycle. The proposition passed by a close margin, 52.2 per cent versus 47.8 per cent, thus ending the practice of same-sex marriage at the time. It was widely speculated in the media that the success of the ballot measure was attributable to the high turn-out from impoverished African American voters who enrolled primarily to elect Barack Obama, voters whose homophobic tendencies undermined their allies' goal of ensuring same-sex marriage remained legal (e.g. Morain and Garrison 2008). Anti-gay marriage pundits basked in the supposed irony of Barack Obama's victory coming at the expense of queer rights and even in progressive sectors it was not uncommon to hear quiet resentments about African Americans as significant contributors to Proposition 8's success.

There are three things that might be noted about the ugly racism of the situation. First, a study by the National Gay and Lesbian Taskforce indicated that support for the measure among African Americans was greatly exaggerated and roughly in line with the general population (Wildermuth 2009). The equivocation of 'African American' with 'homophobic' is not merely racist, but demonstrably false. Like LGBT interpretation of the Healing of the Centurion's Slave, there is an implied contrast between the sexual enlightenment of the Gentile (read: white) centurion and his homophobic Jewish (read: racial minority) peers. Second, it is important to remember that marriage is a peripheral concern for many queers, who attend to more immediate issues. The Audre Lorde Project – a New York-based organization for queers of colour – devotes its attention to matters more directly relevant: police violence, protections for sex workers, resources for transgender youth, and economic justice, among many other concerns. In other words, gay marriage despite all its importance to certain queer demographics (primarily middle-class, cisgender, white queers) is very low on the radar for others. These other approaches to queer activism tend to emphasize the intersectionality of gender and sexuality with issues like race, socio-economic status, and structural problems. To imply that voting in favour of same-sex marriage absolves one of homophobia overlooks the way in which violence against queers intersects with other identifications. Third, this narrative functions as erasure of the contributions of queers of colour to emancipatory political projects, a problem commonly perpetuated by white queers often referred as 'whitewashing'. People of colour have been central figures in queer liberation at its most significant moments – the two most important figures at the Stonewall Riot were Marsha P. Johnson (a trans Black person) and Silvia Rivera (a trans Latina woman). Retellings of the events at Stonewall, however, are increasingly whitewashed, as appears to be the case in the Roland Emmerich film *Stonewall*, which depicts the riots as primary work of white men. For instance, even though Sylvia Rivera threw the first brick at the riots, the *Stonewall* film appears to attribute this action to a fictional, conventionally attractive Midwestern cisgender gay man. In some ways, the Ethiopian eunuch may be understood as a helpful corrective to the erasure of queers of colour – the eunuch's prominence within the biblical tradition, even though his role is not explicitly political, offers a form of representation otherwise uncommon.

Examples of problematic queer readings advanced by scholars might be understood not as mere aberrations from which 'we' good interpreters are excepted, but rather part of a pervasive cultural logic within which all are implicated. Beyond the fact that it would be inaccurate to characterize the interpreters discussed above as 'racist', this would let ourselves off the hook too easily. To claim to be outside of this interpretive schema would simply involve adopting another form of exceptionalist rhetoric – that we are the exception to sexual exceptionalism. Rather than pre-empting criticism of our interpretive politics, it confronts us with the inevitable shortcomings we make even in the process of trying to improve upon existing methods of interpretation. The act of calling out other scholarly interpretations might thus be understood as a way of working through our own problematic politics. That is, this should not be mistaken for advanced techniques in the game of 'spot the racist'.

Conclusion

Much of the present chapter may seem familiar to those aware of the history of feminist New Testament interpretation. One might recall the tendency among feminist interpreters a few decades ago to depict Jesus as offering an egalitarian alternative to *Jewish* misogyny, to implicitly denigrate sex workers, or to devote disproportionate attention to women of high social classes. The attempt to advance a reading that was 'good for women' came at the expense of a pernicious supersessionism and class politics that were soon recognized as contributing to other problems. It seems that the nascent field of queer New Testament interpretation is presently dealing with similar issues as part of a 'growing pains' process that has an analogous myopia towards what is 'good for (white) gays'. I have suggested that activist work and recent work in gender studies could be productively adapted for New Testament interpretation. In particular, examples from Luke-Acts encourage us to examine both Lukan and scholarly gender politics with an eye towards intersectionality, as there is often a tendency to overlook certain assumptions about who properly represents Christianity. When examined through such a lens, it is clear that Luke-Acts engages in problematic discourses, ranging from settler colonialism to perpetuation of state violence. By identifying these problems, we are better positioned to examine our own participation in analogous practices.

Chapter 5

DIASPORA ACTS: CONTEXTUALIZING A METANARRATIVE SYNTACTS

A. Francis Carter, Jr.

One ever feels his twoness – an American, a Negro; two souls, two thoughts, two unreconciled strivings; two warring ideals in one dark body, whose dogged strength alone keeps it from being torn asunder. … In this merging he wishes neither of the older selves to be lost. He would not Africanize America, for America has too much to teach the world and Africa. He would not bleach his Negro soul in a flood of white Americanism, for he knows that Negro blood has a message for the world. He simply wishes to make it possible for a man to be both a Negro and an American.

W. E. B. Du Bois, *Souls of Black Folk*

The slave-trade was the diaspora of the African, and the children of this alienation have become a permanent part of the citizenry of the American republic.

Charles Victor Roman, *American Civilization and the Negro*

An Introduction in Blackness: Presenting Contexts and Reading Contexts

Race and racialized existence are inescapable and ever-present prisms through which I, however enigmatically, see the world. The intersections of race, national-particularity, and Diaspora-identity are foundational to the formulation(s) and articulation(s) of my own identities, theologies, and politics.[1] Far from an obstacle

---

1. I capitalize Diaspora when referring to an actual group of persons that constitute or live in Diaspora. I use diaspora in the lower-case when discussing diaspora as heuristic or theoretical concept. I reject scholarly constructs of diaspora that presume trauma, desire for return or formulate diaspora as a binary existence in opposition to an ideal-root. See Carter, Jr. (2016) for an extended discussion of theories of diaspora.

to avoid or impediment to negate, I acknowledge and embrace this racialized world view as a historically and culturally informed cache of interpretive tools that enhance my study of early Christian literature. In the following pages, I utilize my own subject-positions within Black America and the African Diaspora to perform a contextual reading of Acts of the Apostles and its ancient historical context(s).[2]

I begin by discussing terminology and my use of the terms 'blackness' and 'Black America'. This discussion gives a general introduction to my interpretive context while also providing an ideological and contextual foundation for my hermeneutic approach. Following this introduction, I use an autobiographical anecdote to illustrate the hegemonic and contextual nature of history writing within a US context and the impact of metanarratives on history. Through this autobiographical narrative, I identify differences between my Black American metanarrative for US history and the dominant metanarrative generally invoked in presentations of American history. As a contextual illustration, this presentation serves as a hermeneutic model for discerning the metanarratives traditionally applied to Acts. Using these contextual insights, the final portion of the chapter appropriates Black American identity and its association with Diaspora to (re)conceive the Acts narrative through my contextually constructed metanarrative of Diaspora. The consequent metanarrative assumes concomitant identities, attends to geopolitical difference and particularity, resists idealizing insiders and refrains from paradigmatically viewing dispersion as synonymous with consumption and conquest. In effect, this chapter employs a contextual description of Black America as a model for a contextual exegesis of Acts' historical setting from the perspective of a diasporic metanarrative. By privileging protean, polyvocal contexts where authors negotiate multiple identities and allegiances, this reading of Acts draws on my Black American and diasporic identities to show how contextual-critical biblical interpretation can illuminate alternative logics, ideologies, and metanarrative substructures that undergird readings of Acts.[3]

2. My preference for the terminology of Black America is one option among numerous possibilities. The nomenclature used to discuss African-descended people in the United States has had its own evolution: Negro, Coloured, *gens de couleur*, mulatto, Afro-American, African-American, African American, Black, and Black American are some of the preferred terms employed over the past two centuries. Long-standing debates centre on what type of entity or identity blackness infers: racial; ethnic; somatic; experiential; socio-cultural; political and ideological; ontological; genetic. Similar questions revolve over whether Black America is a community, people, or demographic group.

3. This chapter's intention is not to replace existing hegemonic metanarratives with my own, nor is it to invalidate the legitimacy of other (re)constructions of Acts' historical context. Instead, I encourage readers to acknowledge the contextual nature of historical reconstruction and advocate for increased attention to contextual critiques of the historical constructions that support biblical exegesis.

Blackness and Black America

Blackness has never been pure, homogenous, or solely 'African'. Like any social construct or process of racialization, blackness is perspectival and context-determined. Maintaining porous boundaries, its essence is always developing. Rather than referring to particular range of skin complexions, blackness is a signifier that constructs meanings across varied experiences, cultures, histories, ancestries, geographies, and somatic features.[4] Appealing to bell hook's call for notions of a post modern blackness that considers multiple aspects of one's identity, my view asks individuals to think in terms of diversity and multiplicity (hooks 1990).[5] No more than nationality, such as American, can singularly encompass one's gender, religious, ethno-racial, and political identity, blackness is one of many subjectivities that mutually inform one another.

While 'blackness' and 'diaspora' function as the principal frameworks that inform my racialized identity, this chapter specifically privileges Black America as the particular socio-political perspective through which I read Acts. Here, Black America describes the particular and racialized geopolitical articulation of the African Diaspora in the United States. Black America, the collectivity of Black Americans, is a myriad of different stories and experiences, ever changing through both memory and discourse and emigration and immigration. Black America originated with the dispersion of Africans into the Americas via Europe's triangular trans-Atlantic slave trade. This trans-Atlantic slave trade, less a single event, is better understood as an era or complex space comprised of myriads of roots, routes, beginnings, and ruptures. And though the trans-Atlantic slave trade is critical for understanding the cultural, economic, and socio-political dimensions of the African Diaspora generally and Black America specifically, it is deficient to reduce the history of Black America to one of bondage. The dispersion of Black Africans from innumerable ethnic, linguistic, and religious traditions throughout the world continues into the present.

This Diaspora has consequently produced a Black America that consists of many nodal points that are responsible for a multitude of narratives of origin and being. As an articulation of the African Diaspora, Black America regenerates and absorbs more diversity as its composite experiences, stories, politics, and demographics change. These two central elements, namely, the trans-Atlantic slave trade's historical and formative impact on the presence of African-descended persons in the United States, and the ongoing human, intellectual, and cultural interchange and migration that occurs across the Black Atlantic and greater African Diaspora are vital to perceiving Black America as a continually transforming Diaspora. In

---

4. This approach attempts to co-opt and reclaim terms such as *nègre* and negro through denotative affinity while discarding their strict associations with the biological and anthropological racial construct negroid.

5. For representative works that theorize, construct, and critique notions of blackness, see Gilroy (1993), V. Anderson (1995), and Wright (2004).

this light, the concepts of blackness and Black America are discursive tools that build connections and enhance relationship through language and discourse. In the midst of a past littered with heinous violence, racialized oppression, and countless endeavours to deny Black Americans dignity as fellow-citizens, respect as fellow-humans, or fidelity as co-creators of America, Black America evolved in response to narratives, memories, and experiences of all types of Black folks striving to exist, survive, and possibly thrive in the 'land of the free'.

Black America and Its Discursive Diversity

Contextual biblical critics, no longer searching for the albatross of one universal meaning, already utilize particularized subject-positions to highlight various dimensions of texts. By recognizing that texts can support multiple metanarratives, critics can further appreciate the potentiality of texts' meaning and disclose their own ideological and epistemological biases. Metanarratives often infer their own axiology and influence what textual features garner signifying-value. The contextual analysis of interpretive metanarratives can thus introduce readers to alternative logics, histories, and meaning. It can also challenge the ways that dominant and hegemonic readings purport to employ the sole correct metanarrative – and consequently logic – for a text.

One consequence of Black America's heterogeneous and nonlinear past is that as individuals identify as Black American and with its historic socio-cultural and political trajectories, they can also individually and corporately narrate histories of recent immigration, non-African ancestors, free antebellum ancestors, or even Black slave-holding ancestors. The diversity found within Black America provides individuals with the ability to identify through a general (meta)narrative of Black American history dating to the sixteenth century, while also identifying as a first-generation Haitian-American striving to maintain certain cultural and linguistic particularity distinct from antebellum or Civil-Rights-era America. The potential co-existence of multiple, and at times, seemingly incongruent metanarratives within Black American discourse is vital to its ongoing negotiation of particularity and difference.

Discussed in more detail below, these metanarratives, or grand narratives, enjoy varying levels of consensus within specific cultural settings and occur as overarching paradigms that use narrative to organize reality through the selective syntactic arrangement of past to present while also foreshadowing that which is to come as logically self-evident. With Black America comprised of such diversity and constantly changing, Black Americans often navigate between multiple narratives of self, community, and nation. The two excerpts that open this chapter highlight Black American contextual concerns with nation, race, history, and authenticity: each concern, a paradigmatically construed social construct deeply anchored in the projection of metanarratives. Du Bois and Roman infer that Black America exists as the embodiment of the seemingly incongruent metanarratives of Black experience and American nationality.

Each author acknowledges prevalent experiences and American notions that associate Black Americans with slavery, alienation, and other. Black people are a problem. America is a nation of violence and injustice. Both Du Bois and Roman juxtapose this reality – that is paradigm – to an America of opportunity, republicanism, citizenship, and home. Instead of privileging one paradigm over the other, these authors participate in a metanarrative that insists on the co-existence of multiple paradigms. From Phillis Wheatley's musing on being brought from her 'pagan land' (Wheatley 1996: 13) to former president of the United States Barack Obama's much cited 'A More Perfect Union' (Obama 2008), this practice of simultaneous appeal to seemingly competing metanarratives is observable throughout Black America's discursive tradition. My heuristic use of racialized 'blackness' and 'diaspora' builds upon this understanding of Black America to demonstrate the implicit role that interpreters' contexts play in framing the metanarratives upon which personal experience, historical reconstructions, and biblical exegeses rely.

Different History, Different Existence: Memory as Context

They say, 'Rely [on], go back to our shared values'. We have no shared values. You can only say something is shared if people come to consensus and agree on [all the] definitions.[6]

Richard I. McDermott

The past is never dead. It's not even past.[7]

William Faulkner, *Requiem for a Nun*

'Nathaniel Turner was a crazed fanatic.' I sat at my desk looking around the classroom examining the faces of my classmates and it felt as though everyone agreed. I was a junior at Walter Hines Page High School in Greensboro, North Carolina, sitting in Mrs Cleary's Advanced Placement US History class. From time to time when I reminisce, I still feel the awe of that moment. With unraised head and eyes focused downwards on my notebook I was feverishly attempting to transcribe all of Mrs Cleary's lecture notes when I heard my classmate's description of Turner. Admittedly, in my youth I at times emitted an air of precociousness and knew moments of hubris, so my initial reaction, a chuckle, was primarily one of derisive humour. I thought my classmate, bereft of American history and negligent in her studies, had failed to closely read our last assignment. Because our teacher, a white, Virginia-native with deep passion and respect for history, was one of the

---

6. Used with the kind permission of Richard I. McDermott, Esq.

7. Copyright 2017, Faulkner Literary Rights, LLC. Used with permission. The Literary Estate of William Faulkner, Lee Caplin, Executor.

school's most respected, feared, and demanding instructors, I waited, sitting with a grin steeped in *schadenfreude,* for the acerbic and corrective rebuke that was sure to follow this classmate's historical misstep. None came.

Reverberations of my classmate's comment echoed in my head, 'Nathaniel Turner was a villainous rogue and murderer: a crazed fanatic.' Honestly, I cannot remember Mrs Cleary's response, but it was not her response that affected me. It was the deafening silence: the tacit agreement and approving nods that I saw around the room. In this room of twenty-some students and teacher, only two of us identified as non-white. My initial self-assured snicker quickly transformed into stupor: confusion, suspicion, uncertainty, self-doubt. I stealthily thumbed the textbook's index to reread the handful of sentences devoted to Turner; I checked the index to make sure Nat Turner was indeed Nathaniel Turner. I remember racking my brain to recall what I read as a child, what I was taught in my church elementary and middle school youth groups, how relatives, books, and television programmes had invoked the name Nat Turner. Though all this angst lasted only a few minutes, the feeling of total and bewildering displacement was intense. History, according to my classmate's statement and the silent approving nods of others, remembered Nat Turner as a savage murderer and violent menace. Even more confusing, it remembered the suppression of Turner's revolt as the restoration of peace, safety, and order.

Before proceeding, it is important to state that the above anecdote is not when I 'began to feel the pressure of the "veil of color"' (Du Bois 1968: 83). This moment was neither my racial awakening nor the first time I recognized cultural difference. It was at a very young age that I became acutely aware of the cultural, political, and social significances of my racialized identity. As the product and beneficiary of numerous Black American institutions, this racialization was important and provided no shame or indignity. Raised in Greensboro, a southern city that is home to two historically Black Colleges, a substantial Black population and the site of the first sit-in during the Civil Rights movement, the racialization of blackness was an early contributor in my upbringing and acculturation. The significance of racialized blackness, however, did not preclude me from also living in an integrated world of school, Scouts, and sports. Existing across a variety of social spaces, I developed respect for particularity and an appreciation for the diverse stories that accompany people in their daily interactions.

It was with this background that I looked at the faces of what seemed to be every classmate, affirming that Nat Turner was indeed a villain; with each nod, I came to a greater appreciation for the depth to which history is a construct of perspective and context, and I better understood that silence, which often accompanies consensus and shared identity, can lead to obscured and distorted perceptions of community, self, and other.[8] The silence that preceded my classmate's comment guarded and nourished the unity with which I self-identified

---

8. I cannot confirm the inner thoughts of my classmates. I am certain that my complicit silence projected a distorted representation of my beliefs.

as a student of American history. Had my classmate's assertion about Turner not disrupted that silence, my presumption that Nat Turner's heroism was universal would have continued to be understood as the self-evident, axiological projection of twentieth-century America's love of liberty and disdain of slavery. The silence that followed my classmate's assertion disrupted the rooted universality of that presumption, requiring that I grapple with my own blackness and its consequent metanarratives.

The Patterns of History: From Discourse to Paradigm

The above-described moment was pivotal in shaping my perceptions of history, voice, and silence. Compelling more thorough engagements of the contextual, ideological, and constructed natures of history and the settings in which history is invoked, this anecdote informs both my approach to contextual biblical criticism, in general, and the particular diaspora-informed, Black American hermeneutic implemented in this reading of Acts. Context not only shapes how past events become historical narrative, it also informs the ideological and cultural paradigms that give historical narratives signifying power. These insights suggest that contextual biblical criticism can benefit from intentional considerations of the impacts of ideology and context(s) on both the reconstruction and interpretation of history.

Narrative presentations of the past, understood here as history, are key components in the production of ideas and meaning. Comprised of contextual recollections, memories, traditions, omissions, and valuations, history is by nature perspectival. On one level, history exists as a freestanding discourse that organizes the past as a chain of events through the patterning of actors, agents, stimuli, consequences, and their relationships; it forms a logically coherent narrative. This form of history presents the past as a peculiar event whose significance points internally towards itself. On another level, these narratives of the past function as hermeneutic intertexts whose significance points externally, giving meaning to other texts and events. In these cases, histories are organizing structures providing semio-syntactic frameworks that interpreters progressively use to construct, decipher, and interpret other texts.

When serving as intertexts, histories can perform two separate roles. In some instances, they act as sources for discerning analogous signs – that is they provide paradigms for delimiting the semantic range of symbols and figures within certain texts and contexts. Alternatively, histories can function as models for the proper arrangement of events – that is they function as a paradigm for syntactically arranging events. Whether historical texts are literary or experiential, their paradigmatic use is critical to the (re)construction of historical contexts. Histories place texts in relation: relation to people, contexts, eras, or any innumerable amount of other texts.

Histories that play a role in the formation and maintenance of group and community identity often garner heightened significance for modelling history.

The paradigmatic value of foundational histories resides in their representational potentiality as they give meaning to specific events, characters, or people. Accompanying their potential for representation, people can reduce these histories into stock narratives and generic patterns. Part of the communicative value of paradigms is their representational and substitutionary ability. Entities in paradigmatic relationship are able to replace either a single entity or an entire semio-syntactic system.

Cursory discussions of Acts 6.8–8.3 and the death of Crispus Attucks will help elucidate my views of history. My use of Acts 6.8–8.3 illustrates the discursive and cultural connection between history and New Testament exegesis, while my discussion of Crispus Attucks' death displays the potential cultural and paradigmatic impact that nation-states play on the formation and interpretation of history. Through these two examples, I show how contextual criticism of history informs my own Black American hermeneutic and further explains the discursive context that resulted in disparate readings of Nat Turner.

Acts 6.8–8.3 recounts the stoning of Stephen. Dividing the narrative into three sections provides a general sequence of events:

- Summary of Stephen's successful ministry and the false-accusations made against him by non-Christ following Hellenist Jews (6.8–7.1);
- Stephen responds to his accusers before the Sanhedrin (7.2-53);
- The stoning of Stephen and his Burial (7.54–8.3).

The first section provides a positive view of Stephen and introduces his opponents as inferior to Stephen in terms of debate and character. Accused by false-witnesses, Stephen is taken before the Sanhedrin where he responds to charges that he speaks against the Temple and the Law. Stephen replies by narrating Jewish history from Abraham to Solomon. Following his recounting of Jewish history Stephen shifts his response from history to a theological assertion about G*d's residing place.

Asserting that the Lord does not live within things made by hand (7.48), Stephen launches into a caustic charge against the people he views as adversaries. The group to whom Stephen addresses this denunciation is obscured by his Hellenist accusers, the scene's semi-public Sanhedrin setting, and use of the second-person plural pronoun. The narrator does little to clarify the situation by ambiguously employing the plural pronoun 'they' (7.51-53). The stoning of Stephen unfolds quickly, and in its aftermath Saul approves of the execution (8.1) and begins to hunt down and imprison male and female Christ-followers throughout Jerusalem. In the midst of this persecution (*diōgmos*) devout men lamenting Stephen's death attend to his burial.

A majority of interpreters read this pericope paradigmatically along the lines of martyrdom and noble death (Barrett 1994: 302–93; Marshall 1980: 128–52; Fitzmyer 1998: 350–86; Johnson 1992: 104–44; Witherington 1998: 251–78). This paradigm rests on contextually determined interpretations that progressively observe and transform an opposition between Stephen and his accusers as follows:

Paradigmatic Model

Stephen versus Stephen's accusers

into

Minister of the Gospel (Stephen) versus Opponents of the Gospel
(Stephen's Accusers)

into

Christians (people like Stephen) versus Non-Christians (people like
Stephen's accusers)

into

People that please G*d (Christians) versus People that misunderstand
G*d (Non-Christians)

into

Noble Individuals (Christians) versus Evil People and murderers (non-Christians)

into

People Like us (Noble Individuals) versus People like them (Evil people
and murderers)

into

Insiders (People Like us) versus Outsiders/Others (People like them)

Construed paradigmatically, this reading provides a pattern for organizing any number of semantic options. As a paradigm, the structural relationship is principally semantic. Thus, interpreters can construct their world, past and present, through the paradigmatic prism of Acts 6.8–8.3 by observing any number of oppositional relationships that revolve around insiders and outsiders.

Paul Walaskay and Shelly Matthews exemplify that divergent interpretations can both rely upon this very paradigm of insiders and outsiders (Walaskay 1998: 68–80; Matthews 2010). Walaskay, by far the more traditional interpretation in this specific passage, identifies the Sanhedrin as Stephen's executioners, asserting that

> the parallel between the death of Stephen and the death of Jesus is clear, and **these biblical accounts become the literary paradigm for future stories about Christian martyrs.** ... Stephen was a Greek-speaking Jew, perhaps a Pharisee, who began to see problems with legalistic religion, and he was finally victim of a legal system that has the shortcoming of all legal systems: it cannot guarantee that passion will be displaced by reasoned discourse. It cannot guarantee that innocent people will not become victims of a system that intend to protect the innocent. (Walaskay 1998: 79, bold added)

Stephen's speech articulates an appropriate critique of unjust systems and human deficiency. The historical implication is that early Jesus followers, at least in Luke's estimation, understood their Christian identity in response to these ancient circumstances and systemic needs.

Shelly Matthews' interpretation strongly critiques Luke's narrative as anti-Jewish in its pejorative use of Jews as a foil to construct an ideal image of Christians. In contrast to Walaskay, Matthews' historical reconstruction reveals ancient Christian identity as polemical, anti-Judaic, and rooted in hyperbolic significations of violence. Arriving at separate historical conclusions, Matthews appropriates a similar paradigm to argue:

> In contrast with the fates of the Lukan Jesus and the Paul of Acts, the martyrdom of Stephen functions perfectly as a means both to vilify the Jews as barbaric and murderous enemies of the Roman order and to bracket Romans out of the originary violence that creates the first martyred Jesus follower and marks the church's first great persecution and expansion. ... In Acts' story, Stephen is the originary martyr. **The particular details of the deaths of all the other apostolic martyrs – including Paul, Peter, and James the brother of Jesus – need no elaboration; they are all superseded by/folded into the type.** (Matthews 2010: 77, bold added)[9]

For Matthews, the Stephen narrative is dangerous propaganda that witnesses the earliest germs of Christian self-identity as an anti-Jewish foil.

It is, however, important to remember that the paradigm rendered above is the interpretive product of Acts 6.8–8.3. Thus, its founding logic and generative roots lie in a specific chain of events. As depicted in my initial presentation of the paradigm, readers can semantically replicate the opposition Stephen versus his Accusers with little to no consideration of the original narrative. Alternatively, the paradigm can also carry both semantic and syntactic representational value. In these cases, any opposition rooted in Stephen versus his accusers implicitly infers the presence of the entire narrative sequence inclusive of its axiology, logic, and understanding of cause and effect. Allusions to Stephen or martyrdom suddenly connote more than notions of insiders, justice, and perseverance. They signify an entire chain of events already semantically coded:

Semio-Syntactic Narrative (i.e. Standard Metanarrative for Acts 6.8–8.3)

  i. A noble individual [Stephen] (subject) proclaims truth (message) in the world (object);
 ii. An evil group [his Accusers] of people (subject) slanders and attacks (message) the noble individual (object);

---

9. Matthews' interpretation is novel in its inversion of the final, insiders/outsiders transformation. While agreeing with Walaskay on the impetus behind Luke's narrative construction, her interpretation rejects such an ideology as that of the outsider. The primary difference between the two readings, thus, results from how each scholar contextually identifies with the ancient author.

iii. Under siege, the noble individual (subject) publicly proclaims truth and wisdom (message) to the world (object);

iv. In response to truth and wisdom the evil group (subject) refuses to listen and assassinates (message) the noble individual (object);

v. The noble individual (subject) dies bravely while forgiving (message) the evil group (object);

vi. The evil group (subject) approves of their evil and replicates actions (message) on a new group (object);

vii. Observers of the noble individual [subject] validate and eulogize [message] the noble individual [object];

viii. Truth and wisdom, the noble individual's message [subject] spreads and defeats [message] the evil group [object].

Instead of merely arranging figures, any iteration of the paradigm can presume the above narrative sequence. As the paradigm, in this case insider/outsider opposition leading to martyrdom and noble death, gains broader cultural applicability, its underlying narrative appears more frequently as the grand story of other historical events and subsequently an entire people's history. It is at this point that a particular narrative syntax – that is semio-syntactic narrative – can function intertextually as metanarrative.

Though specifics of Luke's narrative disappear, the interpreter's metanarrative, in this case i–viii, becomes analogous and applicable to other texts and circumstances – for example, see discussion of Crispus Attucks below. The metanarrative's pattern, even in the loosest construal, functions collectively as a metonymic symbol. As the specific paradigm garners cultural relevance, the affiliate stock narrative begins to appear throughout quotidian experiences.[10] Thus, through its paradigmatic value, the stock narrative transforms into a culturally specific metanarrative. In the case of the Stephen narrative in Acts, the traditional agonistic paradigm of insiders/outsider opposition leading to martyrdom and noble death supports a metanarrative that appeals to Western notions of the nation-state and frequently appears across Western historiography.

Images of martyrdom and steadfast faith in the midst of oppression became prominent motifs during the development of US national identity and continue to inform American historiography. The revolutionary era contains numerous events that contribute to a foundational history that establishes America as the persevering voice of freedom and justice; the killing of Crispus Attucks during is one such event. Contextually framed by a particular metanarrative, the narrative of Crispus Attucks' death is a story of noble Americans pursuing hard work and justice in the face of British imperial oppression in a strikingly similar manner to the way Stephen's narrative (re)constructs Christian identity.

A former slave, colonial America racialized Attucks through a lens of blackness. Described in historical documents as mulatto, scholars believe Attucks' father was

---

10. These interpretations of reality are not inherently good, bad, accurate, or inaccurate. They simply gain meaning based upon culturally privileged metanarratives.

of African descent and his mother Native American. He was the first person killed during an incident in colonial Massachusetts that has come to be known as the Boston Massacre. Under British rule, colonial Boston was the site of significant social unrest in 1770. The British Crown had deployed soldiers to protect British interests and enforce increasingly unpopular tariff and tax policies. On 5 March 1770, a dispute between a British officer, Hugh White, and a Bostonian apprentice, Edward Garrick, escalated into a large, angry, and taunting crowd accosting and throwing objects at a group of nine armed British soldiers. One soldier dropped his weapon after being pelleted by an object. Upon recovering his weapon, a shot was fired. Other soldiers proceeded to fire into the crowd. Attucks, shot twice, died instantly at the scene. The ensuing ruckus left ten other colonial subjects wounded, four of whom died: Samuel Gray, James Caldwell, Samuel Maverick, and Patrick Carr. Following the event, nine British soldiers stood trial for murder. Future president, John Adams, served as their defence attorney, receiving seven acquittals and two manslaughter convictions.

Metanarratives entice interpreters to subjugate narrative details to conform to the metanarratives' internal logic. While the details and trial testimony of this event can support multiple historical interpretations, the traditional insider/outsider metanarrative applied to the Stephen narrative delimits some of these possibilities. The soldiers, though outnumbered and under duress, are synecdochic signifiers for the British Empire. According to this metanarrative, they symbolize one of the world's largest armies, taxation without representation, oppressive government, tyranny, and rigidly repressive class structures. The massive and rowdy crowd symbolizes the dispossessed and marginalized colonies of hard-working and purportedly law-abiding citizens.

The metanarrative's logic privileges the colonial setting and downplays the dispute's more immediate catalyst. In the consequent foundational history (i) the crowd's public confrontation symbolizes their proclamation of truth and wisdom as the right of free speech and public identification of imperial tyranny; (ii) the soldiers' firing on the crowd epitomizes evil as they killed Crispus Attucks and the other individuals; (iii) instead of the mob killing the soldiers and instigating a riot, the noble Americans acted out of forgiveness and justice; they dispersed and appealed to the colonial justice system; (iv) the acquittal of seven soldiers, according to the metanarrative, confirms the lack of justice in Boston; (v) continuing to read the Boston Massacre upon this metanarrative leads to the observation of increasingly tyrannical British politics in the aftermath of the Boston Massacre; (vi and vii) Boston agitators confronted the continuation of evil activity with public demonstration and passive resistance, as witnessed with the Boston Tea Party in 1773 and the eventual signing of the Declaration of Independence; (viii) the Declaration of Independence, thus, represents the height of American embodiment of justice and righteousness. The British Empire rejected the ideals of this public proclamation of truth and wisdom. Their response to liberty and human dignity was military aggression and the ensuing Revolutionary War.

When read upon the insider/outsider paradigm and metanarrative commonly derived from Acts 6.8–8.3, Crispus Attucks' death during the Boston Massacre comports well with traditional historical renderings of early Christian martyrdom and the 'uniqueness' of US national valour. Attucks' death symbolizes persecution of the righteous and signals the impending triumph of righteousness. This reading is one of the reasons US history often remembers Crispus Attucks as the revolution's first martyr. Would-be historians syntactically read the Boston Massacre as pivotal in the sequence of events that culminate with the establishment of the United States of America. By linking Attucks paradigmatically to martyrdom, the entire event gains meaning within the larger syntax of the metanarrative.

Imbedded in metanarratives are values and a logic that render much of the historical details mute. Subtle perspectival change, however, can drastically disrupt the resultant interpretation. The racialization of blackness is often such a disruptor. Crispus Attucks continues to illustrate the contextual nature of metanarrative selection. While traditional histories celebrate Attucks as a national martyr, some historians have bucked at attempts to remember him as anything but a ruffian (Danker 2008; Minardi 2012: 139–49). This alternative history stretches back to John Adams' courtroom defence of the soldiers and exploits an alternative metanarrative: the pejorative racialization of blackness and Black men as threatening. The successful use of racialized blackness, for Adams, invalidated all the values, ideals, and signifying potential inherent in the traditional metanarrative of martyrdom and noble death.

> This Attucks … appears to have undertaken to be the hero of the night; and to lead **this army** with banners, to form them in the first place in Dock square, and march them up to King-street with their clubs; they passed through the main street up to the main guard, in order to make **the attack.** If this was not an unlawful assembly, there never was one in the world. Attucks with his mirmidons [*sic,* myrmidons] comes round Jackson's corner, and down to the party by the sentry-box; when the soldiers pushed the people off, this man with his party cried, do not be afraid of them, they dare not fire, **kill them! kill** [*sic*] **them!** Knock [*sic*] them over! – and **he tried to knock their brains out.** It is plain the soldiers did not leave their station, but cried to the people, standoff: now to have this reinforcement coming down under the command of **a stout mulatto fellow, whose very looks was enough to terrify any person, what had not the soldiers then to fear?** He had hardiness enough to fall in upon them, and with one hand took hold of a bayonet, and with the other knocked the man down: This was the behavior of Attucks, to whose **mad behavior,** in all probability, the dreadful carnage of that night is chiefly to be ascribed. And it is in this manner, this town has been often treated; a Carr from Ireland, and an Attucks from Framingham, happening to be here, shall sally out upon their thoughtless enterprise, at the head of such a rabble of negroes … as they can collect together. … (Adams 1824: 115–7, **bold added for emphasis**)

After reducing the entire event to the actions of Attucks, Adams dehumanizes the victims by privileging racial, ethnic, religious, and national stereotypes.

> We have been entertained with a great variety of phrases to avoid calling this sort of people a mob. … The plain English is … most probably a motley rabble of saucy boys, negroes and mulattoes, Irish teagues and outlandish jack tars. – And

why we should scruple to call such a set of people a mob, I can't conceive, unless the name is too respectable for them. (Adams 1824: 114)

By stressing that the British soldiers acted against mulattos, negroes, and Irish individuals who have no claim on Boston identity, Adams' language seeks to depict the deceased as outsiders. And outsiders, according to the insiders/outsiders paradigm, are ineligible to signify martyrdom and noble death. Drawing on a competing and still present metanarrative that justified the deaths of Blacks in America, such as Emmitt Till, Medgar Evers, Amadou Diallo, Renisha McBride, Kathryn Johnston Walter Scott, John Crawford III, Jonathan Ferrell, Terence Crutcher, Tamir Rice, and Alton Sterling, Adams transforms the events of 5 March 1770 from the seeds of a free America into the unruly, disruption of civil society by a negro-led group of interlopers.

Recognizing the relationship between semio-syntactic paradigms and metanarratives is important to understand this chapter's hermeneutics of diaspora, particularly due to the frequency that American discourse interprets insider/outsider oppositions through the same metanarrative that supports traditional readings of the Stephen narrative. As shown in the above examples, metanarratives, especially when culturally engrained, are critical in the interpretation of history. In no way invalidating the resultant interpretations, this observation further recognizes the contextual nature of the logic and organizing principles underlying many interpretations of the past. While readers continually make interpretive choices that inform the resultant meaning of the text determining the patterns and restricting the signs available for a logical understanding of the text, interpreters maintain the power to give the texts, though with delimited options, meaning.

Metanarratives, like myths, are culturally situated and likely to enjoy consensus meaning within communities. As metanarratives, these texts are also capable of giving meaning to past and present. While beginning as primarily a syntactic pattern, these metanarratives aid in the identification of analogous and corollary traits across diverse texts. The syntactic system is suddenly accompanied by its ideology and axiology and functions semantically as an interpretive paradigm. The above discussions of insider/outsider oppositions and the martyrdom metanarrative applied to Acts 6.8–8.3 frames this contextual reading of Acts within a broader history of reception, while also informing the national and racialized contexts through which I perceive(d) Nat Turner and read Acts as a Black American.

Black America: Sighting Metanarrative in Context

Background and Events

It is through the above description of metanarrative that I am able to reflect on the opening anecdote as an illustration in the power of metanarrative and model for (re)viewing Acts of the Apostles. Nat Turner (1800–31) was an enslaved African who led one of the largest slave revolts in American history. Slavery in the United

States was a part of the larger social and economic institution of the trans-Atlantic slave trade. Codified by the Constitution of the United States of America, slavery was a violent, dehumanizing, and brutal institution rooted in the racialization of descendants of Africa. Enslaved Africans were chattel property stripped by chain, distance, whip, violence, and circumstance of language, religion, family, and ethnic heritage. As such these individuals had no legal rights. Freed persons had few legal protections and very little recourse to secure those they did have. Whether enslaved or free, slavery was a terror-based institution that left countless souls in the waters of the Atlantic Ocean and, in spite of the ideals of the Declaration of Independence or ideology inscribed in the Constitution, preyed indiscriminately on the domination of men, women, and children.

Nat Turner was born on a plantation in Southampton, Virginia. Able to read, Turner was extremely religious and often claimed to having visions from the Lord. At one point, he ran away from his plantation, but returned of his own will after receiving a spiritual vision instructing him to return. These religious visions also prompted him to organize a revolt. On 21 August 1831, Turner led a revolution consisting of enslaved and free Blacks travelling from home to home, emancipating other enslaved Africans, and recruiting individuals to join their fight for freedom. By 23 August, the Virginia citizenry had quelled the revolution. Turner's brigade had grown to include approximately seventy participants who executed approximately sixty women and children – including Nat Turner's eleven-year-old legal master Putnam Moore – in an effort to incite terror and claim their freedom. In the aftermath of Turner's insurrection, Virginian courts executed fifty-six of Turner's co-participants, while white militias and mobs responded to this slave rebellion by killing upwards of 200 Black men, women, and children throughout Virginia and North Carolina. Not captured until 30 October, a court convicted Nat Turner of insurrection on 5 November 1831. He was hanged, flayed, beheaded, and quartered in Jerusalem, Virginia. Virginia along with many of the southern states responded to Nat Turner's revolution by passing strict laws known as Black Codes. Black Codes attempted to suppress Black community-organizing, stifle social advancement, and deter pursuits of freedom via escape or rebellion by prohibiting Blacks, enslaved and free, from meeting without white supervision, worshipping, or acquiring literacy. Within a cultural context that revered the church, learned citizen, and justice system, Black Codes demonized Black religiosity, community, and literacy as rebellious, illegal, and anti-civic. While ultimately unsuccessful, Nat Turner's revolution drastically changed the conversation and climate towards slavery in antebellum America. Some people describe it as an early precursor to the abolitionist John Brown's raid on Harper's Ferry, Virginia, in 1859 and foreshadow of the Civil War.

Reading Turner, Sighting Metanarrative

Like the death of Crispus Attucks, the events surrounding Nat Turner's revolution can support various metanarratives. When growing up, my reading of Nat Turner rested upon a particular paradigm of nation whose roots lay in the negotiation of multiple narratives. A nation-state, like the United States, exists as a composite of institutions and ideologies in perpetual pursuit of a *telos* to which it never arrives. Serving as objective and catalyst, this *telos* is an ideal that infers a multifaceted past of immorality and virtue juxtaposed with a continually imperfect present. Viewing nation-states in this way assumes internal polyvocality and continually shifting allegiances. A corresponding metanarrative needs a nonlinear trajectory that is helical and continually collapsing onto itself in self-reflection and critique.[11]

Drawing on my paradigm of nation, the events of Nat Turner's revolution gain meaning through focused attention on Turner's initial escape, voluntary return, and appeal to spiritual discernment. Additionally, the paradigm rests upon a metanarrative framed by affirmations of hope and justice followed by practices of exploitation and injustice. In this sighting, Nat Turner's actions were responses to an evil that the US government would eventually acknowledge and engage in a civil war to settle.

In my reading, the name Nat Turner signified a quest for freedom, pursuit of justice, and resistance to slavery. Within Black history, these associations identify Nat Turner as a freedom fighter that denounced American slavery as contrary to Christianity. He acted upon his convictions, sacrificing his own individual freedom and localized sense of morality on behalf of the larger Black community. His actions were in service to a greater American ideal. In this reading, the revolt in Southampton becomes an integral event in the history of Black America, the Black Atlantic, and the United States of America, while Turner is a pivotal figure in Black Americans' trajectory from the Middle Passage to Freedom.

Recalling the killing of white women and children by Nat Turner's followers unsettles many would-be historians. During my childhood, recollections and invocations of the Nat Turner event never glorified this particular violence. People often selectively deemphasized this aspect of the story. When overtly discussed, this detail always became part of the contextual dilemma produced by the heinous institution of slavery. Instead of invoking the death of white women and children in a vacuum framed as unprovoked violence against the powerless and innocent, which is one reading, these memories sighted slavery's daily and generational effects on Black women and children, and the inherently sinful nature of slavery which depended on the complicit participation of white women and children. This reality is apparent when considering that the adult Nat Turner attained his temporary freedom only upon the death of his actual owner, the adolescent Putnam Moore.

In fact, following this interpretation these unsettling details are integral to the revolt's meaningful significance. Neither erasing or condoning the mutilation of white women and children, its narrative presence is an indictment of slavery as an institution that eliminates the possibility of localized morality. It remembers Turner and his followers as sacrificing their own respectability and morality. One envisions their success not as an ideal model but in its representation of Black agency and the

---

11. One can envision the helical structure of DNA.

movement's subsequent long-term effects on the conscientization of the American public. History, in this case, was not something easily transferable onto present circumstances and contexts; it, however, contextualized Black America and my own being as indebted to a complicated and tragic past. Though butchered in Jerusalem as a chattel noncitizen of America or Virginia, Nat Turner epitomized what I understood as fundamental American ideals. In his critique of America, he embodied some of America's best ideals of liberty, justice, humanity, sacrifice, and bravery. He also displayed the inherent dilemma of living in the midst of social evil.

It was this contextualized view of Nat Turner that confronted my classmates' depiction of Turner as crazed. For me, Nat Turner's blackness connoted racial connection, marginalization, injustice, and inhuman torture. For my classmates, his blackness signified various things ranging from generic otherness to dirty, unintelligent, and dangerous. In addition to the potential for negative racialization of Nat Turner, the representative value of the United States as nation-state worked along with certain contextually determined self-evident realities to buttress their reading. Many of my classmates understood the United States as the model embodiment of justice. They also employed a metanarrative that perceived the present as an articulation – at the very least a partial articulation – of the *telos* and the past as an exemplary model. The conflation of present and *telos* results in the idealization of the present as a positively viewed benchmark. Consequently, while the future entails growth and expansion, the present already embodies the teleological paradigm that secures future augmentation. Here, my classmates' metanarrative views the nation-state as the guarantor of right and justice: the fullest expression of corporate being and ideological identity.

Pulling from discourses such as the Declaration of Independence, the Preamble to the US Constitution, the Star-Spangled Banner, and Emma Lazarus' 'New Colossus',[12] the metanarrative of the United States follows the pattern of

i.   identification of ideals generally absent from the world;
ii. existence amid circumstances or adversaries that conspire to thwart ideals;
iii. perseverance through courageousness and humble collaboration;
iv. expansion and growth as perseverance leads to prosperity and the conversion of outsiders; and
v.   transformation into a model for the world that provides peace and justice for both insiders and outsiders.

This metanarrative is linear, agonistic, and relies on binary subjectivity. When this pattern is observable, it paradigmatically symbolizes freedom, democracy, justice, representation, inclusion, perseverance, and prosperity. The United States, and nation-states in general, exist as euphoric entities that advocate on behalf of their citizenry. Implicit in this metanarrative is the desire for transformation of the universe from a heterogeneous and flawed origin to a homogeneous and ideal

---

12. Lazarus (1903) is a poem inscribed on the Statue of Liberty.

telos. The agonistic nature of this metanarrative necessitates a view of expansion and growth as a zero-sum game dependent on the eradication of the other.

As a result of this metanarrative, my classmates had to negotiate two texts, Nat Turner's actions and the event's national and historical setting. Both texts resulted in depictions of Turner as dangerous because the agonistic and binary character of their metanarrative inhibited sympathetic readings of Turner. Instead of reading Turner's actions as an attempt to find space for co-existence, they read his rebellion as an attempt to eradicate the nation-state and its citizens from the world. This slave revolt is the paradigmatic antithesis to the nation-state's quest to provide justice to the world.

As a result of the idealization of the nation-state, law and order function as the mechanisms that secure justice and safety. Law and order exemplify a society's civility and an individual's humanity. This paradigm establishes the United States as their nation, the Declaration of Independence and Constitution as the law of the land and rebellion as disruption of civic peace and subversion of law and order.[13]

They read slavery as a past institution and historical setting. As an abolished institution, slavery is fundamentally detached from the present, and though unfortunate, was destined to end in its own time. Add to this setting Nat Turner's engagement in the unsanctioned and deviant religious practices of the slave church, which also subvert local law, and Nat Turner's rebellion represents an illegal assault on democratic order, the murder of law-abiding Americans, the slaughter of white innocence, the exclusion of white participation and agency, and the inhumane actions of an impatient individual attempting to rush the obvious *telos* of history. Whereas my rendering of the Nat Turner revolution identifies the underlying hope as freedom rooted in justice, my classmates read the underlying goals as rooted in fanaticism and hate. My classmates and I approached this event as Americans, yet, we were invoking two very different metanarratives of America, specifically, and nation-states, generally.

Depending on the context and metanarrative, history can support divergent meanings. Informed by my Black American and other subject-positions, my predisposition is to invoke metanarratives that problematize and displace the nation-state from its centre as exemplar. Instead, the nation-states' narrative can negotiate an origin that flees from religious persecution while engaging in the genocide of indigenous peoples and duplicitous making and breaking of treaties. Nation-states might espouse that

> we hold these truths to be self-evident, that all men are created equal, that they are endowed by their creator with certain unalienable Rights, that among these are Life, Liberty and the pursuit of Happiness.

13. Amplifying the discursive power of this nation-state paradigm, the West, often synonymous with whiteness, regularly draws on Hegel's depiction of Europe and America as the height of Universal progress. Juxtaposing white Americans in antebellum America as the height of freedom to savage descendants of Africa who are outside of history further contributes to dysphoric readings of Nat Turner as fanatic.

while codifying the institution of slavery in governing documents. A nation-state, even after passing the Thirteenth (abolishing slavery), Fourteenth (granting citizenship and equal protection under the law for Black Americans), and Fifteenth Amendments (guaranteeing suffrage for Black American males) could deny suffrage to women and endure nearly a hundred years of Jim Crow segregation and lynching. A nation-state could exhort the world to

> give me your tired, your poor, your huddled masses yearning to breathe free, The wretched refuse of your teeming shore. Send these, the homeless, tempest-tost to me, I lift my lamp beside the golden door!

yet, craft xenophobic immigration policies with the express purpose of constructing a 'melting-pot' void of Asians, Latina(o)s, and Blacks. Still, nearly four decades after the Civil Rights movement, a nation-state such as the United States could gut the Voting Rights Act of 1965 while politicians nation-wide attempt to suppress access to voting in largely poor and Black neighbourhoods.

The metanarrative supporting my classmates' reading of Nat Turner lacked the contextual or logical validity to give meaning to the events at Southampton, Virgina, in a way that made sense to me. Viewing nation-states as complex programmes of vice, virtue, hope, and failure makes more sense of the apparent contradictions between the rhetoric and practice of nation-states. Perceived through my Black American context, I encounter the contradiction of rhetoric and practice neither as failure nor aberration but as a reflection of the logic and complexity expected from nation-states.

As seen in the divergent historical memories of Nat Turner, the presumption of metanarratives and paradigms are vital to the interpretation of history. More than intellectual and philosophical musings, metanarratives can involve life and death. While my selected anecdote of Nat Turner involves the writing of history, the dominant metanarrative involved in reading Turner as a dangerous fanatic continues paradigmatically to find currency in people's daily interactions. While discerning the words, actions, and intensions of Black peoples in America, no small number of citizens readily interpret unarmed Black folk as threats. Whether considering the arrest of Harvard professor Henry Louis Gates Jr. in his own home, the beating and torture of Abner Louima, or the tragic killings of countless unarmed individuals such as Trayvon Martin, Rekia Boyd, Carl Hopkins Jr, Darrius Simmons, Eric Garner, and Philando Castille or four police cars and multiple armed officers approaching this author while I sat under a starlit Tallahassee, Florida, night doing Physics homework, it is quite possible that uninspected metanarratives are at the heart of (a) unarmed Black Americans being perceived as imminent threats and killed, and (b) many Americans wanting to read these incidents as isolated, non-racialized, and though tragic, justifiable.

Evidenced in the divergent interpretations of Nat Turner between my classmates and myself, communities – that is Americans – are polymorphous, consist of diverse perspectives, and are capable of being polyvocal. Critical appreciation of this polyvocality and an expansion of possible meanings demands both continued inspection of language and final meaning, but also increased inspection of the metanarratives interpreters carry from text to text. The idealization of the nation-state, a central context for identity construction, too often leads to the unilateral projection of hegemonic and exclusionary metanarratives. Intending neither to suppress the use of metanarratives divergent from mine, nor to suggest that my metanarrative is universally more legitimate than others, what appears above is an attempt to highlight the effects of metanarratives on historiography and the shaping of experience. The critical inspection of metanarratives is foundational to living in multi-cultural and globalized worlds and as such, useful for critically evaluating New Testament scholarship among an increasingly diverse academy.

Metanarrative and Context: Critical History and Metanarrative in Biblical Studies

New Testament critics underappreciate the syntactic and intertextual use of history as a pre-figured metanarrative. The significance of metanarratives on history writing and exegesis becomes more evident when considering the practice of metanarrative projection and its place in critical biblical studies. The origins of criticism in the Western scholarly tradition rests largely upon a process that contextually develops methodology, establishes scholarly consensus, and then invokes said metanarratives in the production of general histories of the world. One need only consider Hegel's dialectics or Marx's material criticism to appreciate this practice.

In discussing critical theory and history, nineteenth-century biblical scholar Ferdinand Christian Baur acknowledges that 'the abstract possibility of this and that detail can never be disproved', but suggests that critical theory

> appeals to its broad general truth, to which details are subordinate, and on which they depend: to the logical coherence of the whole, the [preponderating] inner probability and necessity of the case, as it impresses itself quietly on the thoughtful mind. (Baur 1876: 1:vii)

Baur's readings of early Christianity, especially Acts and the Pauline corpus, hold a founding place in biblical criticism. As the historical-critical process shifted, scholars' interpretive focus from shaping the future to using analysis of the past to view history as a progressive construct that explains and gives meaning to the present generality played a vital role in validating certain histories over-against alternative perspectives (Baur 1876: 1:1–3).[14]

---

14. Ernst Troeltsch (1865–1923) presented historical criticism as a tripartite construct composed of Criticism (Assumption of Approximation), Analogy, and Correlation (Troeltsch 1913a, 1913b). Following these principals, scholars perceive the present as paradigmatic in its semantic and signifying effect on interpretations of the past. The general

The impact of this practice of historical criticism has had devastating effects on the African Diaspora in general and Black America in particular. More than simply an intellectual enterprise, the partnership of historical criticism and modernity created realities that legitimated practices that resulted in the social, economic, and political pillaging of Africa and its descendants. Displaying this very process, George F. Hegel's *Philosophy of History* envisioned that 'the History of the world is none other than the progress of the consciousness of Freedom; a progress whose development according to the necessity of its nature, it is our business to investigate' (Hegel 2001: 33). However, predicated on his Eurocentric context Hegel perceived Africa and its descendants as outside of history. As a consequence, the evident unsophisticated baseness of Africa explained why Africa is devoid of history, the unsuitability of Africans for freedom, and the obvious European, Asiatic, and non-African essence of Egypt throughout history. Hegel's history offered a metanarrative that inscribed Africa and Africans as generally other, inhuman, and inconsequential to the study of humanity. This metanarrative continues in various manifestations into the present. With the exclusion of African persons denotatively from history, the appropriation of their world views and realities as potential metanarratives for biblical interpretation has been greatly ignored. This brief discussion of the origins of scholarly criticism helps view this chapter's interest in contextual and critical metanarrative analysis as, though stimulated by my Black American context, an act of historical retrieval and self-investigation for biblical critics connected to the Western tradition.

Diaspora Acts

Traditional Renderings of Acts

As shown above, metanarratives are central to narrating and interpreting history. Just as I viewed Nat Turner differently than my classmates, nontraditional metanarratives may provide alternative frameworks for interpreting Acts. The narrative begins with the end of Jesus' earthly ministry and then revolves around the activities of his disciples, the early growth of their movement and the proclamation of Jesus' message in diverse contexts across the Roman Empire. Unique among New Testament texts, Acts contains the lone canonical depiction of the earliest stages of the Jewish-Galilean, Messianic movement that in one century morphed into the Gentile-dominated Christian church.

The events narrated in Acts cover a lacuna in the history of early Christianity that peaks the historiographic interest of scholars. Richard Pervo pointedly admits that 'the major but almost never stated reason for reliance upon Acts is that without it *we should have nothing else* – that is no sustained account of Christian

truths that historical-critical analyses presume are the products of the particular: contextual convictions, ideas, and experiences.

origins' (Pervo 2008: 5). History and historiography have long been central issues that direct Acts scholarship. Many readers draw on their pre-knowledge of late second- and third-century Christianity to understand Acts as the syllogistic and intermediate step connecting Jesus' ministry to an orthodox, Gentile Christianity. During the pre-critical era of biblical studies, scholars viewed Acts' narrative as the precise and official history of primitive Christianity. Since Ferdinand C. Baur (1792–1860) and the rise of critical biblical studies, scholars glean information about early Christian history by using the text's surface narrative to discern the author's agenda, concerns, context, sources, biases, and theology. Despite the various ideological and methodological approaches employed in the critical study of Acts and the divergence of their resultant interpretations, a scholarly consensus agrees on many aspects of the narrative. A number of these findings involve scholars' reliance upon a common metanarrative of early Christianity:

i. Jesus of Nazareth's Galilean-based, Jewish Messianic movement began as a small sectarian movement of Jews;
ii. The movement's expansion into the Diaspora resulted in its transformation as it began the active inclusion of Gentiles;
iii. As the church and synagogue became increasingly separate, the church experienced significant growth becoming a majority Gentile movement;
iv. Christianity becomes a Gentile-dominant institution that views itself as the true Israel while holding prominent anti-Judaic characteristics.

Just as Matthews and Walaskay use a single metanarrative to produce divergent interpretations of Acts 6.8–8.3, this stock metanarrative of Christian origins can support a range of divergent interpretations that are variations on a single paradigmatic view of history. One reason for this consensus is the observation of common paradigms. The presumption of a Gentile Luke is one such self-fulfilling prophecy that contributes to the metanarrative that undergirds research on Acts. In addition to an ethno-cultural designation, Gentile paradigmatically signals notions of Pauline Christianity over Petrine Christianity, which can infer adoption of Jewish scripture and rejection of Jewish practice; conciliation to Rome and polemic against Jews; and Christian expansion versus Jewish 'sectarianism'.

A related and frequently invoked paradigm deals with the figure of Christian expansion in Acts 1.8. Scholars regularly identify 1.7-8 as Luke's programmatic verses and anchor their interpretations by projecting it onto the entire narrative (Conzelmann 1987: 7; Johnson 1992: 12; Gaventa 2003: 54):

And he [Jesus] said to them, 'It is not for you to know the times or seasons that the father has established by his own authority, but you will receive power after the Holy Spirit has come upon you and you will be my witnesses in Jerusalem, in all of Judea and Samaria, even unto the end of the earth'. (Acts 1.7-8)

The syntactic pattern of Jerusalem, Judea, Samaria, and end of the earth provides a neat linear programme when read with the dominant metanarrative of the nation-state. Using this reading, Jerusalem functions as a historical point of origin that, due to the metanarrative, signifies dysphoria and minority-status. In contrast, Rome carries associations with an idealized *telos* and transcendent success. A subsequent reading of Acts can quickly locate parallels between 1.8 and Acts' narrative:

   i.   Ministry activities in Jerusalem (Acts 1.12–7.60)
  ii.   Ministry activities in Judea and Samaria (8.1–8.40; 9.31)
 iii.   Ministry activities unto the ends of the earth (8.1-40; 9.1–28.31)

Following Acts 8.40, Luke oscillates the geographical setting of his narrative, which gradually covers larger geographic areas while constantly returning to Jerusalem.[15] In lieu of viewing the narrative trajectory as cyclical or helical, interpreters view the narrative trajectory as an outwardly pointing line away from Jerusalem to Rome.

The dominant metanarrative uses linear history to broadly envision Acts as narrating a unique and fledgling minority group through a period of persecution into a global and transcendent movement offering salvation to the world and virtually every event in the Acts narrative becomes an extension of the same logic: Luke's explanation of the church's defeat of its adversaries. As a consequence, 1.7-8 frames Acts paradigmatically along the lines of the dominant metanarrative of nation-states by

   i.   assuming preference for binary subjectivity;
  ii.   invoking an agonistic character of history; and
 iii.   expecting a homogenous *telos*.

Due to the assumption of binary subjectivity, interpreters establish a number of binary categories: Jerusalem/Rome; Jew/Gentile; non-believer/member of the Assembly. Each of these binaries inform one another while extending the agonistic character of the Acts narrative. Jerusalem and Rome represent two competing metropoles: Jerusalem, the ethno-cultic centre of Jewish tradition, and Rome, the centre of the Roman Empire. As the new cosmological centre of the universe, readers can construe of Rome as the idealized *telos* of Christian history. The dichotomy of Jew/Gentile represents the ideal object of evangelization. The potential converts in Jerusalem were Jewish, while the potential converts in Rome are understood as Gentile. Here, interpreters regularly invoke Paul's closing statement in 28.28 'So, let it be known to you that this very salvation of G*d was sent to the Gentiles. They too will listen!' to indicate a final and fundamental change of the Gospel's target audience. Jews represent the detached past and Gentiles the present-future.

---

15. Thus, 8.1–8.40 presents ministry activities in Samaria and Judea. Damascus (9.1-25); Jerusalem (9.26-31); Judea (9.32-43); Syria (10.1-48); Jerusalem (11.1-18); Antioch (11.19-30); Jerusalem (12.1-25); Antioch, Cyprus, and Asia Minor (13.1–14.28) Jerusalem (15.1-29) Syria, Asia Minor, Greece (15.30–21.14) Jerusalem (21.15–23.22), Caesarea, Malta, Rome (23.23–28.31).

Ultimately expressed by the binary non-believers/members of the Assembly, the reading aligns well with the rigid, agonistic character of the dominant nation-state metanarrative.

The underlying metanarrative that produces this reading is one embodied in the language of mission. The wording invoked in 1.8, witness, becomes secondary to the notion of mission. Closely aligned with imperial ideology, mission infers systematic propagation and is often *telos*-oriented. As a consequence, growth and conversion become integrally identified with the fundamental task. The notion of witness on the other hand depicts a role and identity that entails the personal and perspectival telling of one's observations. The role of witness is distinct from that of judge. Consequently, the witness is not responsible for growth or expansion because the witness is unable to judge. Shifting language from 'witnessing unto the ends of the earth' to 'propagating to the ends of the earth' shifts the burden of responsibility and fundamental responsibility. Because of this metanarrative, the Acts narrative reads the history of Christianity as a persevering nation-state. Some scholars defend this reading by contextualizing Luke's intentions as inclusive, radical, and anti-imperial. The anti-Judaic consequences of the narrative, while unfortunate, were unintentional. Other scholars attack this narrative as the exploitative and supersessionist co-optation of Jewish scripture and tradition. Informed by Roman imperial ideology and prevalent anti-Jewish sentiment, Acts illustrates the exclusionary rhetorical practices of identity formation that resulted in the creation of a Gentile-dominant Christianity. Regardless of the reading, both parties generally inscribe Acts with the same metanarrative.

Reading Disruptions in Acts

When read from a Black American context that privileges Diaspora-identity, there are numerous narrative points of dissidence that impede the direct application of the dominant metanarrative. First among these interpretive roadblocks are observations that deter readings that immediately view Acts as the missing link between Christianity's Jewish origins and Gentile Christianity. Luke's preferred terminology appears to differ from that of late second- and third-century Christianity. For instance, aware of the movement's connection to the name Christian (11.26; 26.28), Luke refers to the teachings of this Jesus-movement as the Way (ὁδός, *hodos,* road, way, or path) and its corporate community as the Assembly (ἐκκλησία, *ekklēsia*).[16] Also, the geopolitical and ethnic composition of Luke's Assembly is drastically different from the entirely Gentile church depicted

16. I use the term 'assembly' instead of 'church' to maintain semantic ambiguity as to the nature of these followers' relationships as well as to avoid overly simplistic anachronistic projections of twenty-first-century notions of the Christian church into the late first- and second-century world of Luke's narrative. For references to the Jesus-movement as the Way, see Acts 9.2; 18.25, 26; 19.9, 23; 22.4; 24.14, 22 cf. 2.28; 16.17. For references to the

by second- and third-century apologists. While Gentiles can receive the Holy Spirit, attain Christ's salvation, and enter into the ranks of the Way (10.34-48; 14.24–15.35; 28.23-28), they are absent from the ranks of evangelists, ministers of the Gospel, or public preaching and acting protagonists. In contrast, the predominate composition of Luke's Assembly were Judean and Diaspora Jews, and the leadership is solely Jewish. The thematic emphasis on Gentile inclusion actually resembles Luke's other thematic emphases on female presence and advocacy for the poor. In each case, the discursive emphasis on inclusion fails to result in actual narrative depictions of extensive participation by gentile, female, or impoverished characters.

For instance, scholars regularly note the increased presence of women in Luke-Acts. However, female narrative presence is not proof that the author is female or even 'feminist' oriented (D'Angelo 1990; 2002; Levine 2002; Karris 2002; J. C. Anderson 2004). Throughout Luke-Acts, women frequently appear alongside male parallels and function as providers, not actors. The repetitive depiction of women in domestic, subordinate, or socially marginal positions for some interpreters prevents the description of even a progressive Luke. Amid Luke's consistent acknowledgement of female presence in the Way, he obscures female action and provides no female equivalents to actors who publicly proclaim the Gospel such as Peter, James, John, Barnabas, Silas, Stephen, Philip, and Paul.[17] Following the same pattern used with women, Luke contextualizes the Gospel as having an emphasis on the responsible use of material resources and concern for the poor but erased their presence from the narrative.[18]

Engaging in a discursive strategy similar to the themes of women and the poor, Luke's model image of Gentile inclusion presents them as supportive, subordinate but largely silent.[19] The most prominent, positively presented Gentile actors in Acts are Cornelius (10.1–10.1-48), Lydia (16.11-15), and a jailer (16.25-34), which depict the incorporation of entire Gentile household into the Way by focusing on

community of believers as the Assembly, see 5.11; 7.38; 8.1, 3; 9.31; 11.22. 26; 12.1, 5; 13.1; 14.23, 27; 15.3, 4, 22, 41; 16.5; 18.22; 19.32, 39, 40; 20.17, 28.

17. Tabitha, Priscilla, and Lydia are possible exceptions. Tabitha, who Luke calls a disciple, is the strongest candidate (9.36-43). Priscilla is a co-teacher alongside her husband (18.1-4; 18–28) while Lydia is a business woman and house-holder that is able to overcome Paul and persuade him to reside with her in Philippi (16.13-15).

18. Luke inserts topics of wealth, poverty, and alms-giving into Acts' narrative through depictions of community ideals (2.44-45; 4.32-36); idealized characters (Barnabas, 4.36-37; Tabitha, 9.36; Cornelius, 10.2-4, 31); negative characters (Ananias and Sapphira, 5.1-11; Aramaic-speaking members of the Assembly in Jerusalem, 6.1; Simon Magus, 8.14-24; Philippian owners of a slave girl, 16.16-18; Demetrius, 19.23-27).

19. Luke's depiction of the Assembly as financially self-sustaining and Diaspora Jews as potential property owners (4.34-36) and Roman citizens (16.37-39) diminishes the socio-political and material significance of Gentile inclusion. Consequently, Gentile inclusion becomes primarily a cultural and ethno-cultic signifier.

the ministries of Peter and Paul. Despite the lack of Gentile models for the type of Gentile church leadership that became prominent with individuals like Ignatius of Antioch (died ca. 117 CE), Marcion (died ca. 154 CE), Valentinus (died ca. 160 CE), Justin Martyr (died 165 CE), and Irenaeus (d. 200 CE), Acts' thematic focus on Gentiles has contributed to a consensus among most modern scholars that view Luke as Gentile. (Re)viewing Acts without presuming a traditional metanarrative moves the narrative beyond simple binaries and gives readers more freedom to perceive Lukan themes as multifaceted and nonlinear.

Reviewing from Diaspora

My conception of diaspora and nonlinear approach to historicizing nation-states prefers using twoness and polyvolcality as ways of conceiving identity. Subsequently, I view first-century CE Jewish identity through the lens of Diaspora by (re)imagining Jewish identity as capable of being fully embodied as Hellenistic and Jewish simultaneously. Jewish Philosopher Philo of Alexandria was a Roman citizen and came from an influential family in Alexandria.[20] Philo's description of Jewish identity and the Diaspora appears incongruent with rigid dichotomies. Within Philo's world view, Jews claim their place of residence as their fatherland [πατρίς, *patris,* fatherland, native land] because it is the place where their fathers, grandfathers, great-grandfathers, and more ancient ancestors were born and raised. Rather than dismissing the significance of Jerusalem or Jewish identity, Philo explains that the Holy City, Jerusalem, serves as their *mētropolis* [μητρόπολεις, metropolis, mother-city] (Philo, *Flacc.* 46).[21] This expression of Jewish identity suggests polyvocality and an emphasis on relatedness across diverse communities. His depiction emphasizes the diversity and mutability of Jewish identity in Diaspora.

Diaspora identity, according to these depictions, does not necessitate alienation or fragmentation; particularity matters. Much like individuals of the African Diaspora in the United States can embrace a racialized or diasporic identity and still identify as American, individuals of the African Diaspora from France can identify as French, Jamaica as Jamaican, or Ghana as Ghanaian. In a similar manner, Josephus explains that Jews in Ephesus consider themselves Ephesians and those in Antioch, Antiochians (Josephus, *Apion* 2.39). Josephus further describes internal Jewish identity in his autobiographical *Life of Josephus* as extremely diverse and consisting of various sects [*hairesis,* αἵρεσις, sect or

---

20. Philo addressed Rome's imperial court in-person on behalf of Alexandrian Jews; his brother, Alexander, held an imperial post as one of the wealthiest individuals in Alexandria. Philo's nephew served as Procurator of Judea, Prefect of Egypt, and an influential Roman General during the First Jewish War.

21. Philo also calls Jerusalem the *patris* and *mētropolis* not only for Judea, but for Jews living throughout the Diaspora (Philo, *Leg. Gai.,* 281).

party] such as Pharisees, Sadduccees, Essenes, and an unnamed ascetic group in the Judean desert (Josephus, *Life* 10). Employing similar language, Luke describes Sadducees (5.17), Pharisees (15.5; 26.5), and the Way (24.5, 14; 28.22) as variant articulations of thought and practice within Jewish diversity.

With such models available, the frame of Diaspora crystalizes a Lukan attentiveness to Jewish geopolitical diversity. Acts repeatedly insists on identifying geopolitical particularity. Luke expressly has the original disciples addressed as Galileans (1.11; 2.7) alongside geopolitical descriptions of Barnabas with Cyprus, Paul with Cilicia, Priscilla and Aquila with Pontus via Rome, and Apollos with Alexandria. Luke describes Antioch as the first location where participants in the Way ministered to Gentiles. He specifies, however, that the evangelists were Cypriot and Cyrenian Jews (11.20). In the midst of repeated, negative uses of the term 'Jews', Luke subverts a flat myopic vision of Jewish identity by encouraging his readers to acknowledge Jewish particularity.[22]

Reading from Diaspora also reframes debate and difference from signifying Other to being a perpetual component of polyvocality. Diaspora metanarratives must acknowledge the often tenuous socio-political realities of Diaspora-life. The tenuousness of Diaspora means that the life-death nature of Diaspora discourse always consists of internal debate and self-critique. The dominant nation-state metanarrative presupposes that narratives uniformly depict insiders in positive ways and outsiders in negative ways.

Luke's decision to include unflattering narratives about the Assembly (*ekklēsia*) elucidates this point. Ananias and Sapphira are insiders who drop dead after lying against the Holy Spirit (5.1-11). As members of the Assembly, this couple withheld proceeds from the sale of their property. Traditional readings demonize this couple as ultimate outsiders, failing to appreciate how viewing them as insiders alters Luke's vision of the Assembly. Another critical point in the Acts narrative revolves around an argument that arose within the Assembly because Assembly leaders neglected widows from Greek-speaking Jewish families (6.1-7). Similarly, Luke has few qualms depicting Paul, who excises a slave girl due to annoyance (16.16-18) and refuses to listen to the Spirit during a trip to Jerusalem (21.4), as temperamental and stubborn. Readers who invoke traditional nation-state metanarratives often essentialize Luke's presentation of members of the Way and non-believers. My reading, however, approaches Luke's vision of the world as much more nuanced.

Many interpreters read Luke's negative descriptions of Jews as condemning all non-believing Jews (Sanders 1987; Farmer 1999; Fredriksen and Reinhartz 2002; Donaldson 2010). I suggest that Luke's focus on particularity permits an

---

22. Luke's narrator uses the first person plural 'us' and 'we' in 21.17-36 to depict the narrator as one of Paul's travel companions to Jerusalem (21.17-19). By implying that Trophimus was Paul's lone Gentile companion in Jerusalem, the narrator suggests that he is Jewish. This interpretation is not a claim of historicity but one way to (re)construct Luke's narrator.

alternative reading. Saul/Paul enters Acts as a strident enemy of the Way (8.1-3). Yet, Luke dedicates the second half of Acts' narrative to Paul and his travels. In addition to Paul, Luke places a short speech in the mouth of a Pharisee named Gamaliel (5.27-39). In this speech, Gamaliel defends Peter and the Apostles from an assassination attempt. While being described as respected, Luke refrains from any insinuation that Gamaliel is a member of the Way.[23] Paul's transformation alongside the presence of non-Christ following Jews encourages interpreters to resist static perceptions of identity or judgement within Acts.

The final aspect of Acts that I attend to is Luke's internal allusion to the Way as inclusive of diverse and polymorphous expressions of thought. Invocations of the dominant metanarrative result in the assumption that divergent practices are perversions or inferior. However, Luke consistently describes the Way as adapting and debating in thought and practice. The schism depicted between Hebrews and Hellenists in 6.1-7 results in the appointment of six Diaspora Jews and a proselyte. The Apostles appoint these seven to serve tables and do tasks that the twelve deemed menial. Luke immediately describes them as proclaimers of the Gospel and witnesses to the world. The actions of the seven, not the twelve, result in the increasing numbers of people witnessing throughout the world.

In line with the unexpected differences between the seven and twelve, Acts consists of numerous differences in practice and thought between the Diaspora and Jerusalem that result in meetings, debates, and compromise. The cantankerous Paul engages in disputes with Gentiles, non-Jesus following Jews and Barnabas (15.39-40). It is worth noting that the majority of Paul's Jewish disputes occur over issues of authenticity with other Diaspora Jews and not Jews from Jerusalem. While Luke refrains from negatively describing Barnabas, he clearly states that Paul and Barnabas have an argument that they could not resolve. Add to these examples Luke's definitive description of Apollos of Alexandria as 'accurately speaking and teaching things concerning Jesus' (18.25) despite having only heard of the Baptism of John the Baptist and a metanarrative that endorses polyvocality can easily find the logical coherence within these descriptions.[24]

Though beyond the scope of this chapter, a fuller exposition of these narrative observations will greatly enhance the interpretation of Acts. These narrative points simply serve to highlight aspects of the Acts narrative that are often ignored in subordinate service to hegemonic and dominant metanarratives. In line with my alternative reading of the Nat Turner narrative, the logic of assumed binary subjectivity, preference for an outwardly linear trajectory, and the assumed idealization of insiders and *telos* are incongruent with my invocation of Diaspora-identity. Since the majority of the actors in Acts are Jewish, particularly

---

23. A Pharisee, Gamaliel (5.34-39), and synagogue ruler, Sosthenes (18.17), offer two neutral-oriented depictions of Jews in Acts.

24. While Priscilla and Aquila enhance Apollos' teaching, Luke is intentional in describing Apollos' initial teaching as acceptable, powerful, and engaged in the spirit (18.24-25).

Jews in Diaspora, my nonlinear metanarrative discerns many of Acts' seeming incongruences as expressions of Diaspora discourse. Beginning with the dispute between the Hebrews and the Hellenists in 6.1, intra-Diaspora dispute is the primary narrative catalyst. The sources of these disputes, rather than intellectual, are matters of life and death, community maintenance, and community obliteration. In much the same way any invocation of Black folk implies some specific particularity Luke's 'the Jews' are actually Cyrenian, Cypriot, Asiatic, Pharisaic, Herodian, Priestly, Scribal, or members of the Sadducees. Though Luke frequently uses the general term 'Jews', he consistently reminds his audience that the narrative setting is always in context and aware of Jewish particularity.

In an era when Josephus lambasted the Galilean Jews that he once co-served with during Judea's revolt against Rome and brazenly invoked Jewish scripture to identify Vespasian as Israel's divinely appointed Messiah, is it possible to read early Jewish and Christian discourse through a lens of Diaspora? Acts, written in this same post-70 CE context appeared amid a diverse polyvocal Jewish-world who's political and geopolitical reality had been drastically shaped by Empire and Diaspora. Though traditional approaches to Acts produce diverse interpretations, they largely reflect reliance on a linear paradigm that resembles dominant Western metanarratives of the nation-state. This metanarrative's representation of history is a contextually legitimate and useful way to read Acts as a discourse that legitimates, defends, and emphatically centres Christianity upon Gentile identity. However, because metanarrative selection is always contextually situated, readings dependent on any one metanarrative should only be understood as a reflection of possible patterns and logics.

When engaged from my self-understanding of Black America, Luke's thematic concentration on Gentiles becomes an issue of Diaspora existence. By invoking a metanarrative situated within the logics of Diaspora, the Jewish and Cilician Paul's pronouncement in 28.28 need no longer be conceived as Luke's declaration of THE univocally expressed Way nor as the hegemonic call to eradicate expressions of the Way articulated by Peter, Barnabas, Phillip, Apollos, or even Timothy. With Acts no longer restricted to being the self-evident twin history of Gentile Christianity and Anti-Judaism, this contextual reading attends to numerous textual signs that appeal to my own Diaspora context. Luke's thematic focus on Gentiles can indeed function as a historicized *apologia* of Diasporic existence in the midst of diverse disputes about Jewish memory, Jewish authenticity, and Israel's future. Like reading Nat Turner, the invocation of alternative metanarratives can situate both history and Diaspora as complex matrices characterized by countless roots, routes, ruptures, self-critique, and generations.

In this chapter, I have used my own Black American identity to highlight the contextual nature of metanarratives and their important role in the construction of history. Within dominant US culture, traditional metanarratives have a tendency to privilege insider/outsider oppositions, linear development, and homogeneity. My discussion of Nat Turner illustrates the ease with which people project, unconsciously, their own contextual presumptions onto history. Through discussion of Crispus Attucks and early American history, I outlined a dominant US metanarrative that functions along a paradigm similar to traditional readings of the Stephen narrative, thus, arguing that these metanarratives are cultural and appear across disciplines. Analysis of the insider/outsider, martyrdom metanarrative helped explain why my classmates perceived Nat Turner differently than me. Through my brief discussion of diaspora and my reading of Nat Turner, I was able to identify polyvocality, non-linearity, difference, and concomitant identities as key aspects of my diaspora-informed Black American metanarrative. With two alternative metanarratives outlined, I was able to (re)view the Acts narrative and identify various elements that disrupt the traditional metanarrative. These disruptions correlate with ancient notions of Jewish Diaspora-identity and negotiation. Exhibiting narrative sensitivity to particularity and multidimensionality, the Acts narrative can support a diaspora-informed metanarrative. This exercise, as an initial reading of Acts, argues that many of the narrative events and activities depict a perspectival story of diaspora acts. While focused on metanarrative, I do not offer a single interpretation of acts but a diaspora-informed metanarrative that can support multiple interpretations and historical (re)constructions.

Chapter 6

THE EMPIRE AS LOCAL CONTEXT IN ACTS

Néstor O. Míguez

The tension between the local site and what might be called the global context must be taken into account in the hermeneutical task. This is especially true in situations in which the presence of foreign domination, through economic, political or armed power, shades the local context; this is more significant when that dominion comes from a global power. Contextual hermeneutics tend to emphasize the immediate situation, the cultural milieu, the socio-political circumstances of the readers of the texts, and how their particular circumstances tend to make visible, emphasize or, on the contrary, conceal some aspects of the message.[1]

This is my particular case. Latin America has, as indicated in the way it is named, entered into Western history as a subject of conquest and domination. Before Columbus' arrival it was neither Latin nor America. A long history of colonization, partial liberations, neocolonial enterprises, frustrated hopes and new oppression, and violence punctuate this history. Even for those of us who descend from the different migration waves experience the pressure of the colonial situation, because it is embedded in the system, in the power structures of exploitation, in the cultural ambiguity. When we think of ourselves as people, in the midst of the global scheme of power we cannot but realize that we are submitted to the *arbitrium* (arbitrary judgement) of foreign powers. No Latin American country is free from direct or veiled intervention of the great superpowers, of the spoliation of its resources by international corporations supported by their government, by the use of force when they consider it necessary. The imposition of the neoliberal ideology and free market economy (that in the last analysis is nothing but corporative monopolies)

---

1. It is common to look at a contextual reading as the readings from outside the Western academy. Yet the so-called 'scientific' criteria of the Western academy, its presumed objectivity, are also a contextual reading. Because it is generally unaware of its context, and especially of the power games and the role it plays in them, it tends to ignore or hide certain aspects that might question its naïve or common sense approach to certain issues of the text.

thwarts any democratic intention to change the situation, and the dominant media bias the culture with foreign influence. It is not a cultural exchange – exchange is domination in such an asymmetrical situation. It is not the hybrid culture of a fragmented postmodern world – an economic, political, and military imperial power underlies and supports the total scheme of concentrated global power.

A contextual reading must also look at the context in which a text has been woven. This is certainly necessary in order to relate the conditions in which the text was originally written and the circumstances of the reader. A certain match between them helps and validates the hermeneutical task, even if the differences must be clearly and explicitly established, in order to avoid an easy 'concordism' that ignores the historical development and cultural environment (Croatto 1987).

In times when empires force their demands, ways of life, and power over the local, the *ethos* of the foreign, the pressure of the imposition, introduces the need to consider its incidence in the construction of any given culture, hence, any text produced amid this cultural situation. The text will clearly express the local, and the local concern; it will also show in which ways that location is affected by the presence of what is beyond the visible context. In some cases this can be clearly appreciated; in others, it takes a more careful and detailed analysis to perceive that the local is also the global. And this is true for both, the *Sitz in leben* of the original text and the perception and interpretation of the readers.

But the texts, its narratives, and the performances that the text conveys are woven in the womb of the local, but also a local that is inside the body of a bigger body, of the empire and its culture. So, when the readers of a text that was written under imperial rule are also themselves under the same kind of oppression, a particular sensitivity grows towards the text and its original authors and readers, an empathy that creates a particular understanding of the stories and feelings expressed (or sometimes concealed) in the Scriptures. Living under imperial conditions creates a sensitivity that enhances our perception of the influence and presence of domination even when it is intentionally or unintentionally concealed. Thus, reading in a situation of imperial subordination provides an awareness of the particularities of living under foreign rule when read in the biblical (or other) texts. That which might seem normal or naturalized for those who enjoy the power structure of imperial domination, or have not suffered the cultural estrangement that it purports, is rapidly noticeable by others who carry the experience of oppression.

In this sense, we have to consider the relationship between hermeneutics of suspicion, contextual hermeneutics and liberation hermeneutics. Paul Ricoeur's approach to hermeneutics clearly indicated that in every text, and in every hermeneutics, there are explicit and hidden interests, biased understandings, and partial perceptions. Part of the task of hermeneutics is to bring to light these elements, in order to discover the real meaning and orientation of the text and its interpretations. In following Ricoeur's method, awareness of contextual hermeneutics comes to life, not only because of the theoretical contribution of the French scholar, but also because of the growing awareness of cultural differences, brought up in the struggles for independence and autonomy of Third World nations and societies. Local culture was promoted and the idea of a universal Western culture, the superiority of progressive positivistic rationality, was brought to question. Among the features that are brought up this way are the particularities of the local context, since every text and all interpreters are socially, culturally, and ideologically situated, and that is revealed in the hermeneutical task.

But, when the local context and the social situation is that of oppression, not only cultural issues come forth, but the political and power games concealed in the text and in the interpretations take a new meaning. The hermeneutical task is to show how the mechanisms of social, racial, economic, gender, or other forms of oppression have played in the content and form of the text, and also how previous interpretations have used the text to reinforce domination. Liberation hermeneutics is not only about a more or less particular approach to Scripture, nor does it simply consider the contexts. It is also about engagement; thus, hermeneutics also has the purpose to free the text and the interpretation of its oppressive charge and become a tool in the struggle for liberation. Liberation hermeneutics, the biblical bases, and companion to liberation theology,[2] is not only a method of interpretation or a particular approach, and even less a fad in biblical interpretation, but also the pertinence of faith in situations of oppression, prejudice, and injustice is at stake. But not only for those who live in these oppressive contexts, the context of the oppressed is the global context, related to those who are beyond that specific location, since oppression is related to global systems, and not strange to the reality of the powerful but also to those, even if they realize it or not, who consider themselves 'in the middle' (Rieger 1998: 124–41). That is the real difference between a naïve 'contextual hermeneutics' and a true liberationist reading of the Bible. The fact that most (if not all) biblical texts found their final forms under imperial rule make liberation hermeneutics the clue for a profound understanding of what is at stake in the Scripture stories.

In the following pages it is my intention to show how the confrontation of empire and people (in the sense of *populus*) – the contradictory interests at stake, the legal and political impositions – come alive in a new way when the imperial context of the narrative and the imperial context of the contemporary interpreter are called to enter in the game. For that purpose I will venture into the reading of two pericopes in Acts: the story of the slave girl exploited as diviner in Philippi (Acts 16.16-24), and the following account of Paul's missionary visit to Thessalonica (Acts 17.1-9). In both I shall stress the way in which the empires place the global as part of the local context. I will also need to define what I understand for empire,

---

2. In the case of Latin America, the book by Gustavo Gutiérrez that gave birth to the name of Liberation Theology (1971 in Spanish; 1973 in English) was immediately followed by a liberation hermeneutics approach to the book of Exodus by J. Severino Croatto (1972 in Spanish; 1981 in English). Yet, both books are not the origin of Liberation theology and hermeneutics: 'Popular reading of the Bible' was already a practice in base communities and Christian student's movements in the early sixties. See my 'Lectura Latino Americana de la Biblia: experiencias y desafíos' (2001 in Spanish; 2006 in English).

and why I call imperial domination the present situation at the global level. Let us start with this.

Recognizing Empire

In order to set my hypothesis, let us begin with some concepts about what we might call 'empire'. I do not want to make a former definition to embrace all empires of all times, but to enumerate some characteristics of the kind of political entente that we might name properly as empire. To that end I will recall some of the features expressed in *Empire*, the now classic book by Hardt and Negri (2000). According to them, the empire is a network, a configuration of power that, without a unified centre, constitutes a way of exercising power that extends globally. We might discuss the concept of a lack of a unified centre. It is true that an empire acts as a network, but it is also true that not all the knots in that network have equal power or are equally strong. The global extension of the empire imposes cultural and economic patterns that reflect the imposition of the original force that developed in the imperialist thrust.[3] It subsumes and syncretizes the societies it integrates; it is undoubtedly also influenced by the subaltern in many aspects, but the imperial elite, that might be or might not be geographically unified, constitutes a centre of power that dominates the whole formation.

Just to mention one aspect in this sense, even if the postmodern empire is global, and its network includes financial capitalist knots throughout the world – from China to Brazil, from South Africa to Norway – international businesses are conducted mostly in English, and the US dollar is the reference currency. That shows that not all the knots have equal power. For those of us for whom English is a foreign language, but have to speak or write in English to reach the international public, imperial imposition cannot go unnoticed. When you have the possibility of travelling, and your local currency is accepted for change at less than 30 per cent of its value, the economic consequences of empire become evident. If you have a passport from the United States or the European Union, you can travel around the world with little problem, but if your passport is from Uganda or Nicaragua, you can expect problems in every custom or migration entry point, showing that not every nation is equally considered within that network. Globalization is not the same for everyone.

---

3. The difference between empire and imperialism is a matter of controversy. The empire is mostly considered a consolidated formation that is able to extend and integrate in itself the plurality of conquered societies, especially by integrating its elites. Imperialism is the force that moves some to construct an imperial dominion. There are in history imperialist enterprises that never succeed; but when we consider that a situation of empire has been at least partially achieved, the power that initiated the imperial construction imposes its characteristic and force beyond the fact that other forces have been assimilated to the empire. See Boron (2002).

Social location is also affected by imperial domination. This is especially true for what we might call (though the ambiguity of the expression) 'lower classes' or 'the excluded'. They do not suffer oppression or impoverishment only from the local elite, but also from the domination of the foreign powers, not to mention the ecological consequences of the exploitation of nature. In a situation of empire – and the biblical example of Nehemiah or the Sadducees can certainly illustrate this point – local elites and imperial powers become allies, for they share similar interests, even if there are particular shades in the way they consider power and they have to deal with the local situation. When the poor and the oppressed make their claims, they have to confront in their struggle not only with the vernacular exploiters, but also with the forces of international domination. The local elites are also culturally affected, because even though they benefit from this alliance, they know that, in the last analysis, they are puppets in the hands of the really powerful ones that are beyond the scene. It is pathetic to see how presidents and aristocrats of Third World countries, and their business men and women, shamelessly incline to the requirements of the dominant world leaders and the financial global system. If they do not, they are included in the 'axis of evil'.

The World Alliance of Reformed Churches (WARC) has, among other Christian organizations, considered the matter. It is worthwhile to quote their understanding of what an empire is:

> Empire is the convergence of economic, political, cultural, military and religious powers in a system of domination that imposes the flow of benefits from the vulnerable to the powerful. The empire crosses all borders, distorts identities, subverts cultures, subordinates nation-states, and marginalizes or co-opts religious communities. (Empire Task Group 2007: 5)

In this other approach, the stress is put on the economic exploitation and the strong power asymmetry of the imperial societies. Already Polybius, that visionary Greek historian who in the second century BCE, foresaw the rise of Rome to a world empire, noted the 'ecumenical' expansion of Rome as a matter of hegemony with a utilitarian goal (Musti 1978). The WARC definition also stresses the religious aspect of empires. Empires create their own religion; they erect themselves as godly and transcendent. Empires are built on the ideology of worldly transcendence, and thus, are idolatrous (Míguez, Rieger, and Sung 2009).

Clearly, this is the case of the Roman Empire with the cult of the emperor, but it is also the case of other empires. Christopher Columbus, taking occasion of the meaning of his name (Christopher, the Christ bearer), claimed that it was his duty by divine will to submit the discovered land to the Catholic Church. His claim was ratified by a papal bull (*Inter caetera*, 1493) as the Spanish and Portuguese crowns were assigned to Christianize, civilize, and subdue the native population in the name of God. This ended up in the cruellest genocide in history, since fifty years later the native population of the Americas was reduced to less than half. Five centuries later, in what is now called 'Latin America' (a clear legacy of the empire), we still suffer the consequences of this divine/imperial enterprise.

How can we otherwise read the British 'God save the Queen' said in the Malvinas Islands, more than 8,000 miles from England, in the southern part of the Atlantic, and in the coastal platform of Argentina? How to interpret 'God bless (the United States of North) America' sung in Puerto Rico? God is invoked as warrantor of the colonial enclaves.[4] It is not only blessing the head of the empire, but also requiring the divine to support what it represents: the occupation of a foreign land.

Even more, the imperial system itself becomes godly (Míguez, Rieger, and Sung 2009: Chs. 3–4) for it considers itself limitless and all-powerful in its own right. There is nothing over it to judge or limit its desire. Imperial policies allow the empire to go anywhere, to decide and impose, to control, to kidnap, to torture and kill, to make war, and to ignore local or international laws. It is not by chance that they also consider God as their possession. Empires claim to be the earthly expression of the will of the deities, to be backed by divine powers, the concretion of the will of God, the supporters of godly reign. Since they consider themselves the true bearers of peace,[5] anything or anyone that opposes its power is to be condemned, for it is not only a political enemy but the enemy of humanity and divinity, which, of course, they represent.

Living in the Postmodern Empire

The expression 'postmodern empire' is taken from Robert Cooper, foreign policy adviser to British prime minister Tony Blair. Cooper was influential in the European Union, justifying the involvement of Europe in the imperial wars in Afghanistan, Iraq, and others. In his book *The Breaking of Nations* (2003), he advocates for a postmodern 'soft' imperialism of the West in order to deal with the chaotic and violent nations of the 'premodern' world. The European Union, he claims, is the model of a democratic, tolerant, peaceful, and free society, which should be imposed on the rest of the world, even through non-democratic warfare and forced imposition.

4. The Malvinas (Falkland) Islands are considered colonial possession by the United Nations Special Committee on Decolonization ('Special Committee on Decolonization' 2015).

In the case of Puerto Rico, even though it is not named as a colony, its legal status is similar to those of colonial rule, since its government is submitted to the power and government of a foreign state.

5. We can find claims of imperial dominion as peace makers from the times of the Babylonian kingships until today. The most explicit expression was that of the Breton Chief Calgacus to the Roman General Agricola: 'The Romans create a solitude and call it peace', as registered by Tacitus ('Calgacus' 2016). Today, imperial wars are also 'peace wars' under the ridiculous motto of a 'preventive war' (as if a preemptive war was not already a war).

What is really veiled behind this postmodern imperial thrust is late financial capitalism, based on the neoliberal free global market economic theory. This was clearly exposed more than once by the spokespersons of the empire, like President G. W. Bush, and Condoleezza Rice, to name two of the most vociferous examples: Free society is free market. The only problem is that nothing is free in the free market. For them, freedom is captivity to one and only one possibility of being, what Margaret Thatcher called 'the only way' – an expression with clear religious overtones. The receipts of the International Monetary Fund, the World Bank, and other similar organizations (lately, the European 'troika') go the same way. We can see the consequences not only for Third World nations, with the increase of poverty, unemployment, cut to social welfare programmes, and the like, but for countries like Greece and Spain, and for the lower classes even in the most affluent nations.

The restrictions to personal liberty and rights that we enjoyed [*sic*] in the Third World with the application of the Doctrine of National Security by cruel dictatorships, necessary in order to impose a 'free society', have also now reached the people of the so-called affluent nations. The so-called 'Patriotic laws' and even the unlawful practices that come to light through the 'wikileaks' permit us to realize that the empire applies its espionage not only to its subordinates but also to its own population as well as its allies. With the excuse of 'security' we are controlled in many ways by those who can never be controlled. To live under the empire supposes that we are permanently in danger – the question of security is put in the first place in order to repress any possible threat to the imperial policies. But there is very little security to protect the common people from the arbitrary ways of imperial powers, or the vindictive violence it unleashes as its counterpart.

To chastise without trial, force into exile and banish, to seize and kidnap, to maintain in captivity without judgement, to torture, to assassinate, to suppress evidence, to make people disappear, and to suppress their corpses, all those crimes attributed to terrorists are performed in even a larger scale by imperial states. Thousands and thousands of innocent civilians have been killed without consideration, and sardonically called 'collateral damage'; no one is impeached for those crimes because they are the crimes of the empire. If any of the political, military, or financial leaders of the imperial powers would have to face an impartial court, they would not be able to escape the hardest sentence. Yet, they proudly and arrogantly consider themselves or their professional killers as 'heroes' or 'freedom fighters', while the local population lives in fear. Human beings are nothing, their will does not count if there is oil under their feet, if their elected governments dare to challenge this postmodern 'light' empire.

The imperial dogma presumes to have arrived to the end of history, as one of its ideologues proclaims (Fukuyama 1992). Humanity has no future but its imperial situation, stubbornly nicknamed 'democracy'. This is, to complete the title of Fukuyama's book, the 'last man' [*sic*]. So there is no place for the 'new creature' in Christ, for solidarity instead of greed, for love instead of selfishness, for faith. If this is so, there is no more place for hope, there is no more space for a new way of society. This is the end of all eschatology. This is the true Reign of God, the postmodern empire.

The Empire as Biblical Context

The texts of the Old Testament mostly have been initiated, composed, or written under situations of foreign monarchical rule over Israel, of what may be called expansive monarchies. The Egypt of the Pharaohs, the conquering Babylon, or the Persian rule have been called empires; yet in a nuanced study they do not have all the features of what we will properly name empire in the eyes of careful political distinctions.

The case of the New Testament is different, since there, with Roman rule, we find the kind of political system that can be identified as an empire also in the sense that the word has in the politics of today. As a matter of fact, it is the first political construction that bears that name, and the origin of it. It formulates the model for other formations that are to be called empire.[6]

The New Testament texts convey thoughts and narrative stories in which the influence of the imperial condition is always to be considered. Sometimes this influence is clearly expressed, other times it is to be perceived as powers that move behind the scenes, but that totally conditions the events and the ways they are registered. But it is not only the writing, but also the reading under imperial rule shows this tension between the local and the global. Postcolonial theories and narrative hermeneutics have helped us to see the incidence of the reading context in the interpretation of the text, and how the reading context highlights aspects that remain obscure or pass unawares under other situations or concerns.

I am aware of the discussion about the degree to which the Lukan texts, and especially Acts, have been considered as trying to show a friendlier image of the empire (see, for example, Witherington 1998: 73). It is not my intention to engage in that dispute. What I notice is, whether or not the author of Acts is more pro-empire or not, he[7] cannot avoid being conditioned by the imperial mentality. Whether consciously or not, whether willing or not, the cultural milieu in which we work, the language we use, the understanding of our social location is always imbedded in the dominant pattern of the social formation. Unless we are totally aware of this condition, and permanently struggle to overcome it through an alternative view, we will inevitably reproduce its value system and practices. On the other hand, Luke might try (or not) to play down the aggressive role of the empire, but in telling the stories he cannot escape putting in the picture and exposing the real nature of imperial power, and the constant confrontation of nascent Christianity with the predominant ethos of the empire.

---

6. I will not expand here on the historical difference I see between expansive monarchies of the Near and Middle East in times of the Old Testament and the Roman Empire, though I hope they will be clear, as I clarify what I think are the traits proper to an empire. We have signalled the differences in Míguez, Rieger, and Sung (2009: 3).

7. I am using the masculine for 'Luke', following the traditional view on the authorship of this 'treatise'. But I am not closed to consider any other possibility.

When we mention empire as context, it is not only the concrete details of a given empire, in this case the Roman Empire, but the study of an imperial context brings into the scene what is an empire as such, the imperial ethos, the 'spirit of the Empire', as different from that of other political formations. These become evident in the charges against Paul and his missionary team according to Acts 16 in the case of Philippi and Acts 17 in Thessalonica, and the way the authorities respond in both cases. I will not look at these charges from a legal or a theological point of view (at least in this chapter) since there are sufficient and deep studies and controversies on the matter (Sherwin-White 1963; Ste Croix 1963). I will rather look at them as a display of what is an imperial mind and how imperial power works, influencing the local context.

In the Lukan account of Paul's dealing in his missions in Philippi and Thessalonica, we have two texts that clearly illustrate how the global is present in the local, that is, the global is also the particular context in a situation of empire. In both cases Paul and his companions face the wrath of local authorities, accused by a third party. In the first case, the owners of a slave girl 'when they brought them [Paul and Silas] before the magistrates, they said, "These men are disturbing our city; they are Jews and are advocating customs that are not lawful for us as Romans to adopt or observe"' (Acts 16.20-21).[8] In Thessalonica, some zealous Jews, according to Luke's narrative, 'dragged Jason and some believers before the city authorities, shouting, "These people who have been turning the world upside down have come here also, and Jason has entertained them as guests. They are all acting contrary to the decrees of the emperor, saying that there is another king named Jesus"' (Acts 17.6-7). In both cases we can see how the imperial context is brought to play a decisive role in the narrative of a local incident. In both cases we shall realize the arbitrary nature of imperial power.

Now, let us examine the two accusations mentioned to see how they fit in this scheme.

Roman Empire at Philippi[9]

'And from there [we went] to Philippi, which is a leading city of the district of Macedonia and a Roman colony. We remained in this city for some days' (Acts 16.12). This apparently innocent description of Philippi already states the imperial context. The city, originally built as a consequence of the Macedonian expansion over ancient Thracian territory, became a Roman colony. That is, it is considered an extension, a 'municipality' of the city of Rome, and ruled according to Roman laws. Its authorities were appointed directly from Rome. The place was populated

---

8. Bible quotations are taken from the *New Revised Standard Version* (1999), unless indicated otherwise.

9. For an analysis of the whole episode at Philippi from a socio-political perspective, see Míguez (2012: 160–3).

with retired Roman soldiers. Apparently, Latin was the current language – at least, most standing inscriptions are in that language. The questions are why do we have an extension of the city of Rome, located in the coast of the Tyrrhenian Sea, in the old Thracian region, and with a Macedonian name? Why is it offensive to break Roman customs in such a place? Why are the authorities appointed by the distant Rome and the city guarded by Roman soldiers? These questions can only be answered by the presence of an empire and the reference to imperial policies. While this is not a novelty, it is surprisingly not a matter of consideration in most commentaries. They debate the accuracy of the 'leading city', or recognize the particular character of a colony,[10] but they do not ask what the implantation of an imperial regime meant for the ancient population of the city, for the old peasants of the surrounding farm land, for the religious beliefs and traditions of the region. The presence of the Pythian cult shows the remains of the old culture and population, but now at the service of Roman interest.

The case at Philippi is related to the economic slave system of the Roman Empire (Staermann and Trofimova 1975; Ste Croix 1981). Slavery in Rome is one of the issues that distinguished the empire from previous monarchies. In Egypt, the Persian reign, and in all the antiquity in Middle East, slaves were mostly servants of the state. The slaves were property of the king and employed for the great constructions, roads, and other major enterprises. Serfdom was imposed in the rural areas to cultivate the fields of the royal house. Occasionally the aristocrats were allowed to own some household slaves, but, as we can see in the case of Joseph, in the last analysis they were under the dominion of the kings. This is why when Moses requires the liberation of Israel, the decision lies in the hands of the Pharaoh.

This was different in the West. Already in the Greek city-states, we see that most slaves are private property, as was the case of the *oiketes* (household slaves); yet, they are not the base of production, which resides mostly in the local farmers and the *metoikoi* (immigrant foreigners). But the ownership of slaves and the exploitation of captive work in almost every craft and business becomes the norm for the Roman system. As a matter of fact, it is Roman organization and Roman law that assured private property as the core of society. Most of the legal system of Rome was oriented to deal with property rights, including the ownership of the family and slaves under patriarchal domain. If property was already a concern in classical Athens and spread with the Hellenistic period, it reached its peak in practice with the ascension of Rome. As over against the ancient monarchies, where the land was predominantly in hands of the King, Rome assigned ownership of the land to private persons, mostly the patriarchal families. Even more, the possession of land was a requisite to join the *ordines* (orders) that exercised power through the Senate

---

10. Witherington (1998: 488) signals the fact that Philippi is a colony that depends on Rome, but does not consider the social consequences of this – even when he calls his commentary '*socio*-rhetorical'. Tannehill (1994: 198) doesn't pay any attention to the fact that Roman customs are invoked in the episode.

or the *curiae* (city councils). As the Roman Empire, even in its most centralized period, conceived itself as a republic, the idea of state-owned property in the hands of the *Princeps* was not well considered. The emperor was, undoubtedly, the largest owner of slaves and land, but it was considered his private property, and not to be confused with the state's property.

State slaves were used for the construction of the aqueducts and roads, and to exploit the mines, since metal was needed for the army and the coining of money. The army had a portion of slaves for the service of the troops. Slavery in the mines (in Latin: *ad metalum*) and to the galleys was equivalent to a death sentence, so most mine slaves were rebellious slaves, people convicted for major crimes, or war prisoners. Yet, the bulk of production, which rose mostly from agriculture, rests in the hands of private landlords that exploited slave work. Undoubtedly the case of the farm land around Philippi was organized that way, since Rome distributed the land in that place among its war veterans.

This absolute priority of private property over any other concern, including life, is present in the episode at Philippi. For the sake of brevity I will only look at the episode that led to the imprisonment of Paul and Silas, concentrating on the accusation. More could be said about the event of his liberation, the conversion of the centurion and the debate over Paul's Roman citizenship, but that goes beyond the possibilities of the present work.

The slave girl was the exclusive property of her masters and no one was to interfere in that relationship. The accusation reveals this concept. 'These men are Jews and bring in customs that we, as Romans, cannot accept' (Acts 16.20-21). What can they not accept? Obviously, in the case of Paul it cannot be the Jewish law or circumcision. According to Luke, it is the fact that they cannot obtain economic benefit from that slave girl. The girl had a possession,[11] the *pneuma pythona* (spirit of divination) that allowed the owners to make great profit. In dispossessing the slave from this quality, Paul is putting in jeopardy their business, and for Romans this was a major offence. Any action performed over the property of another was to be considered a breach in the law and an offence to the honour of the owner, more so if that implied an economic peril for the offended party.

The economic aspect of the episode puts in evidence one of the characteristics of empire enlisted in the previous concepts: the flow of benefits from the vulnerable

---

11. Traditionally, this has been interpreted as a matter of demonic possession. But if we analyse this case, it is really the inverse: it is the girl that possesses a particular quality that made her unique, that is, to communicate with this spirit of divination. Paul does not perform an exorcism, in the normal way in which this is understood (against Tannehill 1994: 197), but destroys this capacity in the slave girl. In this case, Paul does not act out of love for the victim, but because he was annoyed of the soothsayers persistent cry. After all, the girl's cry was true: they were the messengers of the Supreme God, the spirit had correctly guessed the nature of the missionaries. Neither can it be said that the girl was 'saved' by this act. To the contrary, her situation after the episode was probably worse than before, and the missionaries take no more care of her.

to the powerful. While some imperial historians and interested exegetes want to convince us that in the Roman Empire there was a flow of money from the powerful to the lower classes through the gifts and other obligations of the patronage,[12] the opposite is true. If something trickled down it was because much more had gone up, as this passage shows us. Imperial *ethos* is always a spirit of accumulation, in politics and in economy, in cultural goods and in symbolic power. Through the ownership of this slave girl, her masters were able to obtain profit, prestige and, indirectly, political influence.[13] Now, all these were gone and the unwritten law of endless gain had been questioned; it is the duty of imperial legates to set it back.

It is interesting in the formulation of the charge that they do not appeal to the law but to the customs. The crowd and the magistrates react, not as guardians of the law (as we shall see in the case of Thessalonica) but as custodians of a certain way of life, of an *ethos*. The immediate alliance of the local authorities with the masters of the slave girl and the support of the crowd shows how this is active in the 'common sense' established by the imperial rule. According to Luke's narrative, there is neither trial nor defence, but an explosion of wrath. Given the public nature of the events, and the fact that probably, because of her activity, the popularity of this girl had spread in the city and region, it became evident that what occurred, however explained, would excite the anger of the surrounding population. For some, it was an attack to their economic stand. For the authorities, it was a breach in their power. For others, it was probably an offence to their ancient beliefs. People in the street would not be much concerned in the nuances of the law, but they could rapidly detect when something could affect the established patterns and beliefs.

Another of the imperial characteristics is also present in this case, the use of religion. The *pneuma pythona* is part of the popular religion of the region. It was related to the cult of Apollo and the Pythia Oracle at Delphi. It is plausible that it also bore some traces of the old Thracian religion, since there is archaeological evidence that the persistence of the Thracian gods was part of the syncretism that formed the divinities worshipped at Philippi. An example of this is the image of the so-called 'Thracian horseman' relief with Latin inscription found at Philippi. These deities fashioned under the disguise of Greek gods and goddesses, together with the Roman religion (including the emperor's cult) and the Macedonian version of the Greek myths, seem to have formed the mixture of beliefs that informed the local creeds. This is also a consequence of imperial politics. Imperial policies in the cultural field

12. This is the case of E. Judge and other representatives of what was called 'the new consensus'. For example, Judge writes: 'But in Greco-Roman society the reverse applies. Money is continually given by the powerful to their dependents, and this transfer of cash downwards in the social scale is the main instrument by which the status of the powerful is asserted' (Judge 1960: 61). The refutation of this strange theory can be found in Míguez (2012: 202, #13).

13. Divination was an important political issue for Roman mentality and it was prohibited outside the imperial control – it implied that someone could predict a future different from the expected.

tend not to combat the local culture but to integrate it at a subordinate level; it is a symbolic demonstration of its power. The so-called 'religious tolerance' is, in the last analysis, part of a conquering strategy. Local religions are to be confronted only when a certain belief demonstrates its capacity to subvert the imperial order, or to excite an identity that sets a risk for the integrative nature of imperial ideology. We can easily see this at work today, for example, in the rejection of the use of the hijab in French schools. Soft versions of the religions should be admitted and cherished, since they can provide symbols that can support the imperial order and show a facade of good will for the conquering power. It was Paul that was 'intolerant' in this occasion and thus brought the conflict. He defied the local religion, and in the same coup he questioned the power of the *Pythia* and the religious policies of the empire. No wonder this brought about the wrath of the legates. The alliance of economic, political, and cultural power, that included the local religion, that constitutes the base of imperial force and the integration of the local elite in it were all contested in this simple act of expelling the spirit of the soothsayer.

One last word related to the fate of the weakest party in this story, the slave girl, that at the end remains in her most helpless position. Paul, according to the Acts narrative, could later claim the protection of his Roman citizenship. This was not available for the girl. She is the real loser in this story, the hidden victim of the whole affair. What would become of her? Nothing more is said about her fate (and this is also noteworthy), but we can guess a very unhappy situation. If she could not provide any more gain for her patrons by fortune telling, she would have to provide it some other way. No one would protect her; no law will take care of her. Not even the missionary team is said to look after her fate. She was devoid of the only power that made her valuable; she was left with no spirit, but the spirit of the empire. As usual, the story (as the imperial history) hides away the suffering of the weakest, the true victims of oppression, the voiceless 'little ones'. For imperial rule (but not only for empires) people are useful while they can provide some profit, but are to be discarded if not. This girl was left exposed to be exploited in some other way or left aside as waste. Empires always behave like that.

Empire at Thessalonica

The case at Thessalonica is slightly different, but it also shows the spirit of the empire in the background of the events. Having studied the episode at length in a previous work (Míguez 2012: 156–72), I will point only to the significance of the accusation as it signals the imperial context and ideology: 'These people who have been turning the world upside down have come here also, and Jason has entertained them as guests. They are all acting contrary to the decrees of the emperor, saying that there is another king named Jesus' (Acts 17.6b-7).

For the sake of brevity, I will point out three issues that reveal how an empire acts. First, the Jews and some ruffians accuse the missionary team that 'these people who have been turning the world upside down have come here also' (17.6). The accusation itself shows the relationship of the global and the local:

the missionary team is *oikoumenen anastatosantes* (turning the world upside down). That is, they are bringing in to the local a revolution that is global. That makes sense if the global is considered as a totality, and stirring the order in a local situation has global background and consequences. To bring in a different world view is to challenge the current, and thus it turns the *oikoumene* (the inhabited world) upside down. The verb used here in qualifying the preaching of the apostles (*anastatoo*), to unsettle, to agitate, to insurrect, has the same root as that of resurrection (*anastasis*). Preaching the resurrection they are provoking a world insurrection. The Christ condemned and executed by the empire was alive. The empire does not have the last word: Affirming the in-resurrection of an executed culprit is a challenge to the self-understanding of any imperial power.

Second, the mob continues in saying 'They are all acting contrary to the decrees of the emperor' (17.7). In addition to the already mentioned legal discussion, what is beyond doubt is that the Thessalonian people consider valid the intervention and laws of the foreign rule. The power network is validated in the *oikoumene*. The local elite is made responsible for the enforcement of a legal power over which they have no say (Thessalonica had its own chosen local authorities, the politarks. That differs from Philippi, that as a colony, had authorities named by the emperor). Obviously, we may say that they were forced to do it. But the literary evidence shows that far from that, they were very willing to see the Roman power and the emperor as their benefactors, as the protectors of their privileges (Hendrix 1984). They were clearly caught into the spirit of the empire, for the decree of the emperor was the fountain of their own strength.

Third, they continue the accusations, 'Saying that there is another king named Jesus' (17.7). In the same line, they legitimate the kingship of the emperor. The two cities we are talking about bear the names of the Alexandrian family: Alexander's father (Philip) and his stepsister (Thessalonike). That is, the Macedonians had a proud history of their own legitimate kings (themselves conquerors of other nations and peoples). But now they acknowledge and accept that a foreign monarch reigns over them. The global has taken over the local, the Macedonian identity dissolved into the imperial thrust. They become proud custodians of their own submission.

Related to that same phrase, considering the Caesar as a king (*basileus*) relates to the particular way in which the subaltern understand imperial force according to their own mindset. It is true that in the east of the Roman Empire, *basileus* was the current title for the emperor. But that title was resisted in Rome itself, since the Senate always refused to grant the title of king (*rex*) to the emperor, in the understanding that the republican rule was still in force. Empire is not a particular system; in the formal understanding of politics, it can operate with diverse institutional forms. We define it as a particular conjunction of forces, a concentration of corporate rule. Such forces, instead of controlling each other to reach certain equilibrium or to avoid abuse, they support each other in their power to impose, to exploit, to exclude. It was not the only time in history when a republic is the base of an empire, and that the so-called republicans sustain the need of imperial rule over others.

This accusation also permits us to see other features of the imperial *arbitrium*. Jason has to take the punishment for housing a relative, blamed with an unproved charge. Once again, as in the case of the slave girl, the charge comes over a defenceless party. We need not linger much with the accusation of 'another king' (17.7). If Paul preached the 'Reign of God in Jesus our Lord' the imperial idea of a worldly eternal power was certainly at stake. Goddess Rome is eternal, and the city under her protection cannot be but eternal. Even today 'Roma aeterna' is one of the mottos of the city. Any eschatology is a challenge to imperial pretensions.

Reading from the Empire

What I have tried to underline in this chapter is the possibility of applying the concept of empire as a hermeneutical tool. It is not the Roman Empire as such, but as a model of imperial rule, that permits us to read these texts as a critique of empire and the imperial spirit, yesterday and today. Paul, whether willing or not, and also Luke as he narrates the events, show the fact that the Christian message defies the spirit of the empire, challenges its customs, its economic and political standards, and affirms another way of understanding power and authority, of understanding human life. It is the account of the presence of another spirit. Contextual reading looks for the empire not only as the context in which the text was written but also as the context in which it may become meaningful today. Certainly, the Roman Empire is not that of today, but the ways of imperial power gives us some categories that can be a mediation to understand the sense of the text today, in its polysemic dimension. The overall search for profit, the sense of endless power which is divinely approved, the legitimacy of foreign rule, the lack of care towards the victims, the conjunction of different elites in their mutual support of power, the forced imposition of cultural standards are common features of empires, yesterday and today, in creating the context at a local level as well as in the worldwide scene.

But, more than that, it allows us to perceive the opposition between any imperial project and the Christian message. No matter how much you try to mellow the contradictions between the imperial policies and the Gospel (if that is what Luke's purpose was, which I doubt), these inevitably show up. Unless, as has happened so many times in history, the Gospel is also rendered captive of imperial interest. Imperial *arbitrium* can never become God's justice, its greed for money and power opposes any understanding of grace, and its killer instinct can never bring life. Empires consider themselves the Absolute, and so they cannot but deny any true understanding of the divine. Empires aspire to perpetuate themselves, making history meaningless and jeopardizing any eschatological hope. Its freedom is captivity to lust, while Christian faith is a call to love. This is why contextual interpretation that takes into account the conditions and sufferings imposed by past and present empires cannot be but suspicion hermeneutics, hermeneutics from below, liberation hermeneutics.

Part III

READING WITH THE CHURCH

Chapter 7

NO NEED TO WORRY, OR IS THERE? A *CAMBA* PENTECOSTAL READING OF LK. 12.22-34[1]

Esa Autero

In media and (Western) popular imagination Bolivia is often equated with snow-capped Andean mountains, coca leaf, and indigenous culture and politics. Nevertheless, nearly two-thirds of Bolivia consists of hot and steamy low lands (Hasbún 2011: 30). Eastern Bolivia or *el Oriente*, as it is locally known, has its distinct culture(s) and customs that differ considerably from the Andes mountain range and the central valleys. Many eastern Bolivians use the word *camba* as a self-designation despite the highly ambiguous character of the term (Waldmann 2008: 37–52). *Camba*s characterize themselves as care-free, hospitable, and happy people in contrast to their rigid and hard-working compatriots, the *collas* (Waldmann 2008: 37–52, 83–94, 140–2, 199–214). Nevertheless, despite the fact that the city of Santa Cruz in the east has become the most prominent economic centre of the country, numerous people in *Oriente* live in abject poverty. Corruption, civil unrest, and the lack of basic services make life difficult for many even in the city. Despite the difficulties, many people in the local Christian communities maintain a care-free and happy *camba* outlook on life.

The purpose of this chapter is to describe and interpret a familiar passage on worry and anxiety in Lk. 12.22-34 as read by two Bolivian Pentecostal communities. The interpretations of the groups give a glimpse on how these ordinary Pentecostal believers understand this passage from the perspective of their unique spirituality, socio-economic location, and life experience. The chapter will conclude with a brief reflection on the method and the role of the biblical scholar in the world of socio-economic inequalities.

---

1. An initial version of this chapter was presented at the SBL conference (2012) in the Contextual Interpretation of the New Testament panel. Parts of the original presentation were later included in my dissertation (Autero 2014) from which this chapter has been adapted. All quotes of Bolivian readers are from Autero (2014) unless otherwise specified. The dissertation was published by Brill Academic with the same title in 2016.

Contexts and Method of Interpretation

Context and Method

I am aware that my own context as a middle-class Finnish-American Pentecostal biblical scholar is very different from the Bolivian one I attempt to describe and interpret. As Daniel Patte has suggested, interpretations involve interpretative choices at all levels (Patte 2011: 199–212). This includes the presentation of my interpretative context as well. Thus, I will briefly highlight the aspects of my context that are relevant for the purpose of this chapter. I have chosen the lens of ambiguity/contradiction to present the multiple levels that make up my context.

As is well known, Pentecostalism has been a movement of the working class and the marginalized since its inception in the early 1900s (Anderson 2004: 39–45; 1979). One of the characteristics of the Pentecostal world view is the belief in spirits, demons, prophecies, and miracles of all sorts, not only in the majority world but also in Europe and the United States (Dayton 1987: 115–41; Hollenweger 1997: 164–72). This distinct world view places Pentecostals into a marginalized position in Western societies. As a result, Pentecostals have often been labelled 'primitive' (Synan 1997: 187–219. See also Duran 2011: 38–40). This was (and is) true of my background in Finnish Pentecostalism as well. Still a few decades ago, academic theology was completely unknown among the Finnish Pentecostals, and there was a polemical relationship between the state-sponsored and dominant Lutheran Church and Pentecostalism. Pentecostals were often, and sometimes still are, marginalized or labelled sectarian, overly emotional, or non-rational. As a student of theology in the early 2000s, this tendency was evident in the university curriculum which was mostly liberal Protestant and Lutheran.

In regard to academic theology, a notion of completely detached and objective research is rather strange to me especially when it comes to reading the Bible. However, the so-called 'spirit-led' or spontaneous Pentecostal hermeneutics that I inherited is something that I cannot uncritically accept either.[2] Further, in some circles of Pentecostalism anti-intellectualism still prevails.[3] These binaries of academic-objective-rational versus spontaneous-subjective-intuitive have led me to inner tensions and ambiguities but also to appreciation of both perspectives and to an attempt to move towards a more integrated approach. As such, my Pentecostal heritage is important to my identity even if I am all too aware of its many weaknesses.

Though a native of Finland, I have had a chance to live on five continents. Most formative have been my years in Bolivia and a six-month stay in India. The variety

---

2. There is a lively and interesting debate among the Pentecostal scholars regarding hermeneutics. For a good introduction to hermeneutics and use of the Bible among Pentecostals, see Spawn and Wright (2012) and Martin (2013).

3. Some preachers discourage studying or demonize academic theology or even seminary education in general.

of cultures and cultural expressions of Christianity have forced me to reflect on my own identity and way of approaching the Bible both as an academic Pentecostal biblical scholar and a member of the socio-economically privileged Finnish-American middle class.

Due to my social location, I have never experienced poverty or extreme economic deprivation. Nevertheless, my work and experiences with the poor communities in Bolivia, India, and the United States have allowed me to see inhumane living conditions of (too) many people. Further, though Pentecostalism has largely attracted the poor and marginalized sectors of the society, the rise of the so-called prosperity theology in recent years within neo-Pentecostalism is an alarming trend. In some of these movements, biblical texts are used to justify socio-economic inequalities, exploitation, mega-temples, and at times lavish lifestyles of the leaders (see further Autero 2014: 20–37). Even with this, one should not lump all Pentecostals or neo-Pentecostals into one mould. The variety of Pentecostal expressions is remarkable as the recent literature on global Pentecostalism indicates (see Attanasi and Yong 2012). One should not forget that on a global scale it is the poor who are particularly attracted to Pentecostalism. In Latin America, the idea may succinctly be captured in the following phrase: 'Liberation theologians opted for the poor but the poor opted for Pentecostalism.'[4] Yet, this does not diminish the predatory aspects of certain types of exploitative prosperity teachings (see further Autero 2014: 35–8). Nevertheless, the general American (and increasingly Finnish) middle-class lifestyle that is focused on individualism and rampant consumerism does not fare much better – even if it lacked an explicitly religious legitimation. At the same time one cannot but feel helpless in the face of the enormous economic discrepancies as well as the competing socio-political agendas and charities that claim to make a difference or change the system. Is there something that an academically trained biblical scholar can do to alleviate poverty and to improve the lot of the poor in the world?

My context(s) plays an important role in the choice of both text and the methodology. Particularly the tension between objective-subjective and the multiple levels of my own context(s) have not only led me to question the claims for objectivity but also made me ponder the difficulty of defining the concept of context, especially when it involves a representation(s) beyond one's own idiosyncrasies. The deeper issue involves definitions of context(s) and who may represent or speak for whom in a given context (cf. Autero 2014: 55–8, 72–80). The choice of the text in this chapter is connected to my dissertation project which involved investigating the impact of socio-economic status on hermeneutical processes of the two Bolivian Pentecostal groups.

---

4. This is a fairly commonly known saying in parts of Latin America. Mariz states similarly that 'the Catholic church opts for the poor because it is not a church of the poor. Pentecostal churches do not opt for the poor because they are already a poor people's church' (1994: 68–80, esp. 80).

My socio-religious and academic context has led me to search and develop methodologies that would help systematize and define the context and its representation more clearly and allow the combination of socio-economic, cultural, and spiritual realities in one's reading. It is all the more important when the context involves something or someone else than one's own socio-cultural context. That is, one tries to give a portrait, even if only partial one, of 'the other'. In this quest, I have found two approaches helpful. The first approach is dialogical hermeneutics or the 'reading-with' approach (West 1999b; 2000: 595–610; 2007). The second is various empirical methods and more specifically a new approach called empirical hermeneutics (Wit 2004b: 3–53; Autero 2014: 39–58). Empirical hermeneutics combines standard social-scientific field research with biblical studies.

Research and Bolivia Context

As part of my dissertation research, I spent eleven months in Bolivia listening, recording, and observing the hermeneutical processes of two Pentecostal communities in the city of Santa Cruz. The communities were chosen to have a representation from a poor area of the city and from a wealthy area. All groups read several texts from Luke's gospel that dealt with salvation, wealth, and poverty.

With this in mind, I will start the next section by describing the general socio-cultural and historical issues about Bolivia, and then move to describe the contextual realities of the communities. This will be followed by a brief summary of the readings of one passage (Lk. 12.22-34) by both communities. Before the final reflection and conclusion, I briefly compare and contrast the readings of the two communities.

As was mentioned in the introduction, eastern Bolivia does not fit into the general media representation of the mountainous and 'indigenous' Bolivia. Though Bolivian *Oriente,* and particularly Santa Cruz, is sometimes portrayed to be synonymous with white neoliberal oligarchy that opposes the indigenous peoples of the Andean region, the situation is much more complicated than this simple dichotomy allows (Hasbún 2011: 30–2). As I talked to the local people in Santa Cruz and the surrounding villages, both the rich and the poor, Protestants and Catholics, it became increasingly clear that the dislike of the current president Evo Morales (2006-) and his politics concerned above all the deeply rooted socio-cultural values. The antagonism between mountainous west and the eastern lowlands has a long history. Historically, the advance of the Inca Empire was halted by the various indigenous tribes of the Bolivian low land (Klein 2003: 20–3). During the Chaco war (1932–35), many eastern Bolivians felt that they were fighting against their own 'brethren' because they were culturally and ethnically closer to the Paraguayans than their highland compatriots (Waldmann 2008: 25). Recently, the politics of Evo Morales towards *cambas,* and especially the violent suppression of the indigenous people in Tipnis have polarized the situation even more. Ironically many indigenous groups of the eastern Bolivia do not consider Evo Morales as indigenous but rather as *campesino* (Wightman 2008: 94–5).[5] They also do not support Evo Morales' so-called 'indigenous politics'. This cultural rivalry is accentuated by the economic migration of the *collas*, or Andean Bolivians, to the city of Santa Cruz and the surrounding countryside. The migration consists mostly of the poor in search of economic opportunities, but a number of rich *collas* also invest in the lucrative agro-industry and businesses or buy luxurious vacation homes. Many *cambas* see this as a form of internal colonization and a threat to their cultural identity.[6] Ironically, some locals pointed out to me how the president's politics of decolonization of the Western powers (especially the United States) from Bolivia has turned into internal colonization of *el Oriente* by the same president.

Eastern Bolivians often identify themselves as *cambas*. The term is highly ambiguous due to its historical and cultural connotations. In the late nineteenth century, the term *camba* was synonymous with indigenous population of the eastern lowlands and was used as a polar opposite of those who had pure lineage of the Spanish colonizers (Bazán 2006: 25–42). Later on it adopted more positive connotations and finally came to mean broadly people who live in the region of *el Oriente*. Nevertheless, as some of my Bolivian friends suggested, today 'it is all about who says it and how you say it'. To call somebody a *camba* can thus be derogatory or positive. *Camba* identity has been, and is, in constant formation. Recent studies debate the exact characteristics of *camba* identity. The happy and worry-free attitude was pronounced as I visited some of the villages outside the city of Santa Cruz. In one village the pastor said that though the villagers are very poor, they are not worried about their next meal. If there is food for today, tomorrow is not something to be worried about. According to an anthropological study of the upper middle-class *Cruceños*,[7] it is precisely this laid-back attitude to life that distinguishes *cambas* from *collas*. Some *cambas* are even willing to label themselves as lazy though others do not agree with this characterization. In popular imagination the symbol of a man playing guitar in a hammock has become very popular (Waldmann 2008: 140–1).

It seems to me that, in addition to a threat to one's cultural identity, one of the important aspects of the rivalry is access to economic opportunities. According to some recent estimates there are approximately 530,000 people in the city of Santa Cruz who live in poverty ('Hay más de medio millón pobres' 2012). As a result of these (and many other) factors, there is a constant threat of political instability, road blocks, and according to some[8] even threat of civil war. During my stay (2011–12) medical doctors went on strike for nearly fifty days. As a result I heard reports of people dying due to lack of medical services. In addition, *el Oriente* has a number of environmental factors that make living conditions difficult. Recent years have

---

5. This came across also in the discussions with locals and the professors at the ecumenical centre.

6. Cf. Waldmann (2008: 147–59) about losing *camba* identity.

7. People who live in the city of Santa Cruz.

8. The possibility of civil war was mentioned to me by both *cambas* and *collas*.

seen epidemic proportions of dengue fever in the summer due to intense heat, flooding, and poor hygiene. In the winter, the chilly southerly winds make life difficult for those without proper shelter; and in the spring the burning of the nearby fields makes the air in parts of Santa Cruz toxic. Without trying to be overly dramatic, from my socio-cultural perspective there is a whole lot to worry about.

The brief analysis above, regarding the contextual realities in Bolivia, indicates that the socio-political and cultural situation defies simple dichotomies. During the reading of the biblical texts, it was particularly the *camba* identity and socio-economic disparities that emerged with some frequency. In addition, some group members referred to their former affiliation in the Catholic Church, which was generally viewed negatively. Before presenting excerpts of the Pentecostal groups' readings, I will briefly describe the communities that I studied.[9]

The sample churches consisted of two Pentecostal congregations, one of which was from a socially and economically marginalized community and one from a wealthy upper middle-class community. The former will be referred to as the marginalized group (MG) and the latter the privileged group (PvG) throughout the chapter. These designations, albeit somewhat vague, attempt to capture the social locations of both communities in the Bolivian society.

The church of the MG is located in a socio-economically marginalized community and has about fifty members. It is part of a small independent Pentecostal denomination. According to the survey, the income level of the MG participants ranged from 56 to 396 dollars per month for those who were employed. Some were unemployed while others worked as manual labourers, office assistants, and small business owners/vendors, and the like. Most participants were from the surrounding *departamento* (department) of Santa Cruz. Though many have access to potable water and electricity, the income level and the worries they reported during the study suggest that at least some are struggling to make the ends meet.

The church of the PvG congregated in a five-star hotel.[10] It was an independent neo-Pentecostal Church of about one hundred regular attendees on Sunday morning services. The income level of the participants ranged from 460 to 28,000 dollars per month. Most participants were consciously affluent professionals and the group included a corporate lawyer, university professor, and TV reporter.

As I conducted the study, each group was asked to read the text(s) from the perspective of their life context and their experience with God. The group discussion began with an opening question 'What do you think this text is about?' and was followed by text-specific questions.[11] Same protocol was applied to both groups.

---

9. It is not possible to give a full thick description in a scope of this chapter. Rather, I will highlight the most important aspects of each community.

10. The city of Santa Cruz is clearly divided into so-called *barrios populares* and the middle/upper-class areas, though in the latter one can find 'pockets of poverty'.

11. This outline follows roughly the contextual Bible study model developed by G. West (1999b; 2000: 595–610; West and Ujamma Centre Staff 2007) and J. Riches (2010: 3–22, 58–68).

Bolivian Pentecostal Readings of Lk. 12.22-34

Summary of the Marginalized Group's Reading of Lk. 12.22-34

Some of the first things that the MG group members pointed out from the passage were that there is no need to worry about the basic necessities of life, such as food and clothing. God provides for His children because He is a good and generous Father. One group member stated that one should not worry about tomorrow. After all, it is possible to take care of today's problems but tomorrow brings new ones. The pastor summarized the passage as 'security in God'. Other group members also emphasized the importance of 'seeking the kingdom'.

> Daniel[12]: … in the kingdom there is love, there is faith, there is goodness [and] truth. There is humility and forgiveness; [that's] the kingdom of God. But seek first the kingdom of God, incredible, right? I have a Father who loves me and knows my needs. So what should I worry about, because I have a Daddy who knows what I need … [He] gives me those things that I need.

As the study progressed, I asked the group members about the worries they have in life but received few responses. Nevertheless, as we continued the discussion a number of people shared some of their struggles or alluded to how they had overcome them in the past.

> Pastor: … we have always trusted in God. … When I was [first] married with my spouse, eh, God has always sent a person or God has always provided with a raven[13] to provide us … [there was] one brother who cooperated with us economically and then left … and then my wife said to me now what do we do?[14] What was my response? God is going to provide us … don't worry … because with my wife we needed to give food to our children … and God provided.

One person mentioned a past moral problem while another one talked about a sickness and death in the community. When I asked if anybody currently was anxious about the basic necessities such as food and clothing, the pastor immediately answered affirmatively and many others nodded but nobody was willing to elaborate. Later on, the pastor told a story how some years ago his former disciples wanted to borrow three *bolivianos* (about forty-five cents). Though the pastor had to support his family and had no money to lend, he gave since he was certain that God will provide his family. Another group member told a story of

---

12. All names have been changed to protect the anonymity of the individuals.

13. This seems to be an allusion to miraculous feeding of Elijah by the ravens (1 Kgs 17.4-6).

14. One notices the dependence on patrons in the church for financial sustainability.

how he went with a group of disciples to hold a church service with the pastor outside of the city but had no transportation to return to the city.

Perhaps one of the most striking worries was the desire for a better socio-economic status. At first the group was sarcastically criticizing the clothing and the lifestyle of the 'high society', but then the pastor stated that this was their old mentality which they needed to leave behind.

> Pastor: … if I believe that God gives me everything, eh, then I have decided, I Miguel Sanchez, to widen my territory. I believe in God and that He will place me into different environment.
> Pedro: Amen…
> Pastor: … not only other people may wear nice clothes. I also, as a son of the Kingdom able to wear nice clothes and have things that they have.[15] – We will not conform to what we have.

Yet, not long after the pastor's confident statement about the 'better things' he looked at me (researcher) and quietly asked whether he could rise to the same economic level where I am. After my hesitant affirmation, the pastor, who had grown up in the streets and gutters of Santa Cruz, said 'it will surely take a long time'.

As the study progressed, it became clear that certain themes and topics came up frequently, some of which were connected to the themes and flow of the biblical text while others less so. The themes that often came up and were related to the passage were the kingdom of God, seeking/striving for the kingdom, faith and trust, and giving/generosity.

One aspect that the group spent considerable time pondering was contained in vv. 32–34 in which Jesus talks about selling possessions and giving alms. One group member pointed out that first one needs to let go of fear. Others pointed out that the opposite of worry and anxiety is not to fear and to let go of one's possessions.

> Ruben: to give up everything … sell your possessions and give to the poor … to give up or give it…
> Rosa: … to sow into the kingdom of God. That is, to give to the needy and with an attitude of not being afraid.
> Juana: … that we need to give up our things… .

As I asked about how one could apply this teaching of Jesus today, a more realistic approach emerged. One group member said 'there it is, to give up our things … but that is almost impossible but it is beautiful to say it… '. The pastor stated that this passage makes one evaluate priorities. Many agreed but some were certain that this passage means that one should let go of one's possessions and give everything to the poor.

---

15. As the pastor told about this, he was wearing a dirty and worn-out T-shirt with holes in it and ragged old pants.

Two important and somewhat conflicting theological views emerged and merged during the reading. On the one hand, the group emphasized God's love and how the Father delights in His children and therefore wants to bless them. On the other hand, there was a strong emphasis on the importance of actions or living out one's faith. For example, one of the group members stated, 'I have a Father who loves me and makes sure that I have what I need' and little later added, 'I simply need to be in the kingdom and live in its justice/righteousness'.[16] Others, like *pastora*,[17] emphasized the active part to the point where 'seeking' seemed to become a prerequisite for receiving God's blessing. This kind of retribution theology where divine blessing (or curse) is meted on human beings based on corresponding human behaviour or virtue was an important feature in both groups' readings. I prefer to call this kind of retribution action-consequence theology.[18] That is, human action and corresponding divine blessing are intimately connected. Action-consequence theology was used as a theological explanatory lens on a range of issues but was particularly important in matters related to money and possessions. For example, one group member shared how her husband was always ready to give to the needy and share with everyone, even with the drunkards and other outsiders. As a result of the giving, they had received many blessings, such as an expensive machine for her husband's work. The pastor told a story of how he gave three *bolivianos* (about forty-five cents) to a disciple in need, and how the same person later gave him bread that was worth much more than what he gave. While one might have expected a similar action-consequence theology to work negatively as well, there was only one example that pointed to this direction.

The group was also surprisingly explicit about their cultural patterns. For example, one group member stated, 'We Latin people are very careless in a sense to seek; we always want things to be served to us'. The pastor quoted a local saying[19] which emphasized the importance of taking action and the resulting rewards. Another group member emphasized the importance of taking action by stating that 'it is not that everything will fall from heaven'. In these comments, there seemed to be a connection to the cultural stereotypes of *cambas* as lazy and negligent, as was mentioned earlier. Nevertheless, the comments also betray an explicit self-critique of the attitude and an emphasis on overcoming the cultural stereotype. The idea of reciprocity, which is another important cultural value in Bolivia, was mentioned by the pastor and also resonates with

16. Spanish *justicia* means justice but may include the idea of righteousness as well.

17. *Pastora* means literally female pastor. In this community, she thus held the title of 'pastor' alongside her husband and thus considerable authority. Nevertheless, the number one leader seemed to be her husband.

18. That is somewhat similar to the Hebrew Scripture and the Second Temple literature (e.g. Deut. 28.1-45; Prov. 10.2-4; Sir. 12.1-7, 29.8-13; 1 En. 92–105); see further Autero (2014: 289–98).

19. *perro que sale a andar halla hueso que mondar* (a dog that goes out to walk will find a bone to chew).

the action-consequence theology (cf. Estermann 2006). Further, as sociologists have pointed out, communal solidarity among the poor and socially marginalized communities is essential for survival. The most important resource of the people living in uncertain economic circumstances is a network of family and friends who live in reciprocal relationship with each other (Eitzen and Smith 2003; Smith 2010). Theologically, the emphasis on action-consequence is connected to the interpretation of covenant blessings in the Old Testament as understood by the Pentecostal tradition (cf. Macchia 2003: 1129–41).

The MG read the text from the perspective of their Pentecostal and socio-cultural background. Little attention was paid to the text's historical context or narrative structure. The group highlighted themes such as seeking God's kingdom, faith in God's care, provision, and experience of God's love. Giving and sharing featured prominently even as the group exhibited a desire for upward mobility in society. Further, as was indicated, action-consequence theology played an important role in the interpretation of the text as well as the group's experiences.

Summary of the Privileged Group's Reading of Lk. 12.22-34

Many aspects of PvG's reading are strikingly similar to those of the MG's reading. The initial focus was on God's provision and the importance of not worrying about one's livelihood. Seeking God's kingdom and the value people have before God was important as well. The entire group considered God as a source of blessing and goodness.

> Pastor: What is the kingdom?
> Carina: It is His presence, to know the word so that faith grows in us…
> Ruben: … yes, it is, it is …
> *Pastora:* It is, Jesus Christ says seek the kingdom and his righteousness.[20] The righteousness of the kingdom is Christ. And, because [it is] to walk in this righteousness that he has done in us…. So seek Christ and everything that is in the kingdom and his righteousness is going to be impregnated, imparted to us in order to walk in these works of righteousness.
> Ruben: … we know that we have to come to understand that God is going to be our king and he will take care of all of our life and He is going to guide us … –
> Pastor: And here … when it says seek the kingdom of God. There is everything in the kingdom … this is what it says, let's say we seek … not the kingdom of money – that in it [kingdom] there is everything.

God's kingdom was variously equated with the person of Jesus, God's presence, and God's love and care and guidance in the life of the believer. Though no concrete references were mentioned here, it seems that every good thing imaginable is

---

20. *Pastora* clearly connects Jesus' teaching in Lk. 12.22-34 here to its parallel passage in Mt. 6.25-34.

included in the kingdom of God.[21] Additionally, seeking Christ and the kingdom were important for the believer to receive its benefits and blessings.

As one looks at the particular worries that the PvG had, one can see notable difference from the MG. The main worries that came across in the PvG's reading reflected the socio-economic status of the group. These included things such as concern about the future and the future of one's children, children's birthday parties, general worry of increasing violence, the economic situation in general, difficulties with finding a new rental apartment, and a lost suitcase on a business trip to China. The pastor also mentioned how he had learnt to overcome his worry with securing a meeting place for the congregation in the five-star hotel; and how he never had insecurities about basic needs as he grew up.

> Pastor: … I remember for example when I was a boy and never worried what I would eat. I went to the fridge and took, and I never worried for [anything] because my father brought me [food]. –
> Vanessa: … to be preparing for the birthday party of my son and I say to the Lord [that] I do not need to spend so much time in my head [thinking] … – … [worry about] problems and … what is our future going look like, our children, the future we want, inheritance, many things. These [are the things] … that are in our mind all day long … .

An important aspect that emerged throughout the Bible study was what could be termed as a 'money discourse'. There seemed to be a constant tension between whether God would provide what one needs or whether God provides material wealth in response to faith, virtue, and obedience. The desire on the part of some group members, and the pastor in particular, for monetary riches was tempered by warnings against covetousness. After initial comments on God's provision the pastor said:

> We need to be inclined to the kingdom really. When we have the kingdom, God provides, let's say, all the money.

Another group member stated:

> God will provide all that we need physically … you never lack work, roof [over your head], you are not going to be a millionaire but you have all that you need.

The pastor related a little later how he used to accompany millionaires and observed their spiritually and existentially empty lifestyle as a commercial helicopter pilot.

---

21. Another member of the group gave a lengthy testimony on how she had learnt to control her mental anxieties. She explained that God helped her 'renew her mind' through prayer and meditation.

Nevertheless, after an incident that involved an inheritance and a lot of money he told how God spoke to him.

> Pastor: God spoke to me [saying] 'I can make you a millionaire just like that in one day if I want' … when you have nothing … and you get … twenty-one thousand dollars … .

Then he continued 'as we believe, so it will happen to us' and takes a famous American televangelist Creflo Dollar as a model who became a millionaire by faith and obedience. Later on, as the group discussed the connection of the passage to the previous parable of the Rich Fool, the pastor made a clear distinction between people who 'just accumulate riches' and those who were rich because of their obedience to God.

> Pastor: … in reality … riches as a result of a life in God are … it is another perspective and we are never going to accumulate because the one who has, gives … . And that is a principle of the kingdom. –
> Ruben: … to be generous and give what you have … .
> Pastor: … in fact you are increasing in your possessions, right?
> Ruben: Yes, yes … .
> Pastor: … because your company is worth more, you can have the one thousand two hundred apartments like the *Roca*.[22]

The pastor's comments seem somewhat contradictory as he at first equates non-accumulation of possessions and giving, but then he switches to the idea of gaining surplus material wealth as a result of sharing. Thus, despite the initial hesitation, it seems that particularly the pastor connects material wealth with faith and the virtue of sharing. Wealth is a consequence of giving though it is not clear to whom one should give.[23] The pastor also indicated that the 'principle of the kingdom' means that the one who gives also receives. Thus, action-consequence theology is once again the underlying theological principle.

As became evident, the money discourse was an important part of the appropriation of the passage among PvG members. While it is difficult to make sense of somewhat contradictory comments of the pastor, not everybody agreed with the type of prosperity theology that the pastor advocated. The pastor himself freely quoted 1 Tim. 6.10, 'For the love of money is the root of all kinds of evil', and at the same time exhibited a desire to be a millionaire. He seemed to resolve the tension by making a distinction between selfish accumulation of riches and

---

22. *Roca* is a luxury condominium in the city.

23. Though it is not apparent here, earlier (see comments on Lk. 6.20-26) the pastor had stated that giving to the materially poor is not generally beneficial since the real problem of poverty lies in the underlying spiritual problems rather than physical poverty or otherwise (see Autero 2014: 104–9).

accumulation of riches as a result of one's faith and obedience to God. The pastor seemed to particularly emphasize the importance of the purity within one's heart and/or motives.

As was the case with MG, the action-consequence theology played a prominent role in the PvG's reading. While the idea of faith with its resulting rewards was applied to various aspects of life, it was the financial aspect that dominated. Particularly, the pastor gave a number of illustrations and/or 'life lessons' from his own experience and that of the American televangelists to support his position. These were at times peppered with isolated Bible verses, such as the pastor's often-repeated verse that promises riches, honour, and life to the humble (Prov. 22.4). Strikingly, while the MG connected 'seeking the Kingdom' mainly to provision of basic necessities and perhaps a bit more, the PvG leaned (especially the pastor) towards connecting seeking the kingdom and financial wealth. That is, if one has faith and seeks God's kingdom, one will receive monetary blessings possibly to the point of becoming a millionaire.

Perhaps the most interesting feature, and also the most worrisome, was the scarcity of comments regarding generosity to the poor and the possible underlying socio-economic factors of poverty. While there were few general comments about giving and even giving to the poor, this was almost completely overridden by the money discourse as well as the emphasis on the existential and spiritual concerns.

On the whole, it seems that the socio-economic status and access to relative wealth combined with the neo-Pentecostal theology directed the PvG's interpretation of the text. There were no explicit comments or awareness regarding the cultural aspects of one's interpretation or appropriation of the text. Historical context or literary structure of the text was not explored and certain parts were highlighted at the expense of other parts. A notable omission was any comments on 12.32-34. Action-consequence theology framed much of the discussion together with an emphasis on seeking God's kingdom.

A Brief Comparison of the Readings

Both groups focused on similar issues such as seeking the kingdom, the importance of faith, and how to overcome worries in daily life. God was viewed as a Father, provider, and a good King. Both groups also emphasized the action-consequence theology and saw faith and obedience as important virtues that 'moved' God to grant blessings and benefits to the believer. However, whereas the PvG emphasized God's benefits to the faithful, and the possibility of great material wealth (esp. pastor), the MG focused on the provision of basic needs and necessities.

Both groups largely ignored the historical context of the text and lifted the idea of 'seeking the kingdom' rather freely from the historical and literary context. However, at times the MG followed the narrative somewhat more closely than the PvG. This became particularly apparent in 12.33, which focuses on selling possessions, giving alms, and giving to the poor. The PvG ignored nearly the entire section with the exception of few comments on the importance of 'storing treasures in heaven'. As such there were few if any comments on the importance of helping or giving to the poor on the part of the PvG. On the other hand, the MG commented rather extensively on vv. 32–34. They mentioned the importance of faith and not being afraid as well as sharing and giving to the poor and even to the 'drunkards'. This sharing was both individual and communal as the existence of community's soup kitchen indicated. Finally, some group members entertained the possibility that the text refers to the total divestiture on the part of individuals. The PvG did not allude to this possibility. Even though both groups focused on similar themes (kingdom, seeking, worries, faith, etc.), neither of the groups employed significantly different interpretative methods or approaches.[24] Nevertheless, the groups' social location had a rather significant influence on the interpretation of the text. As such the PvG read the text from the perspective of affluence and the MG from the position of socio-economic marginalization. This probably also contributed to PvG's understanding of the text and the importance of material provision; and also possibly to their ignoring the importance of sharing their wealth with the poor.[25]

In PvG's reading of Lk. 12.22-34, the money discourse and prosperity theology were highlighted to the extent that it eclipsed some of the most prominent features of the text such as sharing with the poor, generosity, and community solidarity. These seem, in my opinion, to be some of the most important features of the text for the present-day situation of increasing gap between the rich and the poor.[26] Clearly, there were no poor people within the PvG, neither was there any close connection with the socio-economically marginalized in the community. The pastor's 'money discourse' was largely legitimated by his spiritual and personal experiences, which he used as a hermeneutical key to interpret the passage. Further, the five-star hotel, where the group congregated, effectively excluded any attempts to include any poor into the community. On the contrary, the MG's reading seemed to take into account and support the principles of generosity and solidarity through the practical support of the community members even though (or because?) many members of the community lived in precarious conditions.

The worries that both Pentecostal groups discussed seem to reflect their own socio-economic and communal contexts as well as the Pentecostal theology and spirituality. I was somewhat surprised that many of the worries mentioned in my general description of Bolivia, such as cultural identity, difficult socio-economic and political climate were not emphasized more. This seems to indicate that the spirituality of these Pentecostal groups does not explicitly encourage broader

---

24. Perhaps this should be qualified somewhat. MG seemed to have employed slightly more Scriptural allusions and followed the text a bit more closely than PvG.

25. This conclusion should not be seen too dogmatically, since the group did indicate that sharing with the poor is of some importance later on.

26. However, to be fair to the upper-class group, issues of generosity and social justice did come up when the group read other passages, though the themes never attained high degree of importance in the discussions and did not seem to move the community to take particular action in practice.

socio-political reflection and engagement. The PvG community would have had both the means and avenues to engage (and/or discuss) broader societal issues but tended to focus on the spiritual and individual sphere. The MG did exhibit a sort of protest against the injustices of the society in their reading as they criticized the lifestyle of the 'high society' and talked about their experiences of exclusion and shame. In addition, their 'soup kitchen', mutual support, and communalism do exhibit a sense of solidarity that is sort of social action 'from below'.

Biblical Hermeneutics and Its Effects

As Hans de Wit indicated a decade or so ago (2004a), despite the popularity of Latin American liberation theology and basic ecclesial communities, there exists virtually no *empirical* research on Latin American ordinary Bible readers. Since then, Hans de Wit, together with Edgar López (2013), edited a volume entitled *Lectura intercultural de la Biblia en contextos de impunidad en América Latina*. The volume gives a thorough reading report of eighteen groups of Latin American ordinary readers under the auspices of *Through the Eyes of Another* project. In addition, as mentioned above, my dissertation research investigated two Bolivian Pentecostal groups' readings in depth. Due to the fact that millions of people around the world read, hear, sing, pray, and use the Bible, this kind of empirical investigating is crucial.[27] In locations where the Bible is considered a sacred book by many, such as parts of Latin America, sub-Saharan Africa, and the United States, the Bible's influence is enormous. As such, there is no doubt that biblical interpretation is a contested arena, as the brief summary of the Bolivian groups' readings indicated. The comparison of the Bolivian groups' readings demonstrated how the same texts may be read and used in different ways depending on the group's social location. The way action-consequence theology functioned in each group is a case in point. Overall, the action-consequence theology seemed to function positively in the life of MG; for example, by giving hope and a means to exert some measure of control in life (Autero 2014: 283–4, 303–4). Yet, the same doctrine was used to justify wealth and neglect social concern by some in PvG. This indicates how the Bible may be used to support a certain socio-economic status or elicit hope, solidarity, and self-determination.

As a biblical scholar, I cannot help but wonder what might be the role and responsibility of the biblical scholar in a world of poverty and exploitation? A social activist, economist, or a professional development worker is undoubtedly able to work more concretely and directly in alleviating poverty. Yet, a biblical scholar may be able to make a contribution in the ideological and theological sphere, as many of the liberation theologians have noted. Some exploration has

---

27. This point was explicated by de Wit in the opening speech of my dissertation defence.

been done in this area by Gerald West, Hans de Wit, and others. Taking cues from the Latin American liberation theologians, West has championed the Contextual Bible study method (CBS) and focuses on the importance of social engagement by biblical scholars. CBS is a model that aims to facilitate a liberating encounter between the ordinary and scholarly readers (West 1999b; 2000; West and Ujamma Centre Staff 2007). De Wit's *Through the Eyes of the Another* approach is another example. This inter-cultural Bible reading encounter seeks to involve different types of communities to interact with each other by using biblical texts (de Wit 2004a; de Wit and Lopez 2013). Both are important attempts to engage grassroots Christian communities with critical and pressing social issues. In my own research. I wanted to investigate to what extent socio-economic status influences hermeneutical processes. I also wanted to give a voice to the Bolivian groups, even if this remained my own representation of 'the other'.

It is my contention that the use and influence of the Bible needs to be taken more seriously in regard to the present-day readers, and not just in the past. Empirical hermeneutics is a good methodological approach for this sort of investigation.

Overall, with whom one reads makes a world of a difference. In the comforts of the Western academia, biblical interpretation may come across as a matter of academic preference or theological opinion, but in many places one's hermeneutics may literally be a matter of life or death.

Chapter 8

CONTEXTUAL READING OF LUKE-ACTS WITH PENTECOSTAL WOMEN IN BOTSWANA[1]

Rosinah Mmannana Gabaitse

Introduction

Biblical interpretation in Botswana has always been dominated by men within the churches and academy. The result is that women's interpretive voices remain largely unheard and, in the process, they are disempowered by male biblical interpretation. In an effort to honour women's interpretive voices, I used the Contextual Bible Studies (CBSs) to read selected texts from Luke-Acts with Pentecostal women in Botswana. This was an important exercise because I wanted not only to 'hear' their voices, but to also understand their hermeneutical strategies for reading against patriarchal biblical interpretations. By engaging in a series of research contexts over a period of time (i.e. CBS, focus groups, and one-to-one interviews in reading and interpreting Luke-Acts), Pentecostal women narrated their struggles and their joys within the church and outside of the church. Most importantly, the women revealed their strategies of reading the Bible that confirmed, and at times subverted, the existing male Pentecostal hermeneutic. The aim of this chapter, therefore, is to discuss two main Pentecostal women's reading strategies: (1) interpretations affirming patriarchy through proof-texting or spiritualizing texts and (2) subversive readings by foregrounding the Holy Spirit or through interpreting texts as both social and spiritual. The chapter discusses the status of women within the Pentecostal church, CBS as a research method, Lukan scholars' views on women and the importance of Luke-Acts, and women's hermeneutical strategies.

The research was guided by principles of feminist research which privileges individual experiences and the analysis of the data was guided by a broad feminist hermeneutical approach which aims at exposing patriarchy and androcentrism

---

1. This chapter is based on a section of my doctoral thesis from the University of KwaZulu-Natal which was completed in 2013.

at the level of the biblical text, as well as highlighting the ways in which patriarchy is enacted through biblical interpretation. Feminist hermeneutical approaches critically engage some of the ways in which patriarchal texts can be subverted for liberating purposes by the very people those texts marginalize. Through their reading of Luke-Acts some Pentecostal women revealed ways in which the patriarchy embedded within the Pentecostal spaces through male biblical interpretation can be subverted.

Pentecostal Biblical Interpretation and the Status of Women

Scholars of Pentecostalism have observed that the Pentecostal movement is riddled with contradictions when it comes to the position of women (Alexander 2009: 2). This movement offers women what most call a safe space. Women can prophesy, preach, and teach under the leadership of the Holy Spirit. Further, Pentecostal women are not restrained by Levitical taboos, such as not attending church and not participating in Holy Communion because they have their monthly periods which make them unclean (Mwaura 2008: 279; Kalu 2008: 149). In fact, for decades Pentecostalism was celebrated by both scholars of Pentecostalism and Pentecostal believers for advancing equality between men and women because of foregrounding the Holy Spirit, who enables men and women to be the mouthpiece of God. However, recent studies in Africa and the West reveal that Pentecostalism is a space of both exclusion and embrace (Johns 2009: 174; Salomonsen 2006: 128; Maluleke and Nadar 2002: 11; Yong 2005: 191; McClintock-Fulkerson 1994: vii). Pentecostal movements remain deeply patriarchal and women are still located in 'spheres under male domination' (Yong 2005: 191). The leadership models employed by Pentecostal movements have been described as 'very authoritarian and hierarchical', promoting male authority and hierarchical relationships (Maluleke and Nadar 2002: 11). While the focus on the Holy Spirit has the potential to make the Pentecostal space an egalitarian space, unfortunately it is not, largely because of patriarchal biblical interpretation. Most, if not all, Pentecostal churches, especially in the African context, forcefully teach and advance the supremacy of the male and submission of the female through biblical interpretation (Gabaitse 2015: 115; Masenya 2005: 47–59; Adjabeng 1995; Mate 2002: 549–68; Nadar 2007: 60–78). A negative gender discourse lurks within Pentecostal theology and practice because there is always a scriptural basis for marginalizing and subordinating women (Kalu 2008). Because of its reliance on the Holy Spirit, the Pentecostal church will not overtly prohibit women from preaching and prophesying, but often women are made invisible in these roles.[2] Making women invisible in their roles, the

2. During fieldwork research, I observed that the few times women preached on Sunday in the churches we studied, there was a tendency by the senior pastor or some male elder who came to make anouncements of the church to 'emphasize' her message. They

authoritarian leadership, the supremacy of the male, and the call to have women submit to their husbands are mostly as a result of patriarchal biblical interpretation.

Methodology

My research assistant Maria Mpuse and I conducted research from March 2011 to February 2012 among fifty-one women members of the Pentecostal church and three male pastors.[3] The research was conducted among Pentecostals in three settings in Botswana: urban, semi-urban, and a small village. The ages of the women who participated in this study ranged from 17 to 73. The women were divided into three age groups: 17–39, 40–9, and 50–73. The creation of three distinct age groups was important because of the nature of authority in relationships between younger and older women in Batswana society and the ways in which these dynamics can hamper open engagement between age groups. Further, given the changing social context in Botswana over the last thirty years, older members who grew up in different times have different experiences of being women in church and society. Initially we thought we would divide the groups into two, for women aged 20–34 and 35–73, then we realized early on that the younger women in their late 30s in the second age group were withdrawn because of the age difference between the women. In the Botswana context, younger people must not talk back to elders. Ordinarily, the CBS and focus groups demanded some form of 'talking back' between the participants and this was going to be hampered and the quality of the data was going to be compromised. The educational background, social status, and marital status differed as well, some women especially in the ages of fifty and above had never been to formal school so they did not know how to read, but they knew how to interpret the Bible when it was read for them. The methods we used to collect data included the CBS, focus groups, participant observation, and one-to-one interviews. The research was conducted in both Setswana (the indigenous and official language of Botswana) and English and the sessions were tape recorded with permission from the respondents. Some of the recordings were transcribed into English by me and some by my research assistant.[4] For the purposes of this chapter, I will only describe and analyse the CBS even though I had used several methods of data collection.

would introduce more biblical texts and would take a much longer time emphasizing and 'confirmng' the message preached by the female. In my analysis I believe that this happened because he has more authority than her.

3. The three pastors were interviewed, while we engaged with the women through the CBS sessions, the focus groups, and the one-to-one interviews.

4. The words of the respondents were transcribed verbatim. I use the extracts from the data in this chapter.

Defining the Contextual Bible Study

Over the years, CBS was popularized, defined, and developed by Gerald West in collaboration with the Ujamaa Centre.[5] One of Ujamaa centre's aim is to read the Bible with ordinary readers, a process and an engagement between 'socially engaged Biblical scholars' and 'ordinary readers'[6] from marginalized communities who 'use the Bible as a resource for personal and social transformation' (West 1993: 24; West and Ujamma Centre Staff 2007; West 1999a). The CBS has four commitments. These commitments are to read the Bible from the perspective of the South African context particularly from the perspective of the poor and oppressed. The second commitment is to read the Bible in community with others, particularly with those from contexts different from one's own. The third is to read the Bible critically and, lastly, a commitment to individual and social transformation (West 1993: 12). These four commitments demonstrate that CBS foregrounds the role of the reader, their contexts, and experiences as legitimate spaces for interpreting the Bible. Therefore, CBS is a great resource for engaging with Pentecostal women, whose interpretive voice needs to be heard and validated.

The strength of the CBS is its ability to be flexible and adaptable to diverse contexts; it can be used globally by people dealing with poverty, racial discrimination, HIV and other illnesses, patriarchy and other forms of marginalization. For example, Sarojini Nadar conducted a CBS to find out how women ministers were marginalized among Indian Pentecostal women in Phoenix, Durban. Her conclusions were that 'Bible studies empower rather than oppress women' (Nadar 2003: 210). In addition, Beverley Haddad used CBS among Zulu women living with HIV in South Africa, and the Zulu women freely and safely articulated their experiences of marginalization and theologies of resistance (2000). In Botswana, CBS provided women an opportunity to break male hegemony as well as a safe

---

5. The Ujamaa Centre for Community Development and Research is a project of the UKZN School of Religion and Theology founded during the days of political violence and apartheid in South Africa to facilitate Bible studies with engagements between scholars of the Bible and 'ordinary' people in order to read the Bible together for liberation purposes. The Ujamaa Centre 'is an organisation that locates itself in the interface between biblical studies in academic institutions and ordinary African "readers" (whether literate or not) of the Bible in local communities of faith'. The centre undertakes to conduct Bible studies in communities to 'highlight the ways in which structures and systems may have become corrupt'. See West and Ujamma Centre Staff 2007: 5.

6. The term has been problematized as not appropriate and demeaning towards the people we call ordinary. See for example Nadar 2003: 189–94. Ordinary readers in South Africa refer to people who read the Bible pre-critically – those who are not trained in biblical studies methods of interepretation and exegesis.

space for the women to articulate reading strategies of resistance to patriarchal theologies and interpretation. According to West,

> embodied theologies find their way into the safe Contextual Bible Study site in fragments and in disguised forms, waiting for a resonance with and the recognition of others in a group. (West 2009: 38)

My experience with Batswana Pentecostal women was positive because most of them articulated their theologies and reading strategies freely.

Setting Up the CBS as an Instrument of Data Collection

I introduced myself among Pentecostals as a researcher collecting data to write a PhD thesis. I explained the research process, the study, its objectives, issues of confidentiality, and anonymity. Consent forms were signed and some women gave consent orally before witnesses because they could not write. The studies took place over several days, and lasted around two hours in all the research groups of between 8 and 12 women. The first CBS was on Lk. 4.1-19 followed by Acts 2.1-47, then one on Acts 6.1-7, and the last one on Acts 21.1-14. The text for the day was read slowly and twice in English and Setswana depending on the participants' preferred language. Copies from NIV were also made for the sake of uniformity, even though some women preferred to read their own Bible. The respondents then answered a series of questions which I designed following the general outline of the Ujamaa model. For example, when conducting the CBS on Lk. 4.1-19, I asked questions such as the following:

1. Name the specific ways in which women, men, and children relate to each other in your church.
2. Tell the story in your own words/What is the text about?
3. Who are the characters in this story and what do we know about them?
4. What does Jesus mean by 'setting the captives free'?
5. Focus on vv. 1–2. Are there people who are oppressed in your church?
6. Name them and how they are oppressed?
7. What does the text say to women in your church?
8. How will you read this text to ensure that women are not oppressed in your church?

These questions elicited responses and conversation out of which probing questions were asked leading to deep and wider discussions of other biblical texts that women thought had a bearing in the Lukan text of the day. The Pentecostal women probed each other, further creating more opportunities for engagement as well as revealing diverse and different reading strategies. There was never a time women agreed with each other on one reading strategy because of different personalities and sensibilities. We assured the women that each reading or interpretation was valid.

The women were informed that CBS was not the same as the Bible studies they conduct in their church's weekly meetings, rather, it was a research tool for collecting data on women's approaches to reading the Bible. Often, scholars who use CBS deviate from the Ujamaa model and they adapt it to their contexts and agendas as I did. While the Ujamaa model prioritizes 'issues of vital concern to the group' as identified by the group itself, in my research I (as the researcher) identified the issues regarding the understandings of Pentecostal biblical hermeneutics, gender construction and the marginalization of women in Pentecostal and wider social life in Botswana, and the related biblical texts (West and Ujamaa Centre staff 2007: 5). I was intentional about my interest in conducting the CBS and the research questions were structured in a way that drew attention to my interest in the themes above. It is possible that if I were not intentional about what I asked during the CBS, the questions about gender and the status of women in the church and society may not have come up because my respondents' identities have been constructed through socio-cultural factors and Pentecostal biblical interpretations which promote male supremacy as the norm. I was not expecting them to critically engage with gender issues without me as a researcher probing them through structured questions.

Often, the researcher's agenda determines the questions for engagement with respondents. For instance, when Nadar conducted the CBS among a group of Indian women in Phoenix her agenda and aims were explicitly framed by the conscientization paradigm because she wanted to construct an activist hermeneutic (2003: 13, 14, 188). Her questions were structured in a way that helped her achieve those aims. This deviated from the model proposed by Ujamaa, whose aims for conducting CBS are clearly not to conscientize marginalized groups but to offer interpretive resources which may be useful to the community group (West 2001: 169–84). Therefore, the agendas and aims of a researcher can be legitimate as long as the researcher is intentional about them.

My Role as an Insider-Researcher

Although my goal was not to overtly conscientize, I was not a detached researcher either. I am part of the Pentecostal community and I experience some of the struggles women face.[7] Some interpretations of the Bible offered by women were disheartening and, as an insider-researcher and a woman, there were a few times I had to point out that there are alternative and affirming ways of interpreting texts.

---

7. Even though I am a Motswana Pentecostal woman, bound by the customary law which calls for blind obedience of women to men, I can never absolutely claim to understand the struggles that other Batswana Pentecostal women go through. I am confronted with patriarchy both in the church and wider community; however, I have more space and a stronger voice to speak than most women. When I conducted the study I was pursuing a PhD in biblical studies and I was lecturing at the University of Botswana and that placed me on a different level than the other women in my community, some of whom have never attended formal school.

For instance, I had to offer some sort of intervention/conscientization during the following conversation:

> Woman: If I were to use metaphors to describe men, I will say they are giants, and we [women] are ants and grasshoppers just like the Israelites were as compared to the Canaanites.
>
> Me: What does that mean that you are ants?
>
> Woman: it means that men are better than us, we are nothing as compared to them.
>
> Me: No you are something because you are a child of God and made in the image of God … who skillfully and wonderfully made you. Refuse any interpretation of the Bible that tells you otherwise.

I was mindful though that I was using CBS as a research tool rather than a tool for transformation. Therefore, I had to negotiate how much detachment, attachment, or involvement I had to exercise without influencing the women's narratives too much. If too much conscientization took place, I risked not getting their honest interpretation of Luke-Acts. Many times Pentecostal women affirmed patriarchy and advanced their own marginalization but I held my intense frustrations and biases (in that I had my own ideas about what the interpretation of the texts should be) in tension because I was guided by my research interests, agenda, and aims: to listen to women narrate their strategies of reading and interpreting the Bible. There were times when I was filled with joy when, after careful probing, marginal voices began to emerge. For example, the extract quoted above continues this way;

> Woman: Actually that is what the Bible in Psalms says, I am not sure where it says that I am wonderfully and skillfully made, the text that we read from Acts 2 says that God will give me his Spirit; can God give an ant his Spirit? No, I am a Child of God, loved by God just like God loves the men!

This was an embodied research and my role was complicated. However, being aware and interrogating the complexities of my identity made the research and collecting data on interpretations of specific texts from Luke-Acts successful.

The Importance of Luke-Acts

Research data confirm that Luke-Acts is important for the identity of the Pentecostal believers. Since Pentecostal identity and Pentecostal community revolve around the work of the Holy Spirit, Acts 2 especially takes centre stage among Pentecostal believers in Botswana. The Pentecostals referred to and identified themselves as *Mapentekoste,* meaning the 'people of Pentecost' or as *batho ba Moya o boitshepo,* literally meaning the 'people of the Holy Spirit'. They were able to articulate the importance of Luke-Acts in three main ways. First, it is from Luke-Acts that they are able to defend the baptism and gifts of the Holy Spirit. Second, it is from Luke-Acts that they are able to defend the speaking in tongues which set the Pentecostals apart from other types of Christianity. Third, it is from Luke-Acts that there is evidence that the Holy Spirit is able to transform relationship of inequalities between races and genders. In this sense, Acts is prescriptive and normative for the development of most Pentecostal theologies. In addition to the three reasons advanced by Pentecostals, Luke-Acts resonates with me because it contains many stories about women. At its worst, Luke-Acts is ambivalent towards women; hence, I chose it as a main text for conducting the CBS among Pentecostal women.

The Lukan texts we engaged with were varied and had 'mixed messages'. This was intentional because Luke-Acts is ambivalent towards women so much that scholars of Luke are polarized regarding the status of women in Luke-Acts. For instance, Ben Witherington holds that Luke-Acts is liberatory and positive towards women. Women are affirmed and given more prominence than men. Witherington submits that Luke places women at the centre of God's plan for salvation because the birth narrative is told from the point of view of Mary (1988: 137–8; 1990). The second category of scholars argue that Luke-Acts is a 'dangerous text, perhaps the most dangerous in the Bible' because it has more stories and materials about women, yet, it silences and subordinates them (Schaberg 1992: 275; D'Angelo 2002; D'Angelo 1990: 441–61). Scholars who hold this view agree that Luke-Acts is androcentric. When Luke-Acts is read carefully women are 'models of subordinate service, excluded from the power centre of the movement and from significant responsibilities' (Schaberg 1992: 275). The third category of scholars such as Turid Seim, Gail O'Day, and Barbara Reid maintain that Luke is ambivalent towards women. Turid Seim captures this ambivalence when she argues that 'women are brought to silence, but at the same time they continue to speak through the story' (1994b: 761). Seim's view is that the Gospel of Luke preserves compelling and strong traditions about women (1994b: 761). Women are presented as disciples of Jesus, as active participants in the ministry of Jesus, and as children of Abraham. However, in Acts, the number and roles of women decrease because Acts is dominated by masculinization. Acts becomes the story of men. However, Gail O'Day contends that although Luke is dominated by masculinization, they can never be cloaked into complete silence because Luke has already demonstrated that women were active in the ministry of Jesus. For example, Acts 16 demonstrates that women were active and present even in the work of the church (O'Day 1992: 305–12).

The scholars' views on Luke and women are valid but I tend to gravitate towards views that submit that Luke-Acts is self-contradictory and should be read critically. However, I celebrate Luke-Acts' positive presentation of women much more than I focus on his shortcomings because of the constraints of his context. Considering that his world was steeped in patriarchy, Luke did well by writing stories about women and by presenting the Holy Spirit as a partner to men and women who struggle with issues such as race and ethnicity. Finally, though, it was my intention to choose texts with mixed messages for engagement with Pentecostal women to reflect this ambivalence in Luke-Acts. Some texts have egalitarian and transformative potential (Lk. 4.1-19, Acts 2.1-47), some could be perceived as ambivalent towards women (Acts 21.1-14), and some clearly discourage the leadership of women (Acts 6.1-7).

Women's Reading Strategies

The women's reading strategies were very complex because the interpretations of Lukan texts were not necessarily read in isolation, but were done in relation to other texts and in relation to how they had heard the texts interpreted in different contexts over a period of time. The women offered three types of interpretations. The first category of women offered interpretations affirming patriarchy and advancing their marginalization. The second category offered contradictory interpretations moving from being subversive to subscribing to a patriarchal Pentecostal hermeneutic. The third category, of women's readings offered subversive interpretations of texts. In all three categories there were representations of women from all ages, socio-economic status, and educational background. For instance, there were young educated women living in the city who subscribed to patriarchal biblical interpretation as much as older women living in a village who have never been to school. What is interesting is that some young educated women in their 20s and 30s who lived in the city unreservedly subscribed to patriarchy. This is not surprising because patriarchy is deeply embedded in the language through parables, metaphors, and the culture of Botswana. It is acted upon within families and in schools through subject selection. Hence, most women, even the educated ones, are custodians of patriarchy.[8] However, there were old women, including one who did not even know how to read, who denounced patriarchal biblical interpretations and patriarchal cultures with a passion. A different paper is needed to analyse what makes individual women in a deeply patriarchal setting such as the village to be non-custodians of patriarchy and what makes women in a less rigid setting such as the city to be custodians of patriarchal ideologies.[9] One of the factors that appeared to deeply entrench patriarchy among the women in my study

---

8. For instance, the bride price (*bogadi* in Botswana) is a payment in the form of cattle or cash given to the bride's family by the groom's family before a wedding takes place. It is a cultural requirement that legitimates marriage. Marriage is not complete without the paying of *bogadi*. Studies from Botswana reveal that *bogadi* is essential for the maintenance of male progeny and the main function of *bogadi* is to 'transfer the reproductive power of a woman from her own family into that of her husband' (Schapera 1994: 139). Therefore, *bogadi* is a patriarchal practice and women who are educated know that and very few of them if any can ever marry without *bogadi* being paid. See Kidd and Kidd 2009 and Ministry of Labour 2002.

9. The boundaries between cities and villages in Botswana are not wide because the belief is that people travel to cities to work, but they go back to the villages on Fridays to be home and to be with family. In Botswana a city is not home; rather, an ancestral land in the village is home. A person can work in the city, but when they get married, for instance, they do that in the village. During holidays such as Christmas, Batswana people living in the city travel home and the city is almost always deserted. There is always a concern that an individual person who goes home often might be influenced by 'city life'. This partly explains why Batswana women, even those living in the city, still subscribe to patriarchal ideologies.

was the authority given to the male pastors and the authority of the Bible as the revered unquestionable word of God within Pentecostal spaces. In the following section, I briefly discuss ways in which some women's reading strategies reflected and confirmed patriarchal biblical interpretation and then proceed to focus more on the subversive reading strategies, which is the goal of this chapter. The reading strategies of the women who contradicted themselves reflect the complexity of the Pentecostal space of exclusion and embrace of women. The women's contradictory reading strategies of the Bible demonstrate the ambiguity of the Pentecostal space. I am not discussing their reading strategies because they are captured in the two other strategies discussed in turn below.

Interpretations Affirming Patriarchy: Proof-texting

The women whose interpretation of Luke-Acts affirmed patriarchy as God ordained adopted two main hermeneutical strategies, namely, proof-texting and spiritualizing texts that have egalitarian potential. Proof-texting is a practice of using and reconciling a few biblical texts to support one argument without critically studying the Bible as a whole. Pentecostals adopt this hermeneutical strategy haphazardly to support prosperity theology and the subjugation of women among others. Christopher Thomas can assert this about Pentecostals and proof-texting;

> Many Pentecostal churches have not paid nearly enough attention to the activity of the Holy Spirit in empowering women ... but have allowed one or two texts to undermine the balance of biblical teaching on this topic, as well as the Spirit's own witness. (1994: 56)

As a result, Pentecostal women's use of proof-texting as a reading strategy is reflective of male biblical interpretation and mirrors that of the larger Pentecostal community. The women in this group interpreted Acts 6.1-7 as a narrative about male leadership within the early church community. They recognized that the community at Acts 6.1-7 was made up of Hebraic Jews, Grecian Jews, and other nations mentioned in Acts 2.5-11, showing that so many cultures were represented. Acts 6.1-7 is reflective of what is *normal* and *culturally acceptable* among different cultures since there is no protest about male leadership in the text as it happens in several places in Acts. Because there is no protest, the women then concluded that it is God's plan that men lead and women submit and that the communities of the earth, be they Jewish, Roman, Greek, or Batswana, understand this. The women justified their interpretation of Acts 6.1-7 by going back to Acts 1.21 where a man was chosen to replace Judas and be part of the twelve men leading the community. These two texts affirm each other and affirm that male leadership not women's leadership is the norm. Further, in Acts 2 as a whole it is Peter, a male, who addresses the crowd even though women who were filled with the Holy Spirit were present. The Pentecostal women stated that at that time, it would have been an embarrassment for a woman to address the crowd while there were men within the community. According to the Pentecostal women, the early church women did not see male leadership as oppression because they understood the gender roles. They further pointed out that although Acts 2 seems to imply that men and women existed as a community of equals, it was not so. The early church existed in oneness and in peace because women and men understood their positions as ordained for them by God.

While the Pentecostal women were interpreting the above texts in support of patriarchal biblical interpretation, they also co-opted Gen. 1.27, 1 Cor. 11.3, 1 Tim. 2.9, and Eph. 5.22ff to support male leadership and supremacy. Gen. 1.27 was used to support the submission of women to men. The man was created first and woman was created out of a man so that the woman would submit to him. Therefore, when a few texts from Luke-Acts, Genesis 1 and the above texts are harmonized, they appear to unreservedly support and justify patriarchal biblical interpretations and patriarchal tendencies. The women themselves are convinced that the few texts they refer to provide enough evidence for supporting patriarchy because the *Bible says so.* In fact, patriarchy is not a problem if men and women know their roles and execute them as stated *in the Bible.*

The women's use of proof-texting as a hermeneutical strategy went beyond harmonizing texts to using metaphors to affirm male supremacy. When asked to pick a text that captured the position of men and women in Botswana, one woman said,

> If I were to use metaphors to describe men, I will say they are giants, and we [women] are ants and grasshoppers just like the Israelites were as compared to the Canaanites. … It means that men are better than us, we are nothing as compared to them.

The woman used a story from Numbers 13 that had nothing to do with the status of men and women and co-opted it into advancing the supremacy of the male and the marginal status of women. The use of this image reflects the many times women have been told through biblical interpretation that God ordains hierarchical existence and that women are the weaker vessel. Pentecostal male pastors may not necessarily use this kind of imagery to illustrate the superiority of the male; however, women's images of themselves is constructed through church theology and scriptural interpretation that belittles women. This is then internalized; hence, they imagine themselves as grasshoppers. Not only do Pentecostal women internalize their marginal status, they participate in constructing and sustaining it. This is further fuelled by approaching biblical interpretation with a hermeneutic of trust in addition to the grip that patriarchal culture in the church and society has on them. They are not suspicious of interpretations of the Bible and the construction of images that belittled them further. Through proof-texting, texts that affirm patriarchy are given more interpretive power in order to support hierarchy, the bedrock of patriarchy without proper and critical interrogation of those texts. Ultimately, proof-texting produces erroneous theology about the position and status of women.

Interpretations Affirming Patriarchy: Spiritualizing Texts

The second reading strategy that the women who affirmed patriarchal biblical interpretation adopted was spiritualizing texts. Texts such as Acts 2.17-19 and Lk. 4.18-19, which have the potential for social transformation, were spiritualized. When they read Acts 2.17-19, the women in this group unambiguously acknowledged that the Holy Spirit chooses women and men equally to be God's mouthpiece. Both can be filled with the Holy Spirit and because of that they are made equal on a *spiritual level.* The two extracts below capture this:

> Extract #1: Pentecost makes men and women equal on a spiritual level, women can preach both in the church and crusades, they can lead praise and worship, they preach on Sunday. But the Holy Spirit does not make men equal to women on a day-to-day basis. This means that in terms of authority, men have the authority over women at home and even in the church.

> Extract #2: We are equal before God yes, but because we live in this world that has divisions, and where people are categorized in terms of the titles, the Holy Spirit makes men and women equal in *dilo tsa moya,* (in spiritual things) like prayer, praise, and worship, and speaking in tongues.

The women believe that the Holy Spirit makes men and women equal, when they engage in spiritual things. Prophesying, seeing visions, and dreaming dreams are all spiritual activities which are performed once in a while. A human being cannot perform and execute these duties unless she or he is possessed by a power bigger than themselves, so they need the Holy Spirit. It is important that the Holy Spirit equalizes men and women when they perform spiritual duties because performance of these duties benefits the community in that souls have to be saved. In addition, to spiritualizing Acts 2.17-19, the women also spiritualized the interpretation of Lk. 4.18-19. When asked if they saw the subjugation of women as oppression (that Jesus came to eliminate based on Lk. 4.18-19), the women maintained that the oppression or bondage discussed in Lk. 4.18-19 was spiritual. Spiritual bondage affects the soul and it is caused by sin and demonic attacks. Jesus came to set free anyone whose soul is held captive by demonic attacks (and these are spiritual attacks). One would have thought that the women would name patriarchy as oppression, so that Jesus came to set free anyone enslaved by it. According to the women's readings, Acts 2.17-19 and Lk. 4.18-19 have nothing to do with the social, political, and cultural standings of women. After Pentecostal women complete performing their roles in the spirit, *they return to the normal order where the man is above the woman.* Hence, the women concluded that the work of the Holy Spirit does not result in change in terms of social, political, or cultural standing, men are in authority and women remain under the authority of men.

Spiritualizing texts is applied selectively because texts such as 1 Cor. 11.3, 1 Tim. 2.9, and Eph. 5.22, which became part of our conversations and which clearly elevates the male, are not highly spiritualized. Rather, these texts are read literally to enforce inequality between men and women. For instance, Acts 6.1-7 discussed above and Acts 21.9-12, which endorses male leadership while denying female leadership was not spiritualized. The text authorizes male leadership and the Pentecostal women interpret it as it is. Further, Acts 21.9-12 is silent about the contents of the prophecy of Philip's daughters, while the content of Agabus' prophecy, a male, is narrated and the Pentecostal women read the text to endorse male leadership as well. These texts are seen as *normal, reflecting the way things should be, as cultural* and as *prescriptive*. They are not spiritualized, rather, they are applied to women and men's present social standings. Therefore, the two reading strategies of proof-texting and spiritualizing texts that were adopted by some Pentecostal women did not denounce patriarchy within the text and within Pentecostal biblical interpretation. Instead, patriarchy is strengthened because hierarchy is seen as normal and ordained by God because *the Bible says so* and *that is how the Bible has always been interpreted in my church*. Both strategies are inconsistently applied on texts that seem to subjugate women.

Subversive Readings: Foregrounding the Holy Spirit

The second group of women were rigorous in their interpretation of Luke-Acts as they interrogated, critiqued, and denounced male biblical interpretation. They adopted two strategies: foregrounding the Holy Spirit and interpreting the texts as both spiritual and social. In the first strategy, the women observed that a proper and fair reading of Luke-Acts takes note of the work and role of the Holy Spirit. They made several observations to demonstrate the power of the Holy Spirit to transform people, relationships, and circumstances. First, through the Holy Spirit, Mary, a woman at the margins of her community, is highly favoured by God by carrying the saviour of the world. Since this was a miracle, God could have used a man to carry the saviour of the world. Second, when the Holy Spirit is present, structures of oppression are dissolved. For example, in Lk. 4.18-19 Jesus through the Holy Spirit brings salvation from captivity and oppression from hunger and disease. Third, the Holy Spirit does not respect social boundaries. Any individual, who is open to God can receive the Holy Spirit regardless of gender, class, and ethnicity (Acts 2.1-47 and Acts 15). Lastly, whenever the Holy Spirit is mentioned in Luke-Acts there appears to be an affirmation of life and freedom of existence (e.g. Lk. 1.35; 4.17-18; 10.21 and Acts 2.17-18; Acts 2.38; 6.10). The work and presence of the Holy Spirit is the complete opposite of the presence of unclean or evil spirits. Unclean spirits enslave people with sickness, and make them lose their integrity. For example, some people with evil spirits go out naked in public (Lk. 8.27) but the Holy Spirit sets people free.

It is on the basis of these observations on how the Holy Spirit is transformative that the women's strategy of reading against patriarchy foregrounds the Holy Spirit as a central and necessary guiding principle for life-giving interpretations of the Bible. According to the Pentecostal women in this category, the kind of reading that foregrounds the Holy Spirit is guided by egalitarianism; no race or gender is better than the other, all are equal in all spheres of life. This made their reading subversive because the Holy Spirit is perceived as a power above cultures, ideologies, and patriarchal biblical interpretations. One older woman captured this:

> The Spirit is a power that is beyond us, beyond the laws that we make that says women are weaker, the Holy Spirit has come to destroy the bondage that was imposed on women, culturally and physically, the Holy Spirit sets free. If the Bible says women must be silent and if they must be under the authority of the man, then the Holy Spirit says that all men and women must not be bound by those laws…. . I listen to the Holy Spirit much more than I listen to the Bible and the Pastor, and the church. Plus, I do not know how to read that much, so the voice I hear when I sleep and when I am walking is that of the Holy Spirit. He is with me all the time and I do not carry the Bible with me all the time…. . No culture or church can oppress me, I have been set free. The structures that are controlled by men can marginalise me, but not oppress me.[10]

It is profound that the Holy Spirit is imagined as power above the Bible because some narratives such as Acts 6.1-7 can easily be used to deny women's leadership positions, but the Holy Spirit can critique such texts for they are oppressive. The women demonstrated the transformative work of the Holy Spirit by engaging with the question asked by the crowd in Acts 2.12, 'What does this mean?', in relation to Acts 2 as a whole. They believed that the question is answered by Peter speech's in Acts 2.14-47 and by the end of his speech, the crowd knew what the coming of the Holy Spirit meant. More than anything, it meant that all people have a duty to perform in God's kingdom.[11] They understood that the coming of the Holy Spirit required them to be a new community of believers who fellowshipped with each other. For them to successfully do that, the crowd had to overcome prejudice and exclusion to exist as a community of equals. Therefore, the women pointed out that understanding the transformative power of the Holy Spirit can inaugurate the kind of equality that transcends gender barriers and move men and women into social, cultural, and political equality.

As the Pentecostal engaged with the question 'What does this mean?', they contextualized the question and made it relevant for them: *what does Pentecost mean for Pentecostal women today?* They interpreted Acts 2.17-19 as a narrative about the Holy Spirit who can be experienced at all times by all people, regardless

---

10. These words were uttered by an older woman in her 70s living in a village. The woman's resistance to Pentecostal biblical interpretation and Setswana culture was profound and consistent. She critiqued patriarchy during the CBS sessions, the focus groups, and the one-to-one interviews. This was the kind of subversive reading one would expect from the younger generation who embrace other cultures through television and magazines.

11. Old women are left out in this prophesy and the Pentecostal women made a joke about how the old women were tired because they had been working in the house of God much more than old men. Perhaps old women will be supervising the performance of these tasks in the church. It was profound that they realized that the text leaves them out.

of race and gender. In the Pentecostal tradition, Pentecost is not an abstract event that happened during the times of the early church and ended there. The charismatic manifestations of the Holy Spirit still happen today. Believers are still baptized in the Holy Spirit and women and men still prophesy. The same Holy Spirit who guided Peter to successfully answer the question, 'What does this mean', is the same Holy Spirit who can guide Pentecostals about the creation of life-giving engagements. Therefore, the women stated that through the manifestation of the Holy Spirit, spaces of liberation and freedom remain open so that men and women can occupy the same social status, the same way the early church did in Acts 2.42-47. If the Holy Spirit is allowed by Pentecostal believers to function, a new community of equals can be formed. In addition, the women stated that the events of Acts 2.17-19 mean that the Holy Spirit can come up with a new script of liberating people from the claws of any kind of oppression. Therefore, the Holy Spirit is the one who can guide Pentecostal communities on how to read the Bible in order to affirm life for both men and women equally. The Pentecostal women asserted that *while their own Pentecostal pastors may not know how to use the Bible to advance egalitarian existence between men and women,* the Holy Spirit who does not respect social categories of gender and class can equip them. If Pentecostal ministers listen and discern the Holy Spirit, then there should not be a place for a hermeneutics that still calls women into subordination to men. That there should not be a place for oppression within the Pentecostal church was supported by interpreting Lk. 4.18-19 as denouncing oppression imposed on women through patriarchal biblical interpretation. The women themselves articulated how some Christian women are oppressed by patriarchy as they experience violence, be it financial or physical, because of the use of texts to advance the headship and supremacy of the male.[12] This stands in contradiction to Jesus' proclamation under the influence of the Holy Spirit that he came to set the captives and oppressed free.

Subversive Readings: Texts as Spiritual and Social

The other way women in this group offered subversive interpretations of Luke-Acts was through the interpretation of texts as both spiritual and social. The women made no distinction between equality in the social realm and equality in the spiritual realm. Acts 2.17-18 dissolves inequalities as *all* human beings receive the Holy Spirit. This was indeed a spiritual exercise and the Holy Spirit made men and women equal in the spiritual sense. However, that equality translated into equality in the social, cultural, and political realm as it is demonstrated in vv. 42-47. They argued that the spiritual world is a world where God, not humans, operates, and if God allows men and women to be equal through the Holy Spirit, then, God must desire equality for women and men. It is human beings in their

---

12. Studies on violence against women confirm that violence against women happens within Pentecostal families because of the language of submission that characterizes Pentecostal hermeneutics. See, Phiri 2002: 19–30.

social world who then choose to deny God what God desires for men and women. Acts 2.42-47 gives a glimpse of how God desires God's people to exist as equals. The women further argued that human beings with their sinful nature always devise ways of oppressing others. When they read Acts 6.1-7, the women agreed with the interpretations offered by the women above that the narrative is about what was *cultural and normal*; men occupy leadership positions. However, the women argued that the Holy Spirit does not function and confirm cultural ideologies. Rather, the Holy Spirit transcends normal cultural ideologies so that communities of men and women exist as equals. In addition, God desires a redeemed community, a community not oppressed through patriarchal ideologies, laws, and customs because Jesus came to set the captives free in Lk. 4.18-19. The salvation that Jesus talked about is spiritual as much as it is social, economic, and more.

The readings of Luke-Acts were subversive not only through offering spiritual and social strategies of interpreting texts; they were also subversive because of the women's ability to highlight the problems with only spiritualized interpretations of the Bible. They stated that spiritual equality is problematic because it limits the power of the Holy Spirit to

> transform relationships between men and women, not just at a spiritual level but also at social levels. So that when we attend marriage negotiation for our children, the Spirit is there making us equal to men.

An over-emphasis on spiritual equality denies men and women an opportunity to occupy the same social, cultural, and political space. Hence women are still left on the periphery even though Pentecost is a rejection of exclusion and marginalization. The women emphasized that the Pentecost narrative was communal, *all* are praying, *all* are assembled (2.1), *all* are filled with the Spirit (2.4), the Spirit is for *all* flesh (2.17), the Holy Spirit is given to 'each of you' (2.38). Here, there is no second-class race or gender if the pericope is not spiritualized. Failing to recognize that this text was effecting real social, political, and cultural equality between all people, men and women, because of the spiritual interpretation given to it is tragic because then the Pentecostal church through its hermeneutics is not being true to the Pentecost and Holy Spirit narrative. The Pentecostal church whose existence depends on the Holy Spirit should be characterized by hermeneutics and theology which advance the equal social and political treatment of men and women at home, church, and society, as well as equality between social classes and age groups. Therefore, the Pentecost event and Acts 2 in general stands as a critique to the Pentecostal church for marginalizing women through hermeneutics, thus denying them the 'gladness of heart' (2.46).

In addition, the over-emphasis on interpreting Acts 2 and other texts as effecting spiritual equality only denies the social-political consequence of Pentecost and by doing that Pentecostals fail to transform the gender landscape in Botswana. It is failing to be relevant in a country where gender inequality is a challenge. The women's analysis and observation are profound because in Botswana women are underrepresented in Parliament, in traditional courts, and at local councils. They are also inadequately represented in positions of power in management structures of the private sector (Southern African Research Documentation Centre 2005: 23), and in land boards, brigades, churches, and other community decision-making structures, so that decision-making at higher levels is completely dominated by men (Maundeni 2001: 45). The underrepresentation of women at these higher levels of power means women do not have a good chance of influencing policies that affect their lives. In addition, social systems in Botswana are highly patriarchal as well. For example, marriage endows men with enormous power over women and married women in particular are perceived as unequal partners to their husbands (Ministry of Labour 2000: 3; Ministry of Labour 1998: 10). Under the customary law, a married woman is classified as a jural minor subordinated legally, socially, economically to her husband. There is evidence that 'Botswana marry in accordance with customary rules' (Kidd and Kidd 2009: 80). As a result, women in Botswana are legally incapacitated; they need the consent of their husbands to conduct legal and business affairs. Therefore, if the Pentecostal church was true to the Pentecost narrative and open to the work of the Holy Spirit in effecting equality between men and women, its influence on gender equality could be massive.

Concluding Remarks

It is clear that the Pentecostal church is ambivalent towards women. It has not allowed the Luke-Acts narrative of Pentecost to effect real tangible equality between men and women. It is also clear that Luke-Acts exists in tensions and contradictions. While it anticipates mutuality, equality, and inclusivity, the rhetoric of Luke's story sometimes undermines women and writes them off. Who is silencing these women? According to Luke's admission it is not the Holy Spirit, because the coming of the Holy Spirit makes daughters speak and prophesy. The way Luke narrates his story leaves Spirit-filled women nameless and voiceless. For example, Luke gives a full list of male disciples, but in two or three verses where he alludes to women disciples he does not name them all (Lk. 8.1-3). When the disciples are gathered in the upper room in Acts, the readers are told of the presence of women but they are not named except for Mary. In Acts 1.21-26, the person replacing Judas is the one who has been with Jesus from the beginning of his ministry to the end. Three names are suggested and all of them are male, although there were women who satisfied the criteria for Judas' replacement. Women were present from the beginning of Jesus ministry to the very end but still a male is chosen to replace Judas. In Acts 21.8, a man named Phillip had four daughters who were prophets but we are not told the contents of their prophecy. Rather, Agabus, a male prophet enters their territory and prophesies, so Luke silences the four daughters of Phillip. In addition, Acts 6.1-7 explicitly silences women's leadership by stating that a male is preferred. Therefore, Luke's silencing of prophetic women such as Phillip's daughters demonstrates the limiting factor of his culture and his rhetoric which conceals what the Holy Spirit can do. He has already informed that the daughters will prophesy and he does not give the readers a full narrative report of Phillip's daughters who were prophets. However, when prophetic women are silenced, we are able to read against this silence by using liberating narratives from within Luke-Acts such as the Pentecost event to critique the rhetorical thrust of Luke-Acts. Pentecost tells its own story of women who can speak, who are part of the community of equals that Luke presents in the last verses of Chapter 2. If read critically, Pentecost can explode Luke's very own patriarchal orientation. If the Holy Spirit was able to critique the limiting factors of Jewish culture as demonstrated in Acts 15, the same Holy Spirit does critique the rhetoric of Luke-Acts in its occasional exclusion of women. Therefore, Acts 2 'stands only partially fulfilled' because Luke makes us anticipate daughters who prophesy, but they never do in his story (Gaventa 2004: 60). Until daughters prophesy, the story of Luke is not complete yet.

The Holy Spirit has power to critique manifestations of patriarchy not just within Luke-Acts but within the Pentecostal church as well. Equality between men and women awaits fulfil in the social realm through the Holy Spirit who cannot be constrained and contained by patriarchal structures and cultures. The radicality in which the women perceived the Holy Spirit can continually explode the Pentecostal patriarchal interpretations because Pentecost is radical and transformative. As the women clearly articulated above, if Pentecost is understood as one moment in Luke-Acts where hierarchies are levelled, then there is no place for patriarchal hermeneutics that call women into subordination within the very church that identifies with Pentecost in name and theology. Texts such as Acts 6.1-7 and Eph. 5.22 can be understood within a framework of foregrounding the transformative work of the Holy Spirit for social transformation and critiqued or resisted. Therefore, the Holy Spirit and Pentecost in Acts 2 offer a legitimate reason for Pentecostal men and women to interpret the Bible intentionally with social, cultural, economic, and spiritual transformation as an agenda. This should not be a problem because Acts 2 is already central to Pentecostal theologies in Botswana and elsewhere, what is missing is openness to the Holy Spirit in ways that allow the Holy Spirit to work in dynamic ways within communities to transform them to egalitarian existence.

When women were not proof-texting or over emphasizing spiritual interpretations of texts, they offered interpretations of Luke-Acts that were extremely resistant to the existing patriarchal Pentecostal biblical interpretation. If women can begin to gather together to share their struggles with patriarchy and read the Bible together in the Spirit with the aim of emphasizing liberatory hermeneutics, the women themselves can call the Pentecostal church to accountability. The strategies of foregrounding the Holy Spirit and interpreting texts as both spiritual and social can be advanced and taught to other women during these meetings to counter proof-texting and hyper-spiritualized interpretations of the Bible because these reading strategies are not life giving. The fact that women are at the margins does not necessarily mean that they are completely without power, more so, the Holy Spirit is acknowledged as a power that enables women to thrive in the Pentecostal tradition. The margins can become spaces of power and community from which they can build and effect social transformation and change from the margins to the centre (Draper 1996: 223–9).

Chapter 9

TOWARDS A MORE PERFECT UNION: A SCRIPTURAL READING OF THE PURPOSE OF MARRIAGE IN A CHANGING WESTERN CONTEXT

Rev. Dr Amy Lindeman Allen

Controversy has long swirled around the topic of marriage in biblical studies; however, most discussions focus upon marital prescriptions such as what makes a marriage, what is permissible within or outside a marriage, who can marry, and so on. As a pastor in the Evangelical Lutheran Church in America (ELCA), I have witnessed such preoccupation with prescriptive interpretation of the biblical texts wreak havoc both in individual families and in the family of the church. I am convinced that rather than more prescriptions, the church in my context needs a clearer vision of the purpose and function of marriage.

To this end, I employ Luke-Acts, a corpus often neglected in biblical marriage debates precisely because it lacks much prescription, as a conversation partner with which ELCA families and congregations can benefit from engaging as we seek such a vision. Such a conversation begins with the contextual concerns for marriage and family that have grown out of decade-long conversations in the ELCA around the institution of marriage and the role of a Christian in care for families, individuals, and children involved in such a union and in the life of Christian families more generally.

These concerns raise to the forefront an awareness of the function of relationships in the Lukan text, specifically those of married couples mentioned by name: Mary and Joseph, Elizabeth and Zechariah, Joanna and Chuza, Sapphira and Ananias, and Priscilla and Aquila. The function of these relationships as described variously reflects a movement towards equality and mutuality, care for the vulnerable and the mission of Christ, and redistribution of wealth and resources for the good of the whole community.

Such practices in turn suggest a vision for marital (and all) relationships no longer grounded in secular values of economic and social advancement and stability, but rather in the discipline of discipleship practised throughout the early Christian communities described in Acts. This emphasis on discipleship is seen as these couples subordinate the private interests of their marriages towards equal and mutual treatment of all in the Christian community; protection for and care of the vulnerable; and redistribution of wealth for the provision of all in need.

In light of the role of married couples and families in the Acts community, I suggest that marriage can and should be viewed as a valued means of living into one's discipleship in Christian community. Specifically, in conversation with the Lukan text and my ELCA Lutheran context, I see the marriage relationship as a means by which Christian individuals can engage in proclamation of God's coming Kingdom and service to the oppressed and neglected in communities and a world in need. Such a vision can serve as a valuable model for Christians seeking a new vision for the purpose and function of marriage in our changing social and economic realities.

Recognizing a Paradigm Shift

Although recent decades have witnessed what may feel like more sudden shifts in the definitions and functions of marriage and family, this paradigm shift has actually been developing in Western society for quite some time. Stephanie Coontz explains,

> About two centuries ago Western Europe and North America developed a whole set of new values about the way to organize marriage and sexuality, and many of these values are now spreading across the globe. In this Western model, people expect marriage to satisfy more of their psychological and social needs than ever before. ... Individuals want marriage to meet most of their needs for intimacy and affection and all of their needs for sex. (Coontz 2005: 23)

The shift in recent years has thus not been the values themselves so much as the development of the laws and infrastructures in the United States to support them. Women's liberation, repeals in anti-divorce legislation, an economy and services that are oriented towards a nuclear family, and more changes in the last several decades have now given Americans the ability to realize (or at least seek to realize) more subjective and demanding marriage ideals than ever before. As a result, marriage in the United States is undergoing a paradigm shift. This has impacted the way in which Americans, including those living in a variety of Christian contexts, live out and define the roles of marriage and family.

By reading Luke-Acts from within this new paradigm, I propose that it is possible both to broaden our biblical models of marriage and for such models to provide a way forward for Christians, specifically those in my own denomination, the ELCA, to live into the changing roles and definitions of marriage and family in an authentically Christian way. To set the stage for this reading, I offer first a brief historical overview of the changing realities of marriage and family as they have been experienced first in the broader United States, then in the ELCA, and finally, in the first-century Christian communities to which the two-volume corpus of Luke-Acts is addressed.

A Changing Paradigm in the Twenty-First-Century United States

'In the 1950s married couples represented 80 percent of all households in the United States. By the beginning of the twenty-first century they were less than 51 percent, and married couples with children were just 25 percent of all households' (Coontz 2005: 276). These numbers, however, do not reflect a deterioration in relationships over the past several decades so much as they reflect a shift in the function of marriage as an institution. In the first-century Roman World out of which Christianity emerged, marriage primarily performed economic and social functions – legitimizing children, supporting families, and distributing inheritance. Such functions far predated the time of Christ and spanned many cultures. The same practices also prompted Jewish marital customs such as levirate marriage (the marriage of a sonless widow to her husband's brother in order to produce an heir), which are assumed in Luke-Acts.

These same sorts of economic functions of marriage and, by extension, family, that were assumed in the biblical world, have, according to Coontz, continued throughout most of Western Christian history until roughly the last 200 years. Recently, social, economic, and civic changes in the West have fostered greater equality between men and women, the protection of children previously deemed illegitimate, and increasing options (at least for some) for accumulating and distributing wealth. These forces have combined so that present-day Western society no longer needs marriage to perform the same functions in the same way as it has throughout much of history. Indeed, recent decades have seen a rapid realignment in both the constructions and values of marriage and family in the West, which is just now beginning to stabilize with the legalization of LGBTQ marriage and increased acceptance and understanding of diverse family expressions in the United States.

Such broad social and economic shifts have left some in the church to decry the downfall of the American family, while others, like Coontz, predict a new chapter in Western family life that is both more fragile and more fulfilling (2005: 301). Christians seeking to live faithfully in this 'new chapter', regardless of how they judge it in relation to previous iterations of family life, continue to turn to the Bible for guidance.

Recognizing this Paradigm Shift in the ELCA

In my ELCA tradition, this guidance has primarily come from biblical models of marriage and family devised and interpreted from within the old ideology of marriage. Indeed, while the ELCA has been a leader in accommodating many of the new economic and social realities of marriage and family, as a denomination we have been reticent to live in the accompanying ideological shift necessary to support such change. This has resulted in the application of biblical models and definitions still based in the old ideology, such as the definition of marriage as exclusively between one man and one woman, to couples and families who are living into a new reality in which such definitions no longer apply.

Change in social and economic realities, however, necessitates that the set of ideals that govern them must adapt as well. Hence, ELCA Lutherans must seek a new way of understanding the purpose and function of marriage in light of current social and economic realities – an ideological shift. Such a shift is both necessary in order to remain relevant to the multiplicity of families within the ELCA and in order to continue to model and lead these families forward in lives of faithfulness in the twenty-first century.

Such a move may seem counter-cultural for those still entrenched in the old ideology; however, Christian Scripture has always called the church to be counter-cultural. The ELCA's confession of faith acknowledges the Scriptures of the Old and New Testament, together with other confessional documents, as the basis of its teaching (Evangelical Lutheran Church in America 2017). While twenty-first-century Christians may not find all of their experiences parallel to those of the first-century Christians, when the biblical texts are read from the perspective of our shifting ideology, fertile parallels emerge.

Reading Luke-Acts in Light of a New Twenty-First-Century Paradigm

A careful look at the functions and history of the early Christian communities recorded in Luke-Acts suggests that these communities experienced their own ideological shift in their understanding of marriage in light of their unique social and economic conditions. No longer awaiting an immediate return of Christ, such communities found themselves forced to develop a new vision for their life and relationships in the present in-between time of the building of God's Kingdom. Mention of specific married couples and households in both Luke and Acts, together with Jesus' identification both with his own biological and broader evangelical families, make clear that while Luke does not abandon traditional constructions of family entirely, the Lukan narrative reprioritizes the arrangement of marriage and family relations in light of the family of God embodied by the new Christian community.

Such a vision included experimental practices with regard to a new sense of equality and mutuality among a community that has come to understand themselves as equal in the eyes of God; the protection of the marginalized and vulnerable, such as the widows and orphans in a community oriented towards Jesus' mandate for care; and the distribution of property in these larger communities of equality while coupled with recognition of continued smaller households within the one paradigmatic household of God.

The ideal, if not the reality, of such early communities deemphasized individual or household economics and social status, thus shifting the purpose and function of marriage away from their contemporaries' primarily economic and social focus. In the first century after Jesus' life and death, early Christian communities, such as those described in Acts shifted their ideology of marriage and family (if not always their practice) away from understanding these institutions as primarily economic arrangements towards describing them as an evangelical partnership for the sake of God's Kingdom. Just as the ultimate end of individual life shifted from financial and social security – protecting one's assets and securing one's legacy – so too the ultimate end of married life shifted. Christians in the Acts communities were no longer concerned about themselves and their private relationships, but rather, about their commission to witness to the in-breaking Kingdom of God in all its expansiveness. Thus the risen Christ commissions his apostles: 'You will be my witnesses in Jerusalem, in all Judea and Samaria, and to the ends of the earth' (Acts 1.8b).

In these small, nascent Acts communities, Christians experimented with this new evangelical ideology governing both their individual and corporate relationships (including marriage) in three primary ways: working together towards a sense of equality between men and women; providing for and protecting widows and orphans; and devising an alternate system for the accumulation and the distribution of wealth. All of this occurs in these small remote communities more than millennia before Coontz dates similar social and economic shifts on a larger level.

Although later Christian communities, particularly after Constantine, assimilated back into the predominant social and economic cultural norms of their society, for a time at least, the Christians who comprised or described the Acts communities in Luke's account embraced an alternate ideology. This ideology applied to their marital relationships in the same way that it applied to their communities. This ideology made previous economic and social attachments subservient to the greater goal of entering into and building upon relationships, marital and otherwise, that model service to and proclamation of God's Kingdom as described above.

Constructing a Model for Faithful Living in Light of the Luke-Acts Paradigm

The example of the Acts communities, who modelled their ideology of relationship upon evangelical rather than economic grounds, provides a fertile starting point for the ELCA to begin to reimagine the functional purpose of relationships such as marriage for our church today. Indeed, such an ideology fits with the name 'Evangelical' itself in the ELCA's self-understanding. The words 'evangelism' and 'evangelical', however, have taken on a variety of meanings among first-century Christian communities. Therefore it is worth clarifying how I understand the Lukan author's use of these terms and thus how I hope such an ideology might influence an understanding of mission and agenda in the ELCA.

The Lukan author puts an evangelical mandate on the lips of Jesus in his inaugural sermon in Galilee, when he reads from the scroll of Isaiah, 'The Spirit of the Lord is upon me, because he has anointed me to bring good news to the poor. He has sent me to proclaim release to the captive and recovery of sight to the blind, to let the oppressed go free, to proclaim the year of the Lord's favor' (Lk. 4.18-19). The good news, or in Greek, the *euangelion,* the Gospel, from which we get the word 'evangelism', thus centres around communal experiences of service and caring in Luke's understanding, rather than the preaching of individual salvation or well-being as it has come to mean in some Christian circles today. In Luke-Acts, the good news of God's Kingdom is about service to and care for those in the community who are in need. Jesus further confirms and expands this purpose in Capernaum when the people there seek to prevent him from leaving. Jesus insists that his purpose is 'to proclaim the good news (*euangelion*) of the kingdom of God to other cities also' (Lk. 4.43).

Luke's Gospel is not limited to individual communities, and thus, certainly not to individual partners or families. Rather, it is the calling of all those touched by this Gospel to serve and proclaim God's Kingdom to the outer reaches of the world. So, Jesus commissions his disciples in Acts, 'You will be my witnesses in Jerusalem, in all Judea, and to the ends of the earth' (Acts 1.8). That the same sort of care and community promoted by Luke's Jesus is that to which the apostles are called to witness to the ends of the earth is confirmed in Acts when the first baptisms described result in converts who 'devoted themselves to the apostles' teaching and fellowship (*koinonia*), to the breaking of bread and the prayers' (Acts 2.42). This *koinonia* is defined as a 'close association involving mutual interests and sharing' (BDAG 2000: 552d). In other words, gospel-centred living – evangelism – in Luke-Acts entails the pursuit of mutual interests and sharing, embodied in the living out of gender equality, protection of widows and orphans, and wealth redistribution, as described above.

My twenty-first-century context is dramatically different from the Lukan first-century context and as such lives into this evangelical mandate in different ways. For example, while widows and orphans remain vulnerable groups in the twenty-first century, this is not always the case and in some cases additional or even more vulnerable groups, such as widowers and LGBTQ persons have emerged. Likewise, just as wealth redistribution was an ideal that was never fully actualized in the first century, it remains a difficult if not impractical ideal in ELCA contexts today. Nevertheless, in both instances, the overarching values of protection of the vulnerable and the care and provision for the whole community remain core ethical principles in the present-day ELCA.

As such, I suggest that ELCA Lutherans would be well suited also to learn from the ethical shift of our first-century ancestors with regard to marriage and family, reframing our ideology of these relationships, which has previously been oriented around secular concerns such as wealth and children, in light of the ability of these institutions to serve the gospel-oriented evangelical mission through an emphasis on equality and mutuality, care for the vulnerable, and provision for all. To the extent that the Lukan author portrays marriage as a partnership of equals amid a community of equals, this depiction makes more porous the boundaries of the marriage relationship and invites room for expanded understandings of marriage and family in the current context of the ELCA.

Consequently, this chapter opens a conversation between the experiences of the early Christian communities described in Luke-Acts and current Christian communities in the ELCA. The paradigm shift experienced in the ELCA suggests a new way of reading and understanding the life experiences of married couples in Luke-Acts that imagines these couples as themselves experiencing a paradigm shift in the purpose and function of marriage. This results in these couples and their communities living into (for better or worse) a new ideology of marriage motivated no longer by the consolidation of social and economic power, but rather by the proclamation of and service to the gospel in favour of the marginalized, vulnerable, and poor. Such an ideology, in turn, offers a new biblical model for approaching the purpose and function of marriage in the ELCA's changing twenty-first-century context, such that these two readings mutually inform one another.

The result of my reading these two contexts in conversation with one another is a biblical model for marriage and family based on an ideology of proclamation of God's Kingdom embodied in the principles of equality and mutuality, care, and provision. Such a model is framed in my analysis of Luke-Acts in understandings of marriage as subservient to discipleship, a tool for advancing respect and equality, and as itself a work of the Holy Spirit. In light of the picture of marriage that this frame presents, I suggest that the ideology of marriage and family implicit in the lives and interactions of these couples and households in Acts presents a compelling alternative to the competing secular ideologies of marriage and family that tend to dominate discourse on these topics today and suggests a course for revisioning a more inclusive and evangelical ideology of marriage and family in the ELCA today.

A Twenty-First-Century Lutheran Context

Lutherans have struggled with the place and purpose of marriage in relationship to the church since our very beginnings. In what have been adopted as the formal confessions of our church, Martin Luther writes, 'Because weddings and the married estate are worldly affairs, it behooves those of us who are "spirituals" or ministers of the church in no way to order or direct anything regarding marriage' (Luther 2000: 367–8). Nevertheless, the prayer that Luther suggests pastors pray for the married confirms the worldly ideology of the time. Luther writes:

> Lord God, who have created man and woman and have ordained them for the married estate, have blessed them also with the fruit of the womb, and have therein signified the sacrament of your dear Son Jesus Christ and the church, his bride: We beseech your never-ending goodness that you would not permit this your creation, ordinance, and blessing to be removed or destroyed, but graciously preserve it among us through Jesus Christ our Lord. Amen. (Luther 2000: 371)

Unlike the Christians in the early Acts communities, therefore, Luther recommended structuring and blessing marriage relationships according to the ideology and expectations of the secular world, rather than in contrast to them. Thus the evangelical purpose of marriage as a way to build and support the proclamation of the Gospel in word and deed was left out of Luther's definition and consequently often gets underplayed in the contemporary Lutheran Church, including the ELCA.

Nevertheless, in the last quarter of a century some strides have been made, among them being the description of marriage in the ELCA's primary worship book as 'a gift of God, intended for the joy and mutual strength of those who enter it and for the well-being of the whole human family' (Evangelical Lutheran Church in America 2006: 286). This definition stretches the purpose of marriage beyond a contractual, civic relationship intended for the benefit of two parties to a holistic partnership for the mutual benefit and for the benefit of the broader community – hearkening back to the evangelical centred ideology of the early Luke-Acts communities.

This same language of marriage as gift has since been deployed in crafting a new biblical model for marriage. In 2009, the ELCA Church-wide Assembly, the highest governing board of the church body, approved a teaching document in hopes of addressing growing concerns about family and sexuality entitled *Human Sexuality: Gift and Trust*. In this statement, the ELCA remains true to its Lutheran roots, acknowledging marriage as a temporal estate constantly evolving to 'meet the human needs of protection and flourishing' (Evangelical Lutheran Church in America 2009) and draws upon scripture to propose a biblical model for the living out of marriage in our temporal world. However, this model, while laudable in its attempt to suggest a more holistic approach to marriage that can address our contemporary context, ultimately falls short of making the needed ideological shift.

For its biblical model, *Human Sexuality: Gift and Trust* turns primarily to the creation accounts in Gen. 1–2, finding there God's intent for 'a relationship of trust with humanity' that is both violated and lived out in human relationships with God and one another (Evangelical Lutheran Church in America 2009: 5). In this way the ELCA acknowledges the practical role of marriage within the Christian *koinonia* as always changing. Nevertheless, the model retains the previously dominant paradigm that understands the primary purpose of the marriage relationship within the direct relationship between the two marriage partners – a relationship founded in this understanding through mutual trust. As such, this model ultimately fails in producing a new ideology of how the couple and community ought to think about the marriage relationship, offering instead a new way of framing the previous dialectical ideology – one of a closed relationship, mutually beneficial to two people, now framed in terms of trust rather than economy.

Trust is an important, even necessary, element in human relationship and the basis upon which many Christians place their belief in God. Thus, it is not my contention that trust ought not be a central part of marriage, familial, or community relationships. Indeed, the very function of the *koinonia* in Acts depends upon this, as illustrated by the community's strong response to Ananias and Sapphira in Acts 5. However, following the example of the Acts community, I propose trust as a practical component of Christian relationships, including marriage, not the purpose of these relationships as such.

This practical function of trust within relationships is lifted up in the social statement as reaching beyond the confines of the specific marriage relationship which the statement still defines as between one man and one woman. In practice within ELCA communities, not only has this definition of marriage expanded to include LGBTQ marriages and remarriages, but there are also many nontraditional groups or individuals fulfilling the 'traditional' historical functions of marriage that Coontz defines.

The congregation that I presently serve illustrates this expansion of the function of family in the current ELCA context. A mid-sized church in Reno, Nevada Lutheran Church of the Good Shepherd is affiliated with the growing *Reconciling in Christ* movement within the ELCA. As a Reconciling in Christ congregation, we seek to extend an affirming welcome for all people (and families), with a particular clarity around our welcome for LGBTQ persons to participate in the life of the church. As a result, we serve individuals in a variety of family relationships, including both LGBTQ and straight single persons, LGBTQ persons in both married and unmarried but committed relationships, straight persons in both married and unmarried but committed relationships, divorced persons, divorced and remarried persons, foster families, and grandparents and other caregivers helping to raise children both in and out of their homes – all of which depend upon the same familial trust lifted up by the authors of the social statement *Human Sexuality: Gift and Trust*. Thus, not only have the previous economic and social functions of marriage that Coontz names become, in many cases, outdated in this context, but trust and mutuality have prospered both inside and outside of marriage relationships.

While the demographics in my context are reflective of many ELCA congregations with or without an intentional welcoming statement, the vision for marriage and family in the ELCA has not shifted as quickly as have its practical expressions. Even congregations like my own, which have affirmed a clear intent to welcome couples and families in these changing roles, continue to struggle with defining what such a welcome and, consequently, what married and family ministries look like in this new paradigm. While the ELCA seems to have embraced the cultural shift away from conceiving of marriage and family primarily as social or economic expediencies, the fumbling and ambiguities often encountered in lived experiences of ministry suggest that we have not as yet effectively replaced this old ideology of marriage with a new one.

Since the approval of the 2009 social statement, this statement has been received with mixed emotions among individuals at all levels of the church. This is another demonstration of the extreme gap that exists between individuals on either side of this paradigm shift in marriage mores. ELCA Lutherans, along with much of the rest of Western society in the last 100 years, have experienced a paradigm shift in cultural expectations of the purpose and function of marriage. Many of the life experiences and reactions of individuals to this social statement reflect these changed expectations. However, within the ELCA, both individuals and the community as a whole have failed to shift our vision of the purpose and function of marriage to match the practical changes.

As a church, the ELCA continues to minister to married couples and families as conceived by a former more secular and economically motivated ideology, even while generally affirming the practice of wider expressions of marriage and family in our midst. Thus, while the introduction to the marriage service in *Evangelical Lutheran Worship*, written in 2006, describes marriage with the twin purposes of support for both those who enter into the relationship and for the whole human family with whom they relate, the 2009 social statement returns to a primary focus on how such a relationship of trust is lived out between a couple and their families within a more limited scope.

Examples of this more dated and limited scope of viewing marriage appear in the acclamation of marriage in the same book, declaring that the couple has 'joined themselves to one another as husband and wife', thus leaving little room for same-sex marriage, even where other portions of the service have been edited to be less gender specific (Evangelical Lutheran Church in America 2006: 288). Likewise, the prayer for 'Families' at the beginning of the same worship book asks God to 'bless family life everywhere', but then quickly narrows its definition of family life, praying for God to 'strengthen the commitment of husbands and wives to one another' and 'that through them their children may taste your unconditional love', without similar petitions for those families with same-sex parents, individuals who parent alone, divorcees who co-parent with new spouses, grandparents or other family members who parent, or married couples who choose not to parent (Evangelical Lutheran Church in America 2006: 83).

In more subtle and contextual ways, this old ideology persists in many local congregations as well – sometimes even when such congregations put forth concerted effort to change in at least certain practices. Sermon illustrations tend to utilize illustrations of a heterosexual married couple with children as the norm of family life. Christian Education letters are often addressed to 'the parents of' and church programming labelled as 'Family Ministry' tends to be code for middle-aged parents with child(ren).

If the gulf between vision, as our cultural expectations, and practice, as our lived life experiences, is not bridged in the ELCA, I fear that marriage will become increasingly obsolete or, worse, doomed to fail due to an increasingly outdated or unclear vision with which it is entered into. As the marriages and families in ELCA congregations continue to follow a growing cultural shift away from the largely outmoded property arrangements in which a male husband provides for a female wife, who provides and cares for future offspring, it is necessary to articulate a new vision to take its place.

Following the model of the Acts communities, such a vision as it is applied within our church communities ought not be based on the broader secular world, but rather, rooted in our Christian faith and convictions. If marriage relationships are to play a continued role in ELCA communities, we must be able to re-envision the purpose and function of these relationships in light of Christ's commission in Luke-Acts to proclaim God's Kingdom in such a way that brings good news to the poor, and release to the captive. Such release, in the ELCA context, needs to be experienced across boundaries of space and time as well as across the particularities of our married and family lives. A model for this is articulated in the ideological portrait of married couples and families living into Christ's commission for all his disciples throughout the Luke-Acts narrative. In Luke-Acts, this is seen in an increased equality among genders, protection of orphans and widows, and redistribution of wealth.

In the context of the ELCA, a similar ideology might begin to be reflected in a lived equality among genders and sexual orientations, protection and support of all those who offer care in the context of family broadly defined, and a redistribution of congregational ministries and resources to support marriages as families with or without children across this broadening spectrum.

A First-Century Early Christian Context

The Luke-Acts communities of the first century provide helpful analogues as ELCA communities consider this new ideology for and support of marriage and family in the ELCA. Luke depicts these communities living out a faithful response to their own cultural paradigm shift in the function and purpose of marriage and family. This shift is driven by Luke's depiction of a Jesus who calls for a reorganization of priorities around equality, protection of the vulnerable, and wealth redistribution in response to the in-breaking Kingdom of God (cf. Lk. 9.57-62; Acts 1.3). The communities depicted in Acts have tasted the beginnings of God's Kingdom in their midst and yet await its coming in fullness (Acts 1.6-8). In this in-between time, the Acts narrative thus depicts early Christian communities living into an alternate vision for marriage and family relationships. This vision is centred on the proclamation of and service to God's Kingdom with an outward focused aim of equality among God's children, protection of the vulnerable, and provision for all in the community that serve the whole human family, rather than on the more narrow and internally focused norms of service to the worldly values of property and reputation that serve only the individual married couple and perhaps some of who are close to them.

This reframing of an ideology of marriage in light of Luke-Acts occurs in three stages. First, Luke-Acts portrays early Christians, at least in the ideal, as uninhibited by personal property. As a consequence, economic motivations for marriage are implicitly overturned by an ideology that sets up concern for the discipleship and the community in place of individual economic concern.

Second, Luke-Acts rejects marriage for the purposes of procreation or protection of one's social status in favour of the less patriarchal aims of increased gender equality and protection of and respect for the vulnerable. Increased gender equality and protections for widows and orphans make marriage unnecessary as a means of protection and thus open up possibilities for marriage to take on a more positive function.

Finally, thus re-visioned as one among many of the spirit-filled relationships embodied by the early church, Luke-Acts presents marriage as a relationship that provides couples yet another vehicle by which to subvert the oppressive top-down organization of secular society. The supports and relationships present in marriage as presented by the Lukan author are thus turned on their head in service not to two individuals, but rather to those in the broader community about whom Luke's narrative is concerned. This community, in turn, empowers married and family units to enact the proclamation of the coming Kingdom of Christ central to their communal identity as a whole.

In short, the old concerns of marriage as a means towards property and personal recognition after death are no longer primary for Luke; however, until the fulfilment of the Kingdom, the estate of marriage remains. Those left living in this in-between time between Jesus' birth and the eschaton empirically do not abandon human relationships, among which is the potential for the relationship of marriage. Rather, Christians are called to subordinate themselves and their family relationships of all kinds to the proclamation of and service to the Kingdom for the sake of the broader family of God. To the extent that marriage or family relationships facilitate this work of the Spirit they are to be celebrated and affirmed. This can be seen through a reframing of how one might view marriage and family relationships in Luke-Acts in light of an awareness in the contemporary shift in the purpose and function of marriage, as well as the diversity of expressions of both marriage and family within the ELCA.

Reframing Marriage and Family Relationships in Luke-Acts

Although married couples and families are mentioned in Luke-Acts and form part of the discipleship communities in both books, the verb 'to marry' (*gameō*) never appears in Acts at all. This suggests that the Lukan author is not specifically interested in the daily lives of married couples, but rather, simply assumes these relationships in the overall portrait of early Christian community and discipleship. A similar perspective is also affirmed by later church writer, Tertullian who acknowledges such marital relationships in early Christian communities, while also recognizing them as an anachronism in light of the professed rejection of personal goods. Tertullian writes, 'All things are without distinction [of ownership] among us, except wives' (Tertullian *Apology* 39.11).

What Tertullian recognizes as disjuncture, however, in Luke-Acts serves more as another example of reversal. In typical Luke-Acts form, the structures of marriage are turned on their head. Therefore, in its very subservience to the life of discipleship, the marriage relationship as described in Luke-Acts provides a helpful framework for developing an alternative ideology of marriage as a relationship that no longer sits at the centre of social and economic relationships in the present day.

Marriage Relationships as Subservient to Discipleship

Discipleship, specifically the proclamation of and service to God's Kingdom, is a central value for the Lukan author (Lk. 8.21). In framing an understanding of marriage influenced by Luke-Acts, therefore, it is of primary importance that all relationships, including marriage, ought therefore to be read in service to Luke's evangelical end. The first mention of marriage in Luke's gospel (Lk. 14.20), together with a later mention in Lk. 17.27, however, set a disjunctive tone. In each instance, marriage is portrayed as a hindrance to discipleship. In Luke 14, telling a parable about the Kingdom of God, Jesus illustrates the ease with which human possessions and relationships can get in the way of discipleship. In Jesus' parable, instead of responding to the King's invitation to a banquet, representing God's Kingdom, people give excuse after excuse – including having just been married (Lk. 14.20). Marriage is thus portrayed as one of the material realities that can keep us from living out God's call to discipleship. This is similarly portrayed in Jesus' description of the days of Noah, when people 'were eating and drinking, marrying and being given in marriage, until the day Noah entered the ark, and the flood came and destroyed them all' (Lk. 17.27). In each instance, marriage is not directly condemned, but rather held up as one of many foils and distractions that can keep people from heeding the Word of God. Thus, marriage is seen as getting in the way of discipleship.

At the conclusion of his parable in Luke 14, Jesus exhorts, 'Whoever comes to me and does not hate (*misei*) father and mother, wife and children, brothers and sisters, yes, and even life itself, cannot be my disciple ... . So therefore, none of you can become my disciple if you do not give up all your possessions' (Lk. 14.26, 33). While the strong implications of the imperative *misei* should not be downplayed, it is important to distinguish the term and its affective connotations from an imperative to actively leave or abandon these relationships. Thus, the first priority of discipleship must be service to and proclamation of God's Kingdom and should not be distracted by anything else. Indeed, even the second priority in Jesus' view seems to be towards the human family more generally and the marginalized and vulnerable more specifically. Hence, the use of this strong verb which connotes 'disfavour' or even 'detest' is appropriate as a way of ranking the ideal regard for individuals in these family relationships in juxtaposition for one's regard towards the vulnerable and the poor (BDAG 2000: 652d). According to Luke's Jesus, one's partner in marriage ought not to be favoured over against anyone in need.

Historically, in first-century Galilee, most relationships were governed and often entered into for economic reasons. Marriage was no exception. Countryman explains,

> The standard way of thinking about marriage in both the first-century Greco-Roman and the Jewish cultures they ruled was primarily as a property arrangement. Dowries were exchanged, contracts were signed, and wives were considered the property of their husbands. (Countryman 2007: 148)

All of the marriage laws mentioned and assumed in the text of Luke-Acts hold in common a concern for ensuring the legitimacy of children and the protection of property (cf. Lk. 16.18; 17.27; 20.28-34). This was the premise of all Roman laws of that period concerning marriage and divorce (Treggiara 2004: 33). Similarly, although the Jewish *ketubah* payment (their closest equivalent to a dowry) seems to have had different applications over the years, it always refers to a payment made by the husband or his family to the family of the bride – sometimes, even, returned in the case of divorce (Treggiara 2004: 33). In this way, ancient marriage experienced both its beginning and its end as a financial arrangement – one within which one's concern for the social and economic interests of the other partner were central because they directly affected both parties in the marriage.

However, Luke's narrative portrait of the Christ event and Christ's attendant heralding of God's Kingdom suggests an ideological alternative. Specifically, within the Luke-Acts narrative, Jesus' birth sets the stage for an economic reversal that, even if never fully achieved, was at the centre of the social consciousness of the early Christian communities from whom and for whom Luke-Acts was written.

Luke-Acts describes a conscious rejection of personal property, leading to an ideal of shared resources as a primary aim (Satlow 1993: 133). This begins with the announcement of the virgin birth in Luke 1, which flies in the face of all claims to worldly possession and status. In the birth stories of both Jesus and John, the Lukan author silences the expected male actors – the human fathers and heads of household to whom all property and status belong – and instead sets the scene for Mary to celebrate God who has 'lifted up the lowly' (Lk. 1.52b).

Mary's husband is not even mentioned until the following chapter, effectively nine months from the beginning of the narrative; and Elizabeth's husband is literally silenced throughout her entire pregnancy. In this way, the traditionally powerful male heads of household are obscured and the relationship between these two women – 'and now, your relative Elizabeth in her old age has also conceived a son' (Lk. 1.36) – takes centre stage. Remarkably, though, Luke frames this relationship not primarily on the connection between these women as cousins or the timing of their pregnancies, but rather, in their connection through the power of God through the Holy Spirit. Elizabeth's pregnancy is announced as an answer to prayer (1.13), after which, the Holy Spirit fills Elizabeth through the actions of the infant in her womb (1.41) and likewise, Mary's pregnancy is announced as an experience of the Holy Spirit (1.35). The experience of marriage and family in the Luke-Acts narrative is thus set, from the very beginning, to be dictated by and in service to the work of the Spirit in opposition to previous economic roles.

This shift continues through the life and teachings of Jesus and the early Christian communities after him. In place of the prevailing conception of relationships of economic interest, Acts 2 paints the picture of an ideal community in which 'all who believed were together and had all things in common; they would sell their possessions and goods and distribute the proceeds to all, as any had any need' (Acts 2.44-45).[1] In such a community, relationships such as marriage and family are no longer governed by economic interests, since such interests would be nullified.

Such a radical reordering of relationships in which one partner might even be thought to 'detest' the other is thus necessary in order to provide Lukan disciples the most uninhibited path towards discipleship and the service of God's Kingdom.

---

1. While there is not clear scholarly consensus on the historical existence of a community that fits the parameters Luke describes, most scholars agree that this was an ideal towards which many early Christians strove. Such economic ideals are foundational to the way in which people live and act in relation to one another, often even more so than lived economic reality. Luke-Acts lays out an ideological framework of economic equality that, even if not lived out in its fullness, continued to dictate and inform relational decisions made by the early Christians who accepted these Scriptures as foundational texts for their faith.

Failure to engage in such a shift may lead a would be disciple to hold back his or her goods or service from the community in order to care for a spouse or a child. This is what happens in the case of Ananias and Sapphira, whose deaths the Lukan author directly connects with their collusion to hold back even a small bit of their marital property (Acts 5.3-9). However, in this description, the author simultaneously illustrates how one of the old economic ideologies of marriage is overturned and legitimates the continued existence of marriage under a new evangelical ideology. Just as the Acts communities do not abandon their possessions, but rather, pool their use for the common good (Acts 2.44-47), so too, the Acts communities do not abandon their marriages. Instead, couples like Ananias and Sapphira are asked to live out their marriage relationships for the sake of the common good (Acts 5.1-11).

Failing to grasp the fullness of this new vision for marriage within the Christian community ultimately leads to the tragic downfall of Ananias and Sapphira in this narrative. Ananias and Sapphira secretly retain proceeds from the sale of their land, without disclosing this to the community (Acts 5.2). 'According to the narrative the practice [of retaining some money for themselves] would have been acceptable. What was not acceptable was their deceit' (Pervo 2009: 128). While the contrast between Barnabas' generosity and Ananias' and Sapphira's deceit should not be downplayed, from a family perspective it is also significant that Barnabas' faithful act as an individual is contrasted by the Ananias' and Sapphira's act as a married couple. The boldness that is required of them is thus not only one of individual sacrifice, but of communal reorientation of vision. Ananias and Sapphira act according to their old Roman cultural vision of marriage – one in which, even when they serve the interests of a larger group (such as the apostles), they retain concern for their common interest as a married couple (storing away money to care for themselves). The decisive action taken against this couple when they are both struck down dead suggests a firm break with this previous vision.

Such a break demands a new ideology consistent with the redistribution of wealth that the author depicts as one of the guiding practices for living out the goal of discipleship. Consequently, I suggest that an ELCA context that continues to value marriage in service of the whole human family ought to support an ideal of marriage and practices and policies attendant to it that, through its treatment of married couples and families, serves to support the financial and economic good of the broader community in the church and community at large.

Marriage as a Tool for Living into Equality and Respect

The second time the topic of marriage comes up for Luke's Jesus is in a debate with the Pharisees about faithfulness to the law. Here, as with his healings on the Sabbath, Jesus interprets such faithfulness in light of respect for the equality and well-being of persons, in this case two persons who have entered into a marriage relationship with one another, rather than for rigid or legalistic readings of the law.

The Pharisee's question about divorce comes from an internal dispute within Judaism. The Torah forbids adultery (Exod. 20.13; Deut. 15.18), but in enforcing that prohibition, there was debate among first-century religious scholars including the Pharisees as to whether or not the prohibition of adultery necessarily implied a prohibition of divorce. Luke Timothy Johnson summarizes, 'Although the School of Shammai would allow divorce only on the grounds of fornication, the School of Hillel would allow it simply because the husband found another woman more attractive (*m. Gid.* 9.10)' (Johnson 1991: 251). Jesus weighs in on the conservative side, equating a man's remarriage after divorce or to a divorcee with the act of adultery (Lk. 16.18).

Thus, Luke's Jesus, as in the other two synoptic Gospels, seems to take a fairly strict interpretation of the law. Unlike similar logions in Matthew and Mark, however, Jesus' statement in Luke lacks any further context or rationalization. It seems to have been a part of a larger conversation that the Lukan author felt compelled to recount, but the context of which was either already lost or in some other way irrelevant to the Lukan author. What, then, can this logion reveal about the role of marriage in Luke-Acts? First, the attention within the Pharisaic conversation seems less to be on the morality of adultery as a sexual act and more on its legal and interpersonal implications (Bovon 2013: 468). Second, by focusing not on the act of divorce itself, with its economic and procreative implications, but rather on remarriage after divorce with its interpersonal dynamics, Luke' Jesus seems to be shifting previous legal considerations to considerations for the well-being and respect for relationships. Jesus may not be so concerned with the keeping of the law as he is with the protection of the persons involved – specifically, of the women as a vulnerable class, for whom a husband's remarriage would have led to a decrease in protections and property.

Bovon notes that within the larger context of the logion, this implies a human response to God's Kingdom that is faithful both to the God's coming eternal Kingdom and current legal structures (such as laws against divorce) since these represent 'two distinct periods of time' (Bovon 2013: 469). Thus, Jesus's statement about divorce in this context is centred around a respect both for the furtherance of God's coming Kingdom and for the individual people and relationships of which that Kingdom is made up in the present. Although contemporary legal understandings don't match the Lukan prohibitions against divorce, this move towards holding these two together is modelled here in Luke.

Such adaptation is seen in even sharper contrast in Lk. 20.35-36. Jesus declares, those whom God has 'considered worthy to experience that age and the resurrection from the dead neither marry nor are given in marriage because they are no longer able to die'. While this can be taken as a rejection of marriage, the depictions of the early Christian community do not warrant such a response. Rather, Jesus seems here to be rejecting the previous warrants and purpose for marriage as it was defined within the human condition of this life. There is, thus, a paradigm shift in how the Lukan community is to understand marriage and family life, from an individual protection of property, often to the benefit of the male who retains property rights even in the case of divorce, to a communal concern for the respect and well-being of all – male and female, within and outside the marriage relationship.

The previous vision for marriage, which Jesus cites in Lk. 20.35-36, assumes that the purpose of marriage has something to do with the human condition of death. Indeed, the levirate law cited by the Sadducees that protects a family in case of the death of husband with no heir is based on this reality of death. Because of death, the man's legacy is only guaranteed to persevere if he has an heir to carry his name and care for his property. Likewise, because of death, a widow without a son to provide for her could become vulnerable and fall through the cracks of the patriarchal system.

Levirate marriage is designed to protect against these ills; however, in his response, Jesus refuses to be pulled into the Sadducees' cultural assumptions. Jesus has a new vision for what marriage and family ought to be – one rooted not in the protection of property and prestige in this life, but rather, in Jesus' overarching purpose of proclaiming God's Kingdom and bringing about God's promised justice and release for the oppressed. Eternal life precludes the worldly need to carry on one's name – the Resurrection came complete with the promise for the worthy that both they and their name would literally live forever. Thus, while Jesus does not deny the validity of the scriptural law of levirate marriage and the potential problems that it could create in the resurrection, Jesus asserts instead that its temporal protections will no longer be needed in the eternal Kingdom of God.

The protection of the widow is provided for in the Acts community, not by a forced marriage, but rather, by a pooling of communal resources. In this model, vulnerable individuals are protected regardless of their marital status. Marriage is, therefore, not a cultural mandate for the individual good, but rather, an individual option in favour of the communal good. Couples like Ananias and Sapphira who bring their possessions into the community help to provide for widows and orphans within the community, rather than demand that these persons be subsumed into a marriage relationship for their protections. The implications of this shift remove not only the Sadducee's immediate concerns about the resurrection, but also the potentials for abuse when a widow or any other vulnerable person, with or without children, is forced to enter into a marriage as their only option for survival.

Marriage and Family as Embodying the Work of the Spirit

Luke-Acts, written relatively late in relation to the rest of the New Testament corpus (sometime between 75 and 100 CE) is characterized by an anticipation of God's eternal Kingdom, while still acknowledging the need to live in the present in-between time of God's Kingdom. Whereas earlier accounts, like Mark's Gospel, anticipate that God's Kingdom will come within the lifetime of most believers, by the time that Luke writes the reality of delay is obvious. Therefore, Brian Blount observes in Luke a Jesus 'who proclaims that the kingdom is already among [believers]' and in Acts a community of believers who affirm and live into this belief (Blount 2001: 82). While marriage may not be necessary in the Resurrection life, in this in-between time, it continues to play a valuable role for believers. This section explores that role in its nascent development, empowered by God's Spirit in the Post-Pentecost Church of Acts and then follows these same believers out into the mission field of society at large as they live out the work of the Spirit through their human relationships to the benefit of their communities.

While marriage no longer appears necessary within the Christian community for any economic or social protections, Acts testifies to at least two couples who retain their married relationship with one another nevertheless – Ananias and Sapphira (Acts 5.1-11) and Priscilla and Aquila (Acts 18.18). Although Ananias and Sapphira are unable to live into the new vision for marriage within community, retaining former self-serving economic interests, it would seem that Priscilla and Aquila do not have this problem. Instead, Aquila and Priscilla share their home and their livelihood with Paul while he is in Corinth and later accompany him as far as Ephesus, where Paul entrusts them with the proclamation of the Gospel and service to the community when he moves on (Acts 18.18-19).

This is significant both due to the gender equality expressed in the plural pronouns used to describe Paul's stay with this couple, rather than a patriarchal tendency to ignore Priscilla's part in the household, and perhaps more so, given the couple's willingness to leave behind that household and its material provisions in service to the care of the community and proclamation of the Gospel. In the marriage of Priscilla and Aquila, we see in many ways the opposite of that of Ananias and Sapphira. For the sake of the common good, Priscilla and Aquila work together to achieve more good for the sake of God's Kingdom than they would have been able to achieve alone.

Luke's eschatology, which is implicit in Luke's treatment of marriage and family relationships both broadly in the Kingdom of God, and specifically, in contractual and biological relations, thus emphasizes the present experience of God's Kingdom and of Christ's resurrection while anticipating the full manifestation of the Kingdom and resurrection of all the dead at the eschaton. Believers who live in this in-between time live, in their communities and in their more intimate relationships, in service to both the immediate needs of the whole human community here on earth and the proclamation of and building up of God's Kingdom with its anticipated eschatological end.

The immediacy of this experience is manifested throughout Luke-Acts in the work of the Spirit, most clearly attested in the experience of Pentecost (Acts 2.1-47). This experience of God's Holy Spirit coming into the midst of the apostles is what inspires an influx in baptisms, gives rise to the Lukan author's description of the first Christian communities, and indeed, frames the whole Acts narrative, with Peter's sermon in Jerusalem (Acts 2.14-36) paralleled by Paul's final sermon in Rome (Acts 28.23-28). God's Holy Spirit is thus attached to the proclamation of the Gospel and empowers those, from the first apostles to later witnesses such as Priscilla and Aquila, who would otherwise not be able to accomplish such works on their own.

This current and ongoing work of the Holy Spirit can also be seen in Luke's description of God's work among believers as a thing that is already experienced, rather than for which they are to wait in the eschaton. In Lk. 20.35, the author replaces the future tense verb of the Markan account (Mk 22.30) with an aorist participle for 'those who are considered worthy' (*kataxiothentes*), reflecting such an already experienced action. Luke's version is almost always read in conjunction with the other accounts as a prophetic aorist, which references a future event so certain that it could just as easily be considered as having already happened. However, while this may be the primary sense of the verb, the force of the now and not yet eschatology of Luke suggests that it also means something more. For Luke, those considered worthy of this future experience have *even now* begun to experience its fruits.

In Luke-Acts, God is already at work reversing the structures of power by replacing traditional power bearers (such as displacing patriarchal power with increased gender equality) with an expanded picture of individuals and communities who bear the good news of God's Kingdom – where all power ultimately resides. Thus, while the marriage relationship may not function in the same way (if at all) at the eschaton, it remains a useful means by which to both experience and live out the work of the Spirit in the present. Such usefulness, however, is understood not in the former secular sense of the first-century world that valued influence in terms of power and prestige, but rather, as a gift of God imparted by God's Holy Spirit. So Jesus assures the apostles, 'You will receive power when the Holy Spirit has come upon you' (Acts 1.8) as the precondition for his commission that they be witnesses to the ends of the earth. Similarly, the apostles impart this power on the baptized by the laying on of hands (Acts 8.17) and Peter ascribes the same power of the Holy Spirit to Jesus ministry in his sermon to the Gentiles (Acts 10.38). The power of the Holy Spirit is thus attested as a consistent force in doing the work of God's Kingdom.

Indeed, this is seen even from the first chapter of Luke's Gospel when the angel tells Mary, 'The Holy Spirit will come upon you, and the power of the Most High will overshadow you; therefore the child to be born will be holy; he will be called Son of God' (Lk. 1.35). Mary later celebrates this same empowering work of God's Spirit in her song after Jesus' conception, giving thanks that the Lord 'has brought down the powerful from their thrones, and lifted up the lowly; he has filled the hungry with good things, and sent the rich away empty' (Lk. 1.52-52). That such a song would come from the lips of an unmarried virgin is itself a departure from expectations of marriage and child bearing in the broader culture in which Mary lived. And yet, due to Mary's betrothed status, such a departure remains intricately connected to Luke's broader vision of marriage – suggesting a reversal in which the economy of God's household takes precedence over the economy of their own household in Mary and Joseph's marital relationship.

Jesus was born to serve God and God's Kingdom, for the good of all God's children – particularly the vulnerable and outcast, not to advance Mary's (or Joseph's) social standing or provide economic security for them as a family unit. Indeed, Joseph isn't even mentioned in Luke's Gospel account until the second chapter, after Mary's angelic visit and her subsequent visit with Elizabeth. However, when Joseph does appear, it is in route to Bethlehem with Mary, his betrothed, whom we have already learned is expecting a child by the Holy Spirit (Lk. 2.5). In this way, Mary and Joseph themselves subvert previous expectations of marriage, with Joseph accepting as his son Jesus, an illegitimate heir, and the two of them together providing for and protecting Jesus (described as 'his parents' in Lk. 2.42), whom they are told is destined for bringing about the Kingdom of God (Lk. 1.32-33; 2.10-14).

In this way, Jesus' birth heralds a new beginning for the entire family of Israel – one in which well-being and wholeness, often translated salvation, is determined by the power of the Holy Spirit rather than by the sole acquisition of physical wealth or protection of social status. Mary proclaims, God's 'mercy is for those who fear him from generation to generation' (Lk. 1.50). God's Kingdom in Luke-Acts is rooted in this sort of faithfulness, or divine commitment, which stretches across generations and is fulfilled in the person of Jesus. Indeed, God's faithfulness, embodied in Luke's Jesus, stretches across traditional demarcations of geography and ethnicity as well. This is demonstrated by Jesus' interactions with Gentiles in Luke's Gospel and then systematized by Paul's mission to the Gentiles in the latter half of Acts (Lk. 8.26-37; 10.25-37; Acts 8.5-20; 9.32-11.18; 15.36-21.16). The Holy Spirit rests upon and restores all the baptized without distinction.

While marriage may be one option among many for the living out of Jesus' commission through the power of the Holy Spirit, family more broadly conceived as a relationship of mutual commitment to one another in and through the pursuit of God's Kingdom on earth is lifted up in the Acts narrative as core to the evangelical mission. Indeed, the second-century philosopher, Celsus, observed, 'The Christian family was at the very heart of the growth of [the Christian movement]' (Seim 1994a: 207). Acts both expands expectations of God's faithfulness beyond the chosen Jewish family to also include a larger community of Gentiles across a vast geographic expanse, and retains the rootedness of family in connection with the experience of faithfulness in this new community. So we are told that Cornelius, the Gentile to whom Peter is sent through a vision, was 'a centurion of the Italian Cohort … was a devout man who feared God *with all his household*' (Acts 10.1, emphasis added). And Peter baptized Cornelius, his household, and the other Gentile believers who received the Holy Spirit in Cornelius' household on that day (Acts 10.44-48). Similarly, Lydia and her household (Acts 16.15), Paul's jailer and his household (Acts 16.29-33), Crispus and his household (Acts 18.8) are all baptized. In this way, Peter's experience with Cornelius and these other Gentile believers both confirms the household as a nucleus of faith and expands the idea of household beyond the immediate family unit to all those who are called together in community. Such community is established, however, not for the immediate preservation of the family unit – indeed, particularly for the jailer, a profession of faith may have been dangerous (Acts 16), but rather, in order to hear the good news of God and receive God's Holy Spirit as a commission to bring that Gospel into the world in service of God's justice – including increased equality and mutuality within the family, protection of the vulnerable including widows and orphans, and redistribution of wealth and resources for the common good.

The family unit serves as an ideal starting place to support such faithfulness – as Mary's song, inspired by her encounter with her cousin Elizabeth, illustrates. In fact, the very fact that Mary travels to Elizabeth's home without the accompaniment of a husband (or even her fiancé) and is then empowered in her witness by this female relative illustrates the expansive view of family that is further established in Luke's Gospel. The concern is no longer about a single marriage relationship with progeny that guarantees personal wealth and acclaim, but rather, an expanded sense of family, including such marriage and child relationships, which give acclaim to God and God's Kingdom.

While not directly related to the marriage relationship, these become extensions of Christian living for both those within and outside Christian relationships and expand the concept of family beyond a marriage relationship. The female disciples described in Lk. 8.1-3, particularly Joanna, are an excellent example of this new kinship commitment that, for some, replaces previous kinship relations, and for others, becomes an extension thereof. Two of the three named women – Mary and Suzanna – have no spouse or father mentioned with them, even though women were identified by their male protector in the first-century world. For them, their identity with Jesus and his disciples may well have replaced previous kinship associations.

On the other hand, Joanna's spouse, although remaining distant, is mentioned by name – Chuza. Moreover, that Joanna and the other women are said to have 'provided for [Jesus] out of their resources' (Lk. 8.3) implies an ongoing connection to their previous kinship relations in order to supply such resources. Joanna's resources presumably come from the earnings of her spouse Chuza who is relatively well off, in the service of Herod. Thus Joanna and Chuza, in a relatively untraditional relationship for the time, defined by distance and Joanna's commitment to follow and serve Jesus (we do not know whether she did so with or without Chuza's consent) model a new way of approaching the marriage relationship. They do not dissolve their marital ties; however, neither are they bound by them. Instead, they pool their resources for the furtherance of Jesus' mission to which Joanna, at least, has subscribed.

For those who follow Jesus, the new community of disciples supersedes the previous households of which they each had been respectively a part, as we've already seen in Lk. 14.26. Not surprisingly, then, Jesus concludes his blessings and woes directed to the 'great crowd of his disciples' (Lk. 6.17) and others in the crowd with the admonition, 'But love your enemies, do good, and lend, expecting nothing in return. Your reward will be great, and you will be children (*huioi*) of the Most High; for God is kind to the ungrateful and the wicked' (6.35). Households, or families, may provide fertile ground for the hearing and the doing of the Gospel, but the work of the Spirit must not stop there. Continuing in his Jewish tradition of identifying the Israelites as the children of God (Deut. 14.1), Luke's Jesus affirms that relationships in the Kingdom of God are not defined by marriage contract or biology, or any other household arrangement, but rather by participation in community.[2] The strength and support one receives through the trusting and

---

2. In the Jewish community, one sign of participation in this community became circumcision (Gen. 17.1-27; 34.13). In his depiction of the community of Jesus' followers,

faithful relationships embodied by marriages or families in any variety of forms, thus, serve to further the ends of the Kingdom – including equality and mutuality, care for the vulnerable, and provision for the larger community – rather than to be ends on their own.

Yet, Luke does not abandon traditional constructions of family entirely. The narrative of Luke-Acts repeatedly identifies such relationships as the locus for the work of the Holy Spirit. Instead, Luke reprioritizes the arrangement of marriage and family relations in the Christian community. To this end, Luke's Jesus identifies his family as those who hear the word of God and do it, prioritizing service to and proclamation of the Kingdom, while leaving space for the Kingdom community to include his biological mother, Mary and his biological siblings as a part of it (cf. Acts 1.14; also possibly Lk. 24.10).[3] 'The relationship to the word of the Lord is constitutive for the family of Jesus and the community of the disciples, and transforms the obligations and relationships presupposed by the biological family' (Seim 1994a: 207). The purpose of God's household, embodied by the discipleship community, thus remains the up-building of the Kingdom regardless of traditional kinship identifications. The proclamation of God's Kingdom commended by Jesus to his apostles in Acts 1 and the service thereof modelled by the Acts communities thereafter take precedence above everything else.

Redefining the Vision and Purpose for Marriage and Family Relations in Luke-Acts

Luke-Acts reframes the purpose of family and marriage within a Kingdom-centred rather than self-centred reality. In the absence of traditional economic groundings, the early Christians of Luke-Acts structure their marital relationships on the same ideological grounds upon which they structured their communities. This structure leaves behind previous economic concerns as central and seeks instead to enter into and build upon relationships that model service to and proclamation of God's Kingdom as their aim instead. By recasting the roles of marriage and family within a Kingdom-centred community, the Lukan author breaks down previous boundaries around the patriarchal household by placing both man and woman under the authority of Christ's commission to proclaim the Gospel and treating marriage as a partnership of equals amid the community of equals portrayed in Acts.

---

particularly after his ascension, Luke emphasizes more generally the prescription to hear (understand) and do the word of God than any particular action (Acts 15.1-29).

3. While the demand to place religious loyalties above loyalties to household and kin 'was not unprecedented in the traditions and practices of either Judaism or of the Greco-Roman world as a whole' (Barton 1997: 81), the magnitude with which this relativization was felt within the Jesus-movement due to the demands of itinerancy can still be said to have placed the issue of this conflict at the fore in a way that Greco-Roman and Jewish religious practices did not typically demand.

Thus, while married couples and families do not cease to exist in the communities described in Luke-Acts, their warrant or reason for being shifts to match the new *telos* of the community. The new vision for marriage in Luke-Acts is no longer the protection or procreation of the married dyad. Those who choose to enter into a marriage relationship, or any other kind of familial bond, are instead called together to serve and strengthen the evangelical aims of the discipleship community as a whole – namely, their pursuit of gender equality, protection of the human community, and provision for all as they have need (Acts 2.42-45).

Luke-Acts envisions a new kind of *koinonia* – one grounded in these concerns. Alternative purposes, either for the individual, or for married couples or families, must all be subservient to such evangelical purposes. The purpose of the married couple in the new Christian community is thus to serve the proclamation of the Gospel and provide for the community together. Such relationships of mutuality and service are set up by the negative example of Ananias and Sapphira (in Acts 5.1-9) and modelled by Priscilla and Aquila (Acts 18.1-21), as well as Joanna and Chuza in Luke (8.3).

Two Contexts in Conversation

Although situated in very different contexts, both the first- and twenty-first-century communities we have examined face a shift away from an ethic of marriage based solely on its own narrow ends, such as property, children, and other social considerations. The ELCA context of this ideological shift has provided a new lens through which to consider the experiences described in the Luke-Acts narrative, thus suggesting a broader ideology of marriage and family in Luke's corpus than is oftentimes assumed. At the same time, the picture of marriage and family that emerges from within the discipleship communities of Luke-Acts suggests a gospel-centred starting point for re-evaluating the ideology(ies) of marriage predominant in ELCA communities today.

It seems clear that the lived realities of marriage and family in ELCA communities have already shifted. However, unlike the Acts communities for whom changes in practice seem to be lived out almost immediately in response to an ideological shift, ELCA Christians seem to have shifted our practice without clear thought given to an attendant shift in ideology to nourish and sustain this change. As such, I believe that ELCA Lutherans would be well suited to follow the lead of our first-century ancestors in the faith by reframing marriage and family relationships along the broader standard of discipleship and the pursuit of God's Kingdom. Such a shift moves away from seeing the purpose of marriage as a closed relationship for the sole benefit of the couple and seeks to live out the intent of marriage stated in *Evangelical Worship*, 'For the joy and mutual strength of those who enter it *and for the well-being of the whole human family*' (Evangelical Lutheran Church in America 2006: 286, emphasis added). Such an ideological shift does not necessarily mirror the realities of the Luke-Acts communities, but rather, follows them in principle by trusting and embodying the Holy Spirit in the renewal and protection of the human family, both narrowly and broadly conceived.

The cultural shift away from the old structures of marriage and family has already begun to occur in the ELCA and the broader American culture in which we participate. This can be seen in the exciting and diverse new forms in which families and marriages are lived out in our current congregations. At its best, it is also seen in attempts to broaden and redefine family ministry and expand the entire notion of family within individual church communities. In order to support and grow these important efforts, however, the ELCA as a church body along with the many communities that make up its pulse must recognize the disjunction of its previous secular, internally oriented vision for marriage with this new cultural framework. In its place, the ELCA would be wise to follow its faith mandate to and look towards Scripture for an entirely new way of conceiving the purpose and function of marriage and family – rather than simply a new way to describe the old model, as the 2009 social statement provides. Reading Luke-Acts as a narrative that provides corrective glasses through which to view our present-day reality, this need comes into focus as a vision for marriage as service to and proclamation of God's Kingdom through the trifold goals of equality and mutuality, respect and protection, and communal provision.

Rather than worrying about who is married (or divorced) to whom or which individuals are caring for a specific group of children, the ELCA needs to put more emphasis on enabling individuals engaged in all types of married and family life to live out their relationships as a Christian vocation. As a denomination we got this right when in the same 2009 social statement we affirmed 'what is critical with respect to family is not whether it has a conventional form but how it performs indispensable individual and social tasks' (Evangelical Lutheran Church in America 2009: 23). Although the Lukan author could have in no way anticipated the full multiplicity of forms that marriage and family have taken in the ELCA today, this narrative nevertheless provides a framework for broadening and reorienting our vision. Moreover, I believe, our common tasks remain more similar to those in Acts than we may often admit. Acts suggests that these tasks ought be centred around the proclamation of Christ's name to all ends of the world and the common care of the community, especially widows and orphans and those who are in need. This is the central Christian mission. It is what I believe the evangelical purpose of the ELCA was intended to be.

The dissonance between the vision for marriage and lived experiences of marriage in the ELCA further indicates that many in this context are primed for this kind of teaching. In order to bridge the existing gap between Christian vision and experience, however, like the Acts communities, ELCA Lutherans today must live out their relationships in ritualistic community. Articulating a new purpose alone cannot and has not brought about the needed change. In fact, such statements, when attempted, have been more divisive than unifying in parts of the ELCA. Therefore, it is important that we take seriously the role of the Holy Spirit both in forming new expressions of marriage and family and in using such expressions for the up-building of the Kingdom.

With regard to the specific expression of marriage, such a ritual already exists in the marriage blessing, which implores, 'By the power of your Holy Spirit pour out the abundance of your blessing on [name] and [name]… . Bless them so that their lives together may bear witness to your love… . Finally, in your mercy, bring them to that table where your saints feast forever in your heavenly home' (Evangelical Lutheran Church in America 2006: 289). Such a blessing acknowledges the individual trust and commitment within the marriage as partnership, the broader evangelical commission as disciples to (through their relationship) bear witness to God's love, and finally the hoped for eschaton towards which the entire narrative of Luke-Acts points. Emphasizing both the gift and challenge of this blessing both in the ritual itself and in pre- and post-marriage counselling gives leaders in the ELCA the opportunity to help those entering into marriage reframe their relationship according to this new, externally oriented vision of care.

Moreover, expanding the marriage service to include more than just male and female participants, as Reconciling in Christ congregations have already begun to do, together with a renewed emphasis on the evangelical orientation of this blessing can in turn reorient the broader conversation of marriage away from the particular actors and whether they are male or female or both to the One who empowers *all* the actors – God in the Holy Spirit. Finally, by considering new and creative ways in which additional expressions of family may receive similar blessings, the ELCA could begin to ritualize this gospel-oriented ideology of service at the centre of family life while at the same time giving space for all expressions of families to celebrate themselves as embodiments of the Holy Spirit.

The Acts communities demonstrate how, when the broader vision of proclamation and service is lived out among a group of faithful people in a local community, the power of this new other-centred vision takes root. For the Acts community, this occurred not in marriage rites, which are never explicitly described, but instead in their pattern of temple attendance and ritualistic breaking of bread. This common sharing of the Eucharist by all who desire it, regardless of any external or internal divisions, is also enacted weekly in most ELCA congregations. While not explicitly a common sharing of goods, this ritualistic action levels the playing field, at least for a moment, such that all Christians hold all things – or at least, all things in Christ – in common. In this ritualistic action, we live into the broader vision of family that Luke-Acts presents, even as we come forward to receive this meal respectively as individuals, married couples, and varied smaller family groups. In as much as this meal is provided by a pastor, intended as a servant of the community, it fulfils the reversal of power that Mary's Magnificat proclaims. And, finally, as each individual and family group is sent out from the ritual – be it the ritual of Eucharist or Marriage blessing – they are sent to serve as the disciples in Luke-Acts are sent, in the name of Christ. What unites us is thus not the individual demographic or relational group that we arrive with, but rather, the communal Spirit-driven group we are commissioned together to be.

REFERENCES

Abusch, R. (2003), 'Circumcision and Castration under Roman Law in the Early Empire', in E. Mark (ed.), *The Covenant of Circumcision: New Perspectives on an Ancient Jewish Rite*, 75–86, Hanover, NH: Brandeis University Press.

Adams, J. (1824), 'Closing Defense Speech in Trial of the British Soldiers for the Murder of Crispus Attucks, Samuel Gray, Samuel Maverick, James Caldwell, and Patrick Carr', *The trial of the British soldiers, of the 29th regiment of foot, for the murder of Crispus Attucks, Samuel Gray, Samuel Maverick, James Caldwell, and Patrick Carr, on Monday evening, March 5, 1770, before the Honorable Benjamin Lynde, John Cushing, Peter Oliver, and Edmund Trowbridge, esquires, justices of the Superior court of judicature, Court of assize, and general goal delivery, held at Boston, by adjournment, November 27, 1770*, Boston: W. Emmons.

Adjabeng, J. (1995), *How to Enjoy Your Marriage*, Accra: Olive Publications.

Ahmed, S. (2004a), *The Cultural Politics of Emotion*, Edinburgh: Edinburgh University Press.

Ahmed, S. (2004b), 'Declarations of Whiteness: The Non-performativity of Anti-Racism', *borderlands*, 3 (2): n.p.

Ahmed, S. (2011), 'Problematic Proximities: Or Why Critiques of Gay Imperialism Matter', *Feminist Legal Studies*, 19: 119–32.

Alexander, E. (2009), 'Introduction', in E. Alexander and A. Yong (eds), *Philip's Daughters: Women in Pentecostal-Charismatic Leadership*, 1–15, Eugene, OR: Pickwick Publications.

Allison, D. (1998), *Jesus of Nazareth: Millenarian Prophet*, Minneapolis: Fortress.

Anderson, A. (2004), *An Introduction to Pentecostalism*, Cambridge: Cambridge University Press.

Anderson, J. C. (2004), 'Reading Tabitha: A Feminist Reception History', in A.-J. Levine and M. Blickenstaff (eds), *A Feminist Companion to the Acts of the Apostles*, 22–38, New York: Continuum.

Anderson, R. (1979), *Vision of the Disinherited: The Making of American Pentecostalism*, Peabody, MA: Hendrickson.

Anderson, V. (1995), *Beyond Ontological Blackness: An Essay on African American Religious and Cultural Criticism*, New York: Continuum.

Aune, D. (2007), 'The Problem of the Passions in Cynicism', in J. T. Fitzgerald (ed.), *Passions and Moral Progress in Greco-Roman Thought*, 48–66, New York: Routledge.

Autero, E. (2014), 'Reading the Bible Across the Contexts: Luke's Gospel, Socio-Economic Marginality, and Latin American Biblical Hermeneutics', Th.D. Diss., University of Helsinki, Helsinki.

Avalos, H. (1999), *Health Care and the Rise of Christianity*, Peabody: Hendrickson.

Barrett, C. K. (1994), *A Critical and Exegetical Commentary on the Acts of the Apostles*, Edinburgh: T&T Clark.

Bartkowski, J. (2004), *The Promise Keepers: Servants, Soldiers, and Godly Men*, New Brunswick, NJ: Rutgers University Press.

Barton, S. (1997), 'The Relativisation of Family Ties in the Jewish and Greco-Roman Traditions', in H. Moxnes (ed.), *Constructing Early Christian Families: Family as Social Reality and Metaphor*, 81–102, New York: Routledge.

Battin, M. (1995), *Ethical Issues in Suicide*, Englewood Cliffs, NJ: Prentice-Hall.

Bauer, F. C. (1876), *Paul, the Apostle of Jesus Christ: His Life and Work, His Epistles and His Doctrine. A Contribution to the Critical History of Primitive Christianity*, ed. E. Zeller, trans. A. Menzies, 2nd edn, vol. 1, London: Williams and Norgate.

Bauer, W., F. Danker, W. Arndt, and F. Gingrich (2000), *Greek-English Lexicon of the New Testament and Other Early Christian Literature*, 3rd edn, Chicago: University of Chicago Press.

Bazán, N. J. (2006), "La identidad cruceña a través de la historia", in *Boletín de la Sociedad de Estudios Geográficos e Históricos de Santa Cruz*, 25-42, No: 58. Junio 2006.

Betsworth, S. (2010), *The Reign of God Is Such as These: A Socio-Literary Analysis of Daughters in the Gospel of Mark*, London: T & T Clark.

Betsworth, S. (2015), *Children in Early Christian Narrative*. London: Bloomsbury/T&T Clark.

Beyond Inequalities 2005: Women in Botswana, Southern African Research Documentation Centre, Gaborone and Harare, 2005.

Blount, B. (2001), *Then the Whisper Put on the Flesh*, Nashville: Abingdon Press.

Borón, A. (2002), *Imperio & imperialismo*, Buenos Aires: CLACSO.

Bovon, F. (2013), *Luke*, vol. 2, Minneapolis: Fortress Press.

Briggs, Melody (2017), *How Children Read Biblical Narrative: An Investigation of Children's Reading of the Gospel of Luke*, Pickwick: Pittsburgh; Eugene, OR.

Brock, D. (1992), 'Voluntary Active Euthanasia', *The Hastings Center Report*, 22 (2): 10–22.

Bunson, M. (2002), 'Ethiopia', in M. Bunson (ed.), *Encyclopedia of the Roman Empire*, rev. edn, 200, New York: Facts on File.

Burgress, S. and E. Van der Maas (2003), *New International Dictionary of Pentecostal and Charismatic Movements*, Grand Rapids, MI: Zondervan.

Burke, S. (2013), *Queering the Ethiopian Eunuch: Strategies of Ambiguity in Acts*, Minneapolis: Fortress.

Bush, L. (2001), 'Radio Address by Mrs. Bush', *The White House*, 17 November. Available online: http://georgewbushwhitehouse.archives.gov/news/releases/2001/11/20011117.html (accessed 7 November 2016).

'Calgacus', *Wikipedia*. Available online: https://en.wikipedia.org/wiki/Calgacus (accessed August 2016).

Capps, D. (2008), *Jesus the Village Psychiatrist*, Louisville: Westminster/John Knox.

Carroll, J. (2008), '"What Then Will This Child Become?": Perspectives on Children in the Gospel of Luke', in M. Bunge (ed.), *The Child in the Bible*, 177–94, Grand Rapids: Eerdmans.

Carter, Jr., A. F. (2016), 'Diaspora Poetics & (re)Constructions of Differentness: Conceiving Acts 6.1–8.40 as Diaspora', Ph.D. diss., Vanderbilt University, Nashville.

Collins, J. (2010), *The Scepter and the Star: Messianism in Light of the Dead Sea Scrolls*, 2nd edn, Grand Rapids, MI: Eerdmans.

Conway, C. (2008), *Behold the Man: Jesus and Greco-Roman Masculinity*, New York: Oxford University Press.

Conzelmann, H. (1987), *Acts of the Apostles: A Commentary on the Acts of the Apostles*, Philadelphia: Fortress Press.

Coontz, S. (2005), *Marriage, a History: From Obedience to Intimacy, or How Love Conquered Marriage*, New York: Viking.

Cooper, R. (2003), *The Breaking of Nations: Order and Chaos in the Twenty-first Century*, London: Atlantic Books.

Countryman, L. (2007), *Dirt, Greed, & Sex: Sexual Ethics in the New Testament and Their Implications for Today*, rev. edn, Minneapolis: Fortress Press.

Croatto, J. (1972), *Liberación y Libertad*, Buenos Aires: Bonum.

Croatto, J. (1981), *Exodus: A Hermeneutics of Freedom*, Maryknoll, Orbis Books.

Croatto, J. (1987), *Biblical Hermeneutics*, Maryknoll: Orbis Books. Spanish original: *Hermenéutica Bíblica*, Buenos Aires: La Aurora, 1984.

Culpepper, R. (1995), 'The Gospel of Luke: An Introduction, Commentary, and Reflections', in L. E. Keck (ed.), *The New Interpreter's Bible*, Vol. 9: 1–490, Nashville: Abingdon.

D'Angelo, M. R. (1990), 'Women in Luke-Acts: A Redactional View', *Journal of Biblical Literature*, 109 (3): 441–61.

D'Angelo, M. R. (2002), 'ANHP Question in Luke-Acts: Imperial Masculinity and the Deployment of Women in the Early Second Century', in A. J. Levine with M. Blickenstaff (eds), *A Feminist Companion to Luke*, 44–69, London: Sheffield Academic Press.

Danker, A. C. (2008), 'A Bridge for Crispus Attucks?', *Historical Journal of Massachusetts*, 36 (1): 57–70.

Dart, J. (2002), 'Scholars, Churches Debate: Was Jesus an Only Child?', *Christian Century*, 119 (23): 13–14.

Dayton, D. (1987), *Theological Roots of Pentecostalism*, Grand Rapids, MI: Baker Academic.

Deatrick, E. (1962), 'Salt, Soil, Savior', *The Biblical Archaeologist* 25 (2): 41–8.

Donaldson, T. L. (2010), *Jews and Anti-Judaism in the New Testament: Decision Points and Divergent Interpretations*, Waco, TX: Baylor University Press.

Draper, J. (1996), '"Was There No One Left to Give Glory to God Except this Foreigner?" Breaking the Boundaries in Luke 17:11-19', in L. Hulley, L. Kretzschmar and L. Pato (eds), *Archbishop Tutu: Prophetic Witness in South Africa*, 223–29, Cape Town: Human & Rousseau.

Du Bois, W. E. B. (1968), *The Autobiography of W. E. B. DuBois: A Soliloquy on Viewing My Life from the Last Decade of its First Century*, New York: International Publishers.

Duran, N., T. Okure and D. Patte, eds (2011), *Mark*, Minneapolis, MN: Fortress.

Eitzen, S. and K. Smith (2003), *Experiencing Poverty: Voices from the Bottom*, Belmont, CA: Thomson Wadsworth.

Elkins, K, and J. Parker (2016), 'Children in the Biblical Narrative and Childist Interpretation', in D. Fewell (ed.), *The Oxford Handbook to Biblical Narrative*, 422–33, Oxford: Oxford University Press.

Empire Task Group (2007), *Living Faithfully in the Midst of Empire: Report to the 39*th *General Council 2006*, Toronto: United Church of Canada, https://commons.united-church.ca/Documents/What%20We%20Believe%20and%20Why/Theology%20and%20Mission%20of%20the%20Church/Living%20Faithfully%20in%20the%20Midst%20of%20Empire.pdf (accessed 6 September 2017).

Estermann, J. (2006), *Filosofia Andina: Un Vision para un Mundo Nuevo*, La Paz: ISEAT.

Evangelical Lutheran Church in America (2006), *Evangelical Lutheran Worship*, Chicago: Augsburg Fortress.

Evangelical Lutheran Church in America (2009), 'A Social Statement on Human Sexuality: Gift and Trust', 19 August. Available online: http://download.elca.org/ELCA%20Resource%20Repository/SexualitySS.pdf (accessed 28 March 2017).

Evangelical Lutheran Church in America (2017), 'ELCA Teaching'. Available online: https://www.elca.org/Faith/ELCA-Teaching (accessed 28 March 2017).

Falbo, T. (2012), 'Only Children: An Updated Review', *The Journal of Individual Psychology*, 68 (1): 38–49.

Farmer, W. R., ed. (1999), *Anti-Judaism and the Gospels*, Harrisburg, PA: Trinity Press International.

Fischer, J. (1993), 'Introduction: Death, Metaphysics, and Morality', in J. M. Fischer (ed.), *The Metaphysics of Death*, 3–30, Stanford: Stanford University Press.

Fisk, B. (2008), 'See My Tears: A Lament for Jerusalem (Luke 13:31-35; 19:41-44)', in J. Wagner, C. Rowe, and A. Grieb (eds), *The Word Leaps the Gap: Essays on Scripture and Theology in Honor of Richard B. Hays*, 147–78, Grand Rapids, MI: Eerdmans.

Fitzmyer, J. (1981), *The Gospel According to Luke I–IX*, Anchor Bible, Garden City, NY: Doubleday.

Fitzmyer, J. (1985), *The Gospel According to Luke X-XXIV*, Anchor Bible, Garden City, NY: Doubleday.

Fitzmyer, J. (1998), *The Acts of the Apostles*, Anchor Bible, New York: Doubleday.

Fögen, T., ed. (2009), *Tears in the Graeco-Roman World*, Berlin: Walter de Gruyter.

Franklin, E. (2001), 'Luke', in J. Barton and J. Muddiman (eds), *Oxford Bible Commentary*, 922–59, Oxford: Oxford University Press.

Fredriksen, P., and A. Reinhartz, eds (2002), *Jesus, Judaism, and Christian Anti-Judaism: Reading the New Testament After the Holocaust*, Louisville, KY: Westminster John Knox Press.

Friesen, S. (2010), 'Paul and Economics: The Jerusalem Collection as an Alternative to Patronage', in M. Given (ed.), *Paul Unbound: Other Perspectives on the Apostle*, 27–54, Peabody: Hendrickson.

Fukuyama, F. (1992), *The End of History and the Last Man*, London: Penguin Books.

Gabaitse, R. (2015), 'Pentecostal Hermeneutic and The Marginalization of Women', *Scriptura* 115: 1–12.

Galpaz-Feller, P. (2008), 'The Widow in the Bible and in Ancient Egypt', *Zeitschrift Für Die Alttestamentliche Wissenschaft* 120 (2): 231–53.

Garlington, D. (2011), '"The Salt of the Earth" in Covenantal Perspective', *Journal of the Evangelical Theological Society* 54 (4): 715–48.

Gaventa, B. (2003), *The Acts of the Apostles*, Nashville, TN: Abingdon Press.

Gaventa, B. (2004), 'Theology and Ecclesiology in the Miletus Speech: Reflections on Content and Context', *New Testament Studies* 50: 36–52.

Gilroy, P. (1993), *The Black Atlantic: Modernity and Double Consciousness*, Cambridge, MA: Harvard University Press.

Glancy, J. (2010), *Corporal Knowledge: Early Christian Bodies*, New York: Oxford University Press.

Gowler, D. (2003), 'Text, Culture and Ideology in Luke 7:1-10: A Dialogic Reading', in D. Gowler and L. Bloomquist (eds), *Fabrics of Discourse: Essays in Honor of Vernon K. Robbins*, 89–125, Harrisburg: Trinity Press International.

Green, J. (1997), *The Gospel of Luke*, Grand Rapids: Eerdmans.

Groll, D. (2014), 'Medical Paternalism – Part 2', *Philosophy Compass* 9 (3): 194–203.

Gutiérrez, G. (1973), *A Theology of Liberation*, Maryknoll, Orbis Books. Spanish: Gutiérrez, G. (1971), *Teología de la liberación*. Lima, Perú: CEP.

Haddad, B. (2000), 'African Women's Theologies of Survival: Intersecting Faith, Feminisms and Development', Ph.D. thesis, University of KwaZulu-Natal, Pietermaritzburg.

Hall, A. (2016), 'Heroism', *Word and World* 36: 53–63.

Hall, D., ed. (1994), *Muscular Christianity: Embodying the Victorian Age*, Cambridge: Cambridge University Press.

Hamel, G. (1989), *Poverty and Charity in Roman Palestine, First Three Centuries CE*, Oakland: University of California Press.

Hanks, T. (2000), 'Matthew and Mary of Magdala: Good News for Sex Workers', in R. Goss and M. West (eds), *Take Back the Word: A Queer Reading of the Bible*, 185–95, Cleveland: Pilgrim.

Hanson, K. and D. Oakman (1998), 'The Denarius Stops Here: Political Economy in Roman Palestine', in K. Hanson and D. Oakman (eds), *Palestine in the Time of Jesus: Social Structures and Social Conflicts*, 99–129, Minneapolis: Fortress.

Hardt, M., and A. Negri (2000), *Empire*, Cambridge, MA: Harvard University Press.

Harland, P. (2002), 'The Economy of First-Century Palestine: State of the Scholarly Discussion', in A. Blasi, J. Duhaime, and P. Turcotte (eds), *Handbook of Early Christianity: Social Science Approaches*, 511–28, New York: Altamira.

Harrill, J. (2012), *Paul the Apostle: His Life and Legacy in Their Roman Context*, Cambridge: Cambridge University Press.

Hasbún, P. (2011), 'Regional Identities: Focus on Santa Cruz', *ReVista, Harvard Review of Latin America: Bolivia Revolutions and Beyond*, Fall 2011: 30–2. Available online: http://www.academia.edu/964813/The_Bolivia_issue_of_ReVista_the_Harvard_Review_of_Latin_America (accessed 1 August 2011).

'Hay más de medio millón pobres en Santa Cruz', *La Estrella del Oriente*, 2012. Available online: http://www.laestrelladeloriente.com/noticia_completa.php?idcat=13&idnoticia=29625&fecha=2012-6-13 (accessed 14 June 2012).

Hegel, G. W. F. (2001), *The Philosophy of History*, trans. J. Sibree, Kitchener, CA: Batoche Books.

Hendrix, H. (1984), 'Thessalonians Honor Romans', Th.D. diss., Harvard University.

Hick, J. (1994), *Death and Eternal Life*, Louisville: Westminster/John Knox.

Hollenweger, W. (1997), *The Pentecostalism. Origins and Developments Worldwide*, Peabody, MA: Hendrickson.

Hooks, B. (1990), 'Postmodern Blackness', *Postmodern Culture* 1 (1), doi:10.1353/pmc.1990.0004.

Horn, C., and J. Martens (2009), *Let the Little Children Come to Me: Childhood and Children in Early Christianity*, Washington, DC: Catholic University of America Press.

Horner, T. (1974), *Sex in the Bible*, Rutlant: Tuttle.

Ilan, T. (1989), 'Notes on the Distribution of Jewish Women's Names in Palestine in the Second Temple and Mishnaic Periods', *Journal of Jewish Studies* 40 (2): 186–200.

Jennings, T. (2003), *The Man Jesus Loved: Homoerotic Narratives from the New Testament*, Cleveland: Pilgrim.

Jennings, T., and T. Liew (2004), 'Mistaken Identities but Model Faith: Rereading the Centurion, the Chap, and the Christ in Matthew 8:5-13', *JBL* 123: 467–94.

John, J. (2001), *The Meaning in the Miracles*, Norwich: Canterbury.

Johns, C. (2009), 'Spirited Vestments or Why the Anointing Is Not Enough', in E. Alexander and A. Yong (eds), *Phillip's Daughters: Women in Pentecostal-Charismatic Leadership*, 170–84, Eugene, OR: Pickwick Publications.

Johnson, L. (1991), *The Gospel According to Luke*, Collegeville, MN: The Liturgical Press.

Johnson, L. (1992), *The Acts of the Apostles*, Collegeville, MN: Liturgical Press.

Judge, E, (1960), *The Social Pattern of the Christian Groups in the First Century*, London: Tyndale.

Kalu, O. (2008), *African Pentecostalism: An Introduction*, Oxford: Oxford University Press.

Kant, I. (1990), *Foundations of the Metaphysics of Morals*, trans. L. Beck, 2nd edn, Upper Saddle River, NJ: Pearson.

Karris, R. (1990), 'The Gospel According to Luke', in R. Brown, J. Fitzmyer, and R. Murphy (eds), *The New Jerome Biblical Commentary*, 675–721, Princeton, NJ: Prentice Hall.

Karris, R. (2002), 'Women and Discipleship in Luke', in A.-J. Levine and M. Blickenstaff (eds), *A Feminist Companion to Luke*, 23–43, New York: Sheffield Academic Press.

Kartzow, M. (2012), *Destabilizing the Margins: An Intersectional Approach to Early Christian Memory*, Eugene: Pickwick.

Kedar-Kopfstein, B. (1999), 'סָרִיס', in *TDOT* 10.344–50, Grand Rapids: Eerdmans.

Kidd, P., and R. Kidd (2009), *Situational Analysis of Gender Based Violence in Botswana*, United Nations System in Botswana: Gaborone, Botswana.

'Kids Count Data Center', Anne E. Casey Foundation, Available online: http://datacenter.kidscount.org/ (accessed 23 March 2016).

Kimmel, M., and A. Aronson, eds (2004), *Men and Masculinities: A Social, Cultural, and Historical Encyclopedia*, vol. 2, Santa Barbara, CA: ABC-CLIO.

Klein, H, (2003), *A Concise History of Bolivia*, Cambridge: University Press.

Kodell, J. (1987), 'Luke and the Children: The Beginning and End of the "Great Interpolation" (Luke 9:46-56, 18:9-23)', *Catholic Biblical Quarterly* 49 (3): 415–30.

Ladd, T., and J. Mathisen (1999), *Muscular Christianity: Evangelical Protestants and the Development of American Sport*, Grand Rapids, MI: Baker Books.

Lazarus, E. (1903), *New Colossus*, Monument Inscription, Statue of Liberty, New York City, NY.

Levine, A.-J. (2002), 'Introduction', in A.-J. Levine and M. Blickenstaff (eds), *A Feminist Companion to Luke*, 1–22, New York: Sheffield Academic Press.

Lewis, N. (1989), *The Documents from the Bar-Kochba Period in the Cave of Letters: Greek Papyri*, Jerusalem: Israel Exploration Society.

Lipka, M., and B. Wormald (2016), 'How Religious is Your State', Pew Research Center, 29 February. Available online: http://www.pewresearch.org/fact-tank/2016/02/29/how-religious-is-your-state/?state=alabama (accessed March 23 2016).

Lopez, D. (2008), *Apostle to the Conquered: Reimagining Paul's Mission*, Minneapolis: Fortress.

Luther, M. (2000), 'The Small Catechism', in R. Kolb and T. Wengert (eds), *The Book of Concord*, Minneapolis: Fortress Press.

Macchia, F. (2003), 'Theology, Pentecostal', in S. Burgress and E. Van der Maas (eds), *NIDPCM*, 1120–41, Grand Rapids, MI: Zondervan.

Macleod, D. (1983), *Building Character in the American Boy: The Boy Scouts, YMCA and Their Forerunners, 1870-1920*, Madison, WI: University of Wisconsin Press.

Maluleke, T., and S. Nadar (2002), 'Breaking the Covenant of Violence Against Women', *Journal of Theology for Southern Africa* 114: 5–17.

Mariz, C. (1994), *Coping with Poverty: Pentecostals and Christian Base Communities in Brazil*, Philadelphia: Templeton University Press.

Marshall, I. (1980), *The Acts of the Apostles: An Introduction and Commentary*, Grand Rapids, MI: Eerdmans.

Marshall, I. (1983), *The Gospel of Luke: A Commentary on the Greek Text*, Grand Rapids: Eerdmans.

Martin, D. (2006), *Sex and the Single Savior: Gender and Sexuality in Biblical Interpretation*, Louisville: Westminster John Knox.

Martin, L. (2013), *Pentecostal Hermeneutics: A Reader*, Leiden: Brill Academic.

Masenya, M. (2005), 'The Sword that Heals! The Bible and African Women in African-South African Pentecostal Churches', in I. Phiri and S. Nadar (eds), *On Being Church: African Women's Voices and Visions*, 47–59, Geneva: WCC.

Mate, R. (2002), 'Wombs as God's Laboratories: Pentecostal Discourses on Femininity in Zimbabwe', *Africa, Journal of the International African Institute* 72 (4): 549–68.

Matthews, S. (2010), *Perfect Martyr: The Stoning of Stephen and the Construction of Christian Identity*, Oxford: Oxford University Press.

Matthews, S. (2013), 'The Weeping Jesus and the Daughters of Jerusalem: Gender and Conquest in Lukan Lament', in U. Eisen, C. Gerber and A. Standhartinger (eds), *Doing Gender—Doing Religion: Fallstudien zur Intersektionalität im frühen Judentum, Christentum und Islam*, 381–403, Tübingen: Mohr Siebeck.

Mattingly, D. (2011), *Imperialism, Power, and Identity: Experiencing the Roman Empire*, Princeton: Princeton University Press.

Maundeni, T. (2001), 'Images of Females and Males in Setswana Language: How Females are Disadvantaged', *Gender, Opportunities and Challenges*, 37–48, Proceedings of the 1st National Conference of the Gender Policy and Programme Committee, University of Botswana.

McClintock-Fulkerson, M. (1994), *Changing the Subject: Women's Discourse and Feminist Theology*, Minneapolis: Fortress Press.

Metzger, J. (2010), 'Disability and the Marginalization of God in the Parable of the Snubbed Host (Luke 14.15-24)', *The Bible and Critical Theory* 6 (2): 1–15.

Metzger, J. (2010), 'God as F(r)iend? Reading Luke 11.5-13 & 18.1-8 with a Hermeneutic of Suffering', *Horizons in Biblical Theology* 32 (1): 33–57.

Míguez, N. (2006), 'Latin American Reading of the Bible. Experiences, Challenges and its Practice', *The Expository Times* 118 (3): 120–9. Spanish: Míguez, N. (2001), 'Lectura Latino Americana de la Biblia: experiencias y desafíos', *Cuadernos de Teología*, 20.

Míguez, N. (2012), *The Practice of Hope: Ideology and Intention in 1 Thessalonians*, Minneapolis: Fortress Press.

Míguez, N., J. Rieger and J. Sung (2009), *Beyond the Spirit of the Empire*, London: SCM Press.

Mill, J. (1978), *On Liberty*, Indianapolis: Hackett.

Miller, A. (2014), *Rumors of Resistance: Status Reversals and Hidden Transcripts in the Gospel of Luke*, Minneapolis: Fortress.

Minardi, M. (2012), *Making Slavery History: Abolitionism and the Politics of Memory in Massachusetts*, Oxford: Oxford University Press.

Miner, J., and J. Connoley (2002), *The Children Are Free: Reexamining the Biblical Evidence on Same-Sex Relationships*, Indianapolis: Jesus Metropolitan Community Church.

Ministry of Labour and Home Affairs, Women's Affairs Division (1998), *Report on Review of All Laws Affecting Women in Botswana*, Gaborone, Botswana.

Ministry of Labour and Home Affairs, Women's Affairs Division (2000), *Botswana Country Report on the Implementation of the SADC Declaration on Gender and Development*, Gaborone, Botswana.

Ministry of Labour and Home Affairs, Women's Affairs Division (2002), *Gender Disaggregated Report*, Gaborone, Botswana.

Moore, S. (2003), '"O Man, Who Art Thou… ?": Masculinity Studies and New Testament Studies', in S. Moore and J. Anderson (eds), *New Testament Masculinities*, 1–22, SemeiaSt 45; Atlanta: Society of Biblical Literature.

Morain, D., and J. Garrison (2008), 'Focused Beyond Marriage', *LA Times*, 6 November, Available online: http://www.latimes.com/la-me-timelinegaymarriage-2008nov06-story.html#page=1 (accessed 7 November 2016).

Moxnes, H. (2003), *Putting Jesus in His Place: A Radical Vision of Household and Kingdom*, Louisville: Westminster John Knox.

Musti, D. (1978), *Polibio e l'imperialismo romano*, Napoli: Ligouri Editori.

Mwaura, P. (2008), 'Gendered Appropriation of Mass Media in Kenyan Christianities: A Comparison of Two Women Led African Instituted Churches in Kenya', in O. U. Kalu and A. Low (eds), *Interpreting Contemporary Christianity: Global Processes and Local Identities*, 274–95, Grand Rapids, MI: William Eerdmans.

Nadar, S. (2003), 'Power, Ideology and Interpretation/s: Womanist and Literary Perspectives on the Book of Esther as resources for Gender-Social Transformation', Ph.D. thesis, University of KwaZulu-Natal, Pietermaritzburg.

Nadar, S. (2007), 'On Being the Pentecostal Church: Pentecostal Women's Voices and Visions', in I. Phiri and S. Nadar (eds), *On Being Church: African Women's Voices and Visions*, 60–78, Geneva: WCC.

Neufeld, D. (2014), *Mockery and Secretism in the Social World of Mark's Gospel*, London: Bloomsbury/T&T Clark.

Neyrey, J. (1980), 'The Absence of Jesus' Emotions: The Lucan Redaction of Lk 22:39-46', *Biblica* 61: 153–71.

Nussbaum, M. (1994), *The Therapy of Desire: Theory and Practice in Hellenistic Ethics*, Princeton, NJ: Princeton University Press.

Oakman, D. (1986), *Jesus and the Economic Questions of His Day*, Lewiston, NY: The Edwin Mellen Press.

Obama, B. (2008), 'A More Perfect Union', Speech, Constitution Center in Philadelphia, PA, March 18.

O'Day, G. (1992), 'Acts', in C. Newsom and S. Ringe (eds), *The Women's Bible Commentary*, 305–12, Louisville: John Knox Press.

Olbricht, T. (1964), 'Pathos', in G. Kittel and G. Friedrich (eds), *Theological Dictionary of the New Testament*, 9: 904–39, trans. G. W. Bromiley, Grand Rapids: Eerdmans.

Olyan, S. (2008), *Disability in the Hebrew Bible: Interpreting Mental and Physical Differences*, Cambridge: Cambridge University Press.

Oudshoorn, J. (2007), *Roman and Local Law in the Babatha and Salome Komaise Archives: General Analysis and Three Case Studies on Law of Succession, Guardianship and Marriage*, Leiden: Brill.

Parker, J. (2013), *Valuable and Vulnerable: Children in the Hebrew Bible, Especially the Elisha Cycle*, Providence, RI: Brown University.

Pastor, J. (1997), *Land and Economy in Ancient Palestine*, London: Routledge.

Patte, D. (2011), 'Contextual Reading of Mark and North Atlantic Scholarship', in N. Duran, T. Oklure, D. Patte (eds), *Mark*, 197–237, Minneapolis: Fortress.

Pervo, R. (2008), *The Mystery of Acts: Unraveling Its Story*, Santa Rosa, CA: Polebridge Press.

Pervo, R. (2009), *Acts: A Commentary*, Minneapolis: Fortress.

Pew Research Center, Religion & Public Life (2015), 'America's Changing Religious Landscape', *Pew Research Center*, 12 May. Available online: http://www.pewforum.org/2015/05/12/americas-changing-religious-landscape/ (accessed 17 June 2015).

Phiri, I. (2002), 'Why does God allow our husbands to hurt us? Overcoming violence against women', *Journal of Southern Africa* 114: 18–30.

Prothero, S. (2003), *American Jesus: How the Son of God Became a National Icon*, New York: Farrar, Straus, and Giroux.

Puar, J. (2005), 'Queer Times, Queer Assemblages', *Social Text* 84–85: 121–39.

Puar, J. (2007), *Terrorist Assemblages: Homonationalism in Queer Times*, Durham: Duke University Press.

Puar, J. and A. Rai (2002), 'Monster, Terrorist, Fag: The War on Terrorism and the Production of Docile Patriots', *Social Text* 72: 117–48.

Rachels, J. (1975), 'Active and Passive Euthanasia', *New England Journal of Medicine* 292: 78–80.

Regan, T. (1985), 'The Case for Animal Rights', in J. Van Camp, J. Olen and V. Barry (eds), *Applying Ethics: A Text with Readings*, 10th edn, 466–74, Boston: Wadsworth.

Reid, B. (2007), *Taking up the Cross: New Testament Interpretations through Latina and Feminist Eyes*, Minneapolis: Fortress Press.

Riches, J. (2010), *What is Contextual Bible Study: A Practical Guide with Group Studies for Advent and Lent*, London: SPCK.

Rieger, J. (1998), 'Developing a Common Interest Theology from the Underside', in J. Rieger (ed.), *Liberating the Future: God, Mammon, and Theology*, 124–41, Minneapolis: Fortress.

Ringe, S. (1995), *Luke*, Louisville: Westminster John Knox.

Ringrose, K. (2003), *The Perfect Servant: Eunuchs an the Social Construction of Gender in Byzantium*, Chicago: University of Chicago Press.

Roberts, L. and P. Blanton (2001), '"I Always Knew Mom and Dad Loved Me Best": Experiences of Only Children', *The Journal of Individual Psychology* 57 (2): 125–40.

Saddington, D. (2006), 'The Centurion in Matthew 8:5-13: Consideration of the Proposal of Theodore W. Jennings, Jr., and Tat-Siong Benny Liew', *JBL* 125: 140–2.

Saiving, V. (1960), 'The Human Situation: A Feminine View', *Journal of Religion* 40: 100–12.

Salomonsen, J. (2006), 'The Dark Side of Pentecostal Enthusiasm: Abraham and Sara's Sacrifice in Knutby, Sweden', in S. Stalsett (ed.), *Spirits of Globalisation: The Growth of Pentecostalism and Experiential Spiritualities in a Global Age*, 105–30, London: SCM Press.

Sanders, J. T. (1987), *The Jews in Luke-Acts*, Minneapolis, MN: Fortress Press.

Satlow, M. (1993), 'Reconsidering the Rabbinic *ketubah* Payment', in S. Cohen (ed.), *The Jewish Family in Antiquity*, Atlanta: Scholar's Press.

Schaberg, J. (1992), 'Luke', in C. Newsom and S. Ringe (eds), *The Women's Bible Commentary*, 275–92, Louisville: Westminster/John Knox Press.

Schapera, I. (1994), *A Handbook of Tswana Law and Custom*, Hamburg: International African Institute.

Segovia, F. (2000), *Decolonizing Biblical Studies: A View from the Margins*, Maryknoll, NY: Orbis.

Seim, T. (1994a), *The Double Message: Patterns of Gender in Luke-Acts*, Edinburgh: T&T Clark; Nashville: Abingdon Press.

Seim T. (1994b), 'The Gospel of Luke', in E. Schüssler Fiorenza (ed.), *Searching the Scriptures: A Feminist Commentary*, 728–62, New York: Crossroad.

Seim, T. (1999), 'Children of the Resurrection: Perspectives on Angelic Asceticism in Luke-Acts', in L. Vaage and V. Wimbush (eds), *Asceticism and the New Testament*, 115–25, New York: Routledge.

Seim, T. (2002), 'The Virgin Mother: Mary and Ascetic Discipleship in Luke', in A.-J. Levine and M. Blickenstaff (eds), *A Feminist Companion to Luke*, 89–105, London: Sheffield Academic Press.

Sherwin-White, A. (1963), *Roman Society and Roman Law in the New Testament*, Oxford: Clarendon Press.

Shillington, V. (2001), 'Salt of the Earth? (Mt. 5.13/Lk 14.34f)', *Expository Times* 112 (4): 120–1.

Singer, P. (2003), 'Voluntary Euthanasia: A Utilitarian Perspective', *Bioethics* 17 (5–6): 526–41.

Smith, L. (2010), *Psychology, Poverty, and the End of Social Exclusion: Putting Our Practice to Work*, New York: Teachers College Press.

Southern African Research Documentation Centre (2005), *Beyond Inequalities 2005: Women in Botswana*, Gaborone and Harare: SARDC.

Spawn, K. and A. Wright, eds (2012), *Spirit & Scripture: Exploring a Pneumatic Hermeneutic*, London: T&T Clark.

'Special Committee on Decolonization' (2015), *Wikipedia*. Available online: http://en.wikipedia.org/wiki/Special_Committee_on_Decolonization (accessed August 2016).

Spencer, F. (2004), *Dancing Girls, Loose Ladies, and Women of the Cloth: The Women in Jesus' Life*, New York: Continuum.

Spivak, G. (1988), 'Can the Subaltern Speak?' in C. Nelson and L. Grossberg (eds), *Marxism and the Interpretation of Culture*, 271–313, Urbana: University of Illinois Press.

Staerman, E., and M. Trofimova (1975), *La Schiavitú nell'Italia Imperiale*, Roma: Editori Reuniti.

Ste Croix, G. (1963), 'Why were the early Christians Persecuted?', *Past & Present* 26: 6–38.

Ste Croix, G. (1981), *The Class Struggle in the Ancient Greek World*, Ithaca: Cornell University Press.

Swinburne, R. (1997), *The Evolution of the Soul*, Oxford: Oxford University Press.

Synan, V. (1997), *The Holiness-Pentecostal Tradition*, Grand Rapids, MI: Eerdmans.

Tannehill, R. (1994), *The Narrative Unity of Luke-Acts: A Literary Interpretation*, Volume Two: *The Acts of the Apostles*, Minneapolis: Fortress Press.

Terrell, J. (2006), 'Our Mother's Gardens: Rethinking Sacrifice', in M. Trelstad (ed.), *Cross Examinations: Readings on the Meaning of the Cross Today*, 19–49, Minneapolis: Augsburg Fortress.

Thomas, C. (1994), 'Women Pentecostals and the Bible: An Experiment in Pentecostal Hermeneutics', *Journal of Pentecostal Theology* 5: 41–56.

Treggiari, S. (2004), 'Divorce Roman Style: How Easy and How Frequent Was It?' in B. Rawson (ed.), *Marriage, Divorce, and Children in Ancient Rome*, Oxford: Oxford University Press.

Troeltsch, E. (1913a), 'On the Historical and Dogmatic Methods in Theology [1898]', *Gesammetle Schriften*, II: 728–53, tran. J. Forstman, Tübingen: J.C.B. Mohr [Paul Siebeck].

Troeltsch, E. (1913b), 'The Dogmatics of the "Religionsgeschichtliche Schule"', *The American Journal of Theology* 17 (1) (January 1): 1–21.

Vaage, L. (2006), 'Why Christianity Succeeded (in) the Roman Empire', in L. Vaage (ed.), *Religious Rivalries in the Early Roman Empire and the Rise of Christianity*, 253–78, Waterloo: Wilfred Laurier University Press.

Valantasis, R. (2005), *The New Q: A Fresh Translation with Commentary*, London: T&T Clark.

Velunta, R. (2000), 'The *Ho Pais Mou* of Matthew 8:5-13: Contesting the Interpretations in the Name of Present-Day *Paides*', *Bulletin for Contextual Theology in Africa* 7 (2): 25–32.

Vogels, W. (1983), 'A Semiotic Study of Luke 7:11-17', *Église et Théologie* 14 (3): 273–92.

Voorwinde, S. (2011), *Jesus' Emotions in the Gospels*, London: T&T Clark.

Walaskay, P. (1983), 'And So We Came to Rome': The Political Perspective of St Luke, Cambridge: Cambridge University Press.

Walaskay, P. (1998), *Acts*, 1st edn, Louisville, KY: Westminster John Knox Press.

Waldmann, A. (2008), *El hábitus Camba: Un estudio etnográfico sobre Santa Cruz de la Sierra*, Santa Cruz de la Sierra: Editorial El País.

Walters, J. (1999), 'Invading the Roman Body: Manliness and Impenetrability in Roman Thought', in J. Hallett and M. Skinner (eds), *Roman Sexualities*, 29–43, Princeton: Princeton University Press.

Wasserman, D., and C. Wasserman, eds (2009), *Oxford Textbook of Suicidology and Suicide Prevention: A Global Perspective*, New York: Oxford University Press.

West, G. (1993), *Contextual Bible Study*, Pietermaritzburg: Cluster Publication.

West, G. (1999a), 'Contextual Bible Study: Creating Sacred (and Safe) Spaces for Social Transformation', *Grace & Truth* 16: 51–62.

West, G. (1999b), *The Academy of the Poor: Towards a Dialogical Reading of the Bible*, Sheffield: Sheffield Academic Press.

West, G. (2000), 'Contextual Bible Study in South Africa: A Resource for Reclaiming and Regaining Land, Dignity and Identity' in G. West and M. Dube (eds), *The Bible in Africa: Transactions, Trajectories and Trends*, 595–610. Boston: Brill Academic.

West, G. (2001), 'Contextual Bible Studies in South Africa: A Resource for Reclaiming and Regaining Land, Dignity and Identity', in M. Speckman and L. Kaufmann (eds), *Toward an Agenda for Contextual Theology: Essays in Honour of Albert Nolan*, 169–84, Pietermaritzburg: Cluster Publications.

West, G., ed. (2007), *Reading Other-Wise: Socially Engaged Scholars Reading Together with Their Local Communities*, Atlanta: Society of Biblical Literature.

West, G. (2009), 'The Not So Silent Citizen: Hearing Embodied Theology in the Context of HIV and AIDS in South Africa', in T. Wyller (ed.), *Heterotopic Citizen: New Research on Religious Work for the Disadvantaged*, 21–42, Germany: Vandenhoeck and Ruprecht.

West G., and M. Dube, eds (2000), *The Bible in Africa: Transactions, Trajectories and Trends*, Boston: Brill Academic.

West, G. and Ujamma Centre Staff (2007), *Doing Contextual Bible Study: A Resource Manual*. Available online: http://webcache.googleusercontent.com/search?q=cache:K NGto5ow71YJ:citeseerx.ist.psu.edu/viewdoc/download%3Fdoi%3D10.1.1.458.3779% 26rep%3Drep1%26type%3Dpdf+&cd=3&hl=en&ct=clnk&gl=us (accessed 28 August 2017).

West, M. (2006), 'The Story of the Ethiopian Eunuch', in D. Guest, R. Goss, M. West and T. Bohache (eds), *The Queer Bible Commentary*, 572–4, London: SCM.

Wheatley, P. (1996), *Poems on Various Subjects, Religious and Moral*, Charlottesville, VA: University of Virginia Library.

Wightman, J. (2008), 'New Bolivians, New Bolivia: Pentecostal Conversion and Neoliberal Transformation in Contemporary Bolivia', UMI Microfilm, diss., University of Illinois at Urbana-Champaign, ProQuest.

Wildermuth, J. (2009), 'Black Support for Prop. 8 Called Exaggeration', *SF Gate*, 7 January, available online: http://www.sfgate.com/politics/article/Black-support-for-Prop-8-called-exaggeration-3177138.php (accessed 7 November 2016).

Wilkinson, J. (1977), 'The Case of the Bent Woman in Luke 13.10-17', *Evangelical Quarterly* 49: 195–205.

Willert, N. (2011), 'Martyrology in the Passion Narratives of the Synoptic Gospels', in J. Engberg, U. Eriksen and A. Petersen (eds), *Contextualising Early Christian Martyrdom*, 15–43, Frankfurt am Main: Peter Lang.

Wilson, B. (2015), *Unmanly Men: Refigurations of Masculinity in Luke-Acts*, New York: Oxford University Press.

Wilson, B. (2016), 'Gender Disrupted: Jesus as a "Man" in the Fourfold Gospel', *Word and World* 36: 24–35.

Wilson, B. (2016), 'Sight and Spectacle: "Seeing" Paul in the Book of Acts', in F. Dicken and J. Snyder (eds), *Characters and Characterization in Luke-Acts*, 141–53, LNTS 548, London: Bloomsbury T&T Clark.

Wit, H. de, L. Jonker, M. Kool and D. Schipani, eds (2004a), *Through the Eyes of Another: Intercultural Reading of the Bible*, Vrije Universiteit: Institute of Mennonite Studies.

Wit, H. (2004b), 'Through the Eyes of Another: Objectives and Backgrounds', in H. de Wit, L. Jonker, M. Kool and D. Schipani (eds.), *Through the Eyes of Another: Intercultural Reading of the Bible*, 3–53, Vrije Universiteit: Institute of Mennonite Studies.

Wit, H. de and E. Lopez, eds (2013), *Lectura intercultural de la Biblia en contextos de impunidad en América Latina*, Bogotá, Columbia: Pontificia Universidad Javeriana.

Witherington, B. (1988), *Women in the Earliest Churches*, Cambridge: Cambridge University Press.

Witherington, B. (1990), *Women and the Genesis of Christianity*, Cambridge: Cambridge University Press.

Witherington, B. (1998), *The Acts of the Apostles: A Socio-Rhetorical Commentary*, Grand Rapids: Eerdmans.

Wood, D. (1980), 'Suicide as Instrument and Expression', in M. Battin and D. Mayo (eds), *Suicide: The Philosophical Issues*, 151–60, New York: St. Martin's.

Wright, M. M. (2004), *Becoming Black: Creating Identity in the African Diaspora*, Durham, NC: Duke University Press.

Yong, A. (2005), *The Spirit Poured Out on All Flesh: Pentecostalism and the Possibility of Global of Theology*, Grand Rapids, MI: Baker Academic.

Yong, A. and K. Attanasi, eds (2012), *Pentecostalism and Prosperity: The Socioeconomics of the Global Charismatic Movement*, New York: Palgrave Macmillan.

Young, I. (1990), *Justice and the Politics of Difference*, Princeton: Princeton University Press.

Zeichmann, C. (2015), 'Rethinking the Gay Centurion: Sexual Exceptionalism, National Exceptionalism in Readings of Matt 8:5-13//Luke 7:1-10', *Bible and Critical Theory* 11: 35–54.

AUTHOR INDEX

BIBLICAL INDEX

ANCIENT SOURCES

Lightning Source UK Ltd.
Milton Keynes UK
UKHW020622250320
360829UK00003B/230